Jean Baudrillard
Revenge of the Crystal

Selected writings on the modern object
and its destiny, 1968–1983

Jean Baudrillard
Revenge of the Crystal

Selected writings on the modern object
and its destiny, 1968–1983

Edited and translated by
Paul Foss and Julian Pefanis

PLUTO  PRESS
London • Concord, Mass

in association with
the Power Institute of Fine Arts, University of Sydney

First published in the UK and USA 1990 by Pluto Press
345 Archway Road, London N6 5AA, and 141 Old Bedford Road,
Concord, MA 01742, USA in association with the Power Institute
of Fine Arts, The University of Sydney, Australia

This edition first published in Australia 1990 by
Pluto Press Australia, PO Box 199,
Leichhardt, NSW 2040

British Library Cataloguing-in-Publication data
Baudrillard, Jean
The revenge of the crystal : Selected writings on the
modern object and its destiny, 1968–1983
1. Western culture. Modernism & post modernism
I. Title II. Foss, Paul and Pefanis, Julian
306

ISBN 0 7453 0298 X hb
ISBN 0 7453 0305 6 pb

Printed and bound in UK by Billings, Worcester

Contents

Acknowledgements

This book grew out of the visit Professor Jean Baudrillard made to Australia in 1984 as a guest speaker at the Futur* Fall conference and as inaugural Mari Kuttna Lecturer on Film at the Power Institute of Fine Arts, University of Sydney.

   Thanks are due to the many people who helped ensure this book was published. To Edward Colless and Joan Kerr for their initial conception of the project. To Alan Cholodenko for his support and Rod Ritchie for his help in production. To Philippa Bateman for her assistance. To Ric Sissons of Pluto Press for his patience and advice. To the Visual Arts/Crafts Board of the Australia Council for their financial assistance. Thanks are due to Paul Foss and Julian Pefanis for selecting, translating and editing the texts. Finally our thanks to Jean Baudrillard for permission to translate his work and for his continuing interest in the project.

Michael Carter, Power Institute of Fine Arts, University of Sydney

Envoi

Please follow me.
        Jean Baudrillard

The world is hardly his idea, but Jean Baudrillard alarms us with the thought that the world was seduced before it was ordained, in genesis. What in the world then can be proffered at the beginning, if not the reiteration of this fatal thought? And how does one proceed if from the beginning one is diverted?

Any introduction relies on this presumption: it announces by precedent what follows necessarily. This is its fundamental deception, or its self-deception. In consequence, by a subtle reversal, the outcome of Baudrillard's writing will here initiate an apology; if one had had the insight (or the foresight — same thing), one might have withdrawn before such superfluity (who cares for such needless apostolic emissions?). To say that what leads here followed is similarly excessive. In a fatal reversal, however, any introduction will not literally lead into but will malevolently lead away, detouring that which follows. It would be better, Baudrillard might advance, to acknowledge that initial diversion from the beginning. But this fatal destiny of all things is of course the very thing which Baudrillard's 'theory' prophesies: not only describing *peripeteia* (reversal, metamorphosis) but fatally exemplifying it. 'Either the enunciation of the fatal is also fatal, or it is not'— a dreadful injunction disguising a banal statement of fâct. In any case, this seduction is inescapable. It would be foolish to consider proceeding in any other than an ironic way, in a way acknowledging the conclusion appears to follow.

Would it be proper to follow Baudrillard's invitation? It might be in the shadowy manner of the following, to apprehend him disappearing. And this, in an ironic turn not unlike the fetching Eurydice from hell, summoned from beyond one's prospect by an impossible disregard. (Compelled to avert one's eyes to divert the soul: even the oblique glance will arrest this passage — happening, ceasing — before us.) If one follows then one can only hope not to encounter him; such a meeting would be too cold, too direct, too indiscreet . . . obscene. No proper introduction possible here: etiquette would any way be undone by such contact.

Baudrillard provides the lead: 'Please follow me,' he says. Understand? He appears to mean it, for a successor to keep up with him. 'Please seduce me' is the injunction's foregone conclusion (but a diversion in effect, if this meaning is only a matter of appearances). On any other occasion such importuning would discover improprieties — an indiscretion committed, a responsibility avoided. It is admitted here by virtue of inconsequence — 'Please follow me': it is a belated request that carries a gratuitous implication if we have indeed complied. The pursuit of Baudrillard is no more a matter of concern than his following: 'as if someone behind him knew that he was going nowhere.'

Alan Cholodenko and Edward Colless

Translators' Note

Revenge of the Crystal presents a selection from what could be thought to constitute the 'classic' works of Jean Baudrillard — from his first book *Le Système des objets* (1968) through to *Les Stratégies fatales* (1983). Also included is an interview executed soon after the latter's publication. Altogether these writings comprise a sort of totality: they belong to that period in Baudrillard's endeavour when theory still had a role to play, however circuitously, and with whatever ironic play.

The selection has been constructed with a view to guiding the reader through this period. As a guide, a number of contraints imposed themselves: one chapter from each book over the fifteen year span (excluding works already translated into English or almost entirely so), chosen on the basis of themes that appear to have remained central (consumer society, mass culture, post-capitalism, the loss of the symbolic order, weakening political structures). But if this selection is intended to follow the royal road of classic Baudrillard, then it is just as much directed towards its eccentric meanderings — not only because the result offers a more interesting series of case studies for the operation of his general system (antiques, collections, gadgetry, kitsch, general strikes, feminism, pornography, obesity and hostages, to mention some of those included here), but because such 'diversions' are in fact at the quotidian core of what Baudrillard once tried to counter in the guise of theory.

It seems evident that the work of this time pursues a trajectory pushed along by its own internal momentum. Throughout it, we glimpse signposts in the analysis of a certain defined 'destiny' of Western humankind — that 'system of objects' characterising the art and life of modernity. Yet after 1983 the road begins to veer away from this analysis, preferring instead a more modulated if fatalistic path. As the interview makes plain, the 'system' had run its full course. Henceforth there will appear those *ad hominem* tracts which now form the staple of Baudrillard's account: 'habilitations' (such as the 1987 thesis defence *L'autre par lui-même*), 'travelogues' (like the 1986 *Amérique* and *Cool Memories* of 1987), and 'journalism' (the recent pieces in *Libération* ranging from 'Éloge d'un krach virtuel' to 'Décongélation de l'Est et fin de l'Histoire'). All of this shows every sign of being an apostil to his earlier 'theoretical' regime.

To read classical Baudrillard today is to go some way towards understanding this apparent rehabilitation. And even here, far from attempting to cover the whole 'oeuvre' with a few offerings doomed to raise more questions than they can possibly answer, their value will be better secured in applying them to the reading of recent Baudrillard and beyond.

In this regard, the gradual move from the quotidian towards the fatalistic may indeed be significant. Let us say first that our author has exploited over the years a language of direct idiosyncracy — born less of contemporary European thought (even though his notorious distaste for references conceals a compendium of its achievements) than moulded in a deepening isolation of this cradle of 'civilisation' from its long established aesthetic and political motivations. But it would be a mistake to attribute to his labour a simple effect of cultural bad faith. Baudrillard might even represent a new beginning in the incorporation of popular forms into the tired conceptual machinery of this thought (or an old beginning, since the critique of modernity has always presupposed the failure of philosophical categories to address our modern vicissitudes). This is his real challenge, as much as it is for us. Even so, the steady irruption of deeply nihilistic notions within the narrative of Baudrillard testifies to something more than a frustration with the stagnant ambience of his intellectual milieu. He is indeed concerned with a paradox — that of a time and place in which the centre of experiential gravity has shifted elsewhere.

Where? Into the 'void' according to him, that of global miniaturisation, nuclearisation and satellisation; but equally possible is that it is into a hole in the quite mundane level of critical promiscuity, where everything is governed by the simultaneity of effects and the unanchoring of causes. This is in fact what he also argues: whether through the psychological alienation of *Système* and *La Société de consommation* (1970), the dwindling of symbolic exchange in *L'Échange symbolique et la Mort* (1976), the neglect of seduction in *De la séduction* (1979), or the leap of things into their opposite in *Stratégies*, the same ontic metaphysic and the same political program is fundamentally raised — a paradoxical irresolution of things in the world. And if today this stoic bias is packaged for a more upwardly mobile intelligentsia, one can only assume it is perfectly geared for the morality of our times.

If Baudrillard once opposed seduction to production, then secrecy to visibility, and now tautology to truth, it may all nonetheless signify the crux of this historical aporia to which he has more or less devoted himself: that nothing is so profound as the absence of sense. And yet there remains a true enigma behind all this: doesn't the mirror of Baudrillard curve round on itself and disappear on its own horizon? This is something of which he is fully aware, and even signals in his text. Abyssal logic is tyrannical; far outside the dialectic, here masters and slaves escape the ultimate synthesis of history in favour of an eternal stay of sentence. Ditto, he argues, for the nuclear strategy of our societies — everyone is caught up in the terror and the fascination of imminence. Ditto, one might also say, for a critical endeavour doomed to be nothing more than a distorted mirror of itself.

The question then, if we are to follow Baudrillard along the course thus outlined for us, is to know what challenge we ourselves must hurl in the face of this deadly paradox. Baudrillard himself provides no answer. Either the system is purely descriptive (but to describe is already to carve out a truth), or else it is indulged titration (the neutralisation of opposites — the perfect anodyne for political indifference under the 'softened' but no less effective sublation of differences; in brief, a lie).

Of course, when removed from the circuits of Western dialogue all this begins to look suspiciously ideological. Cultural similitude for 'the suffering pariahs of Calcutta' means little else than the void into which they have been thrown by just this sort of homogenisation of planetary space — whether by the violence of foreign policy, or by the comfort we take in our own benign nihilism. One wouldn't wish to lay any sympathy for this tempered responsibility in the West at the feet of Baudrillard, who at least has helped us to analyse its very operation in our culture. Although, nor could one entirely exonerate him for providing it with yet another example of why it works so powerfully. Is this someone to be followed along a path already much overtrodden?

But then following or pursuing anyone isn't really the way to go. Even if we knew he was going nowhere. Who wants to go nowhere? Far better perhaps would be to do something, to go somewhere, to break the vicious circle which is the bubble of our late modernist apathy. Or to do what should be done with all purloined letters: 'Return to sender, address unknown. No such number, no such zone.'

Paul Foss and Julian Pefanis

Revenge of the Crystal: An Interview with Jean Baudrillard by Guy Bellavance

Just as there is *science fiction*, Jean Baudrillard's *Les Stratégies fatales* (1983) would be a work of *sociology fiction*. 'The revenge of the crystal' the subtitle announces. What is really at issue here is a theoretical narrative in which the object takes revenge. Baudrillard would like the object to speak for itself. And the object accounts for itself by employing the language of paradox. Indeed, he believes that the only antidote to the increasing carcinogenic irreversibility of our contemporary societies would be paradoxical narrative as an instrument of reversibility. This is perhaps what a fatal strategy would be: a theory that turns back on itself to become an object, not a theory of objects, but a theory-object, a theory in which the object would have passions.

Passing through Montreal, he gave this interview only a few days after a public lecture relating to the book. Reactions to it were stormy, if not openly hostile. Aren't these 'fatal strategies' but a flight in advance, a denial of the real and authenticity, a retreat into artificial ecstasy, and an abdication before this new power of objects? It's because Jean Baudrillard seeks a *mode of disappearance* which he would moreover like to substitute for the dominant mode of being that is the *mode of production*. Contrary to the acceleration of communication networks, he thus seeks a slowness: inertia. And yet in the same breath he seeks something faster than communication: the challenge and the duel. This is the whole paradox of his discourse: on the one hand he seeks inertia and silence, and on the other the challenge and the duel. In brief, conflict and seduction in the one alloy, in the one crystal.

He must thus offer himself as a fatal object. When he arrived in Montreal at the beginning of spring, the unseasonably mild weather vanished and winter returned with a vengeance. And at the beginning of the interview the tape recorder wouldn't work, etc. Is it that objects and nature would be aware of this person's 'fatal' imaginary? It is moreover a Principle of Evil that Baudrillard would like to arouse. According to him, it is the only principle that keeps vigil over the present ecstasy. For society has crossed a threshold and moved full stride into permanent ecstasy: the ecstasy of the social (the masses), of size (obesity), of violence (terror), of sex (obscenity), and of information (simulation). This ecstasy is a movement of potentialisation, a rise in power or a redoubling. The mass is 'more social than the social', obesity is 'fatter than the fat', terror is 'more violent than the violent', obscenity is 'more sexual than sex', simulation is 'truer than the true', and fashion is 'more beautiful than the beautiful'. ' "I am not beautiful, I am worse," said Marie Dorval.'[1]

Among fatal objects, the work of art appears to occupy a privileged position. As Baudelaire had correctly seen, art is the *absolute merchandise*, the absolute object. It belongs to those powers of the object which, beyond the ultimate principle of the subject, bring about a fatal reversibility: the power of the pure object to respond to alienation on its own terms. Baudrillard is not, for all that, an 'aesthete'. For him, this power of the work of art has undoubtedly much more affinity with the power of the masses, where he sees an equally strong passion for intensification:

> . . . the human being can find a greater boredom in vacations than in everyday life — a boredom intensified because comprised of all the elements of happiness and distraction. The main point is the predestination of vacations to boredom, the bitter and triumphal presentiment of its inescapability. Do people really disavow their everyday life when they seek an alternative to it? On the contrary, they embrace it as their fate: they intensify it in appearances of the contrary, they immerse themselves in it to the point of ecstasy, and they confirm the monotony of it by an even greater monotony. If one doesn't understand that, one understands nothing of this collective stupefaction, since it is a magnificent act of excess. I'm not joking: people don't want to be amused, they seek a fatal distraction.[2]

The era of transgression thus would be finished. We need to substitute an ironic theory for critical theory. There would perhaps only be but one fatal strategy: theory as objective irony, a theory-object, a theory in which the object is always presumed to be more cunning than the subject, and in which the object always ironically takes the detour of the subject. Faced with this potentialisation and redoubling of things, the subject must learn how to disappear in order to reappear as object. But isn't this a bit banal?

What is the difference between a banal strategy and a fatal strategy?

Indeed, such a detour or opposition is a bit facile. As soon as one draws near it, it becomes much more complicated. This banality of the masses and the silent majorities is all part of our ambience. But for me it still remains a fatal strategy: in other words, it is something unaccountable for itself, inescapable, but also indecipherable, an immanent type of fatality. It is something at the heart of the system, at the strategic core of the system, something like its point of inertia, its blind spot. This corresponds to my definition of the fatal (even though there can be none). For all this behaviour of the masses, mass art, Beaubourg, etc., is the extreme limit of banality, the apogee of banality. Of course, my work used to revolve around these things. But let us say that it was the kind of fatality that takes systems of simulation to their limit and that produces this 'mass' object.

On the other hand, seduction is for me a fatal strategy as well. For me, it is the finest or most beautiful example of a sort of fatality — something quite different, let us say, from the banality of sex, but a wager of another order, an enchanted order; even though, when it comes to the strategy of the masses, it is in fact more disenchanted. But the fatal can cover both aspects. To put it simply, they have no point in common: there is always something like irony behind the fatal. It isn't a tragic, pathetic or romantic type of fatality, nor is it a religious fatalism: it is something ironic. And it isn't even a subjective irony — there is no subject behind it. Perhaps the grand epoch of subjective irony or radicality has now come to an end. It would be the end of an era in which all philosophy had a stake (Kierkegaard as well as the Romantics) and the beginning of a type of objective irony.

It seems to me that behind these strategies there exists something like irony with respect to finalities: not a refusal of finalities, not a transgression of tragedy, not a violent destruction of tragedy, but an ironic deviation of things from the finalities always prescribed by the subject. So, for me, irony would be almost an anti-definition: isn't this the secret, but perhaps the most obvious one . . . of objective irony?

It is the revenge of the object?

Yes, it is. It is what I have called 'the revenge of the crystal', and in reality I started out from that. The book crystallised around this theme. After the title came to me the book happened very quickly. Of course, I already had many of the elements. What is the crystal? It is the object, the pure object, the pure event, something no longer with any precise origin or end, to which the subject would like to attribute an origin and an end even though it has none, and which today perhaps begins to give account of itself. Perhaps there is now the possibility that the object will say something to us, but above all the possibility that it will avenge itself! I was quite happy to see it in a relatively impassioned form, for it may be that objects have passions as much as subjects do: passions not unlike ruse, irony, indifference — indifferential and inertial passions, which are in direct opposition to those tonic and finalistic passions of the subject (e.g. desire, the demand for enjoyment, etc.). The object, on the other hand, is something like indifference. This is also a passion, but an ironic one to my mind. That remains to be explored, perhaps by expanding upon certain chapters in the book. I haven't done that yet. But if I do maybe it would be a theory of *object-passions*, of the object's passions, of objective passions.

It is clear that your relation to the object has changed considerably since *Le Système des objets* (1968) . . .

Yes, it has completely changed! It's no longer even the issue, except as a kind of reference to this obsession with objects. It is the same term. But what really appeals to me — and there's an irony in this, too — is to be completely immersed in objects, to have started from objects, from an obsession with them. Of course, the problem was not immediately one of objects. It was simply a means of moving beyond them. But finally it was nonetheless a departure from objects, and so ends up in . . . the Object! (*Laughter*)

In any case, the analysis of the system of objects was still a round-about way of grasping the problematic, the dialectic of subject-object. There is a system at work here, but something different all the same. There is another logic simply than the alterity of the object, alienation by the object. These are already tired problematics. So the attempt to grasp objects as a system already went a little way towards disrupting the traditional view of things. But ultimately this analysis went off in a different direction.

This object that you talk about seems to be a quasi-subject. It isn't totally passive. And it expresses many things.

No, it isn't passive, and yet it is not a subject in the sense that it has an imaginary. It is without imaginary, but this is its strength, its sovereignty. This is because it is not caught in a system of projection or identification: the mirror stage, desire, or whatever. The object is without desire. It is what in a sense escapes desire, and so belongs to the order of destiny. In my opinion there are only two things: either it's desire, or it's destiny!

It is without negativity as well?

Yes, it is without negativity.

It is always in the superlative?

Yes, certainly. But here it links up with many of the recent trends: not the search for a positivism, but for a positivity, for an immanence of things. With Deleuze for example, even though we are undoubtedly very far apart, there is exactly the same search, one that goes beyond even the most radical kind of subjectivity—to discover what exists there, what the object has to tell us, what the world as such has to tell us. Could it really have no immanent processes? There is no emotivity in it, and yet something comes to pass. It is not passivity. On the contrary, it is playfulness.

What exactly do you mean by this passion for potentialisation and redoubling which you discuss at the beginning of your book— this truer than the true, this more beautiful than the beautiful, these qualities that have entirely absorbed the energy of their opposites?

A fantasy . . . I don't know. Some might even say it is mystical. I don't think so because there is no cosmic principle here. It nonetheless remains a game, and so there must be a rule of play, which precludes unification or a kind of fusion of things. On the contrary, these intensified effects stand out in direct contrast to others things, precisely those things which belong to the order of the mirror, resemblance, and the image. It is strictly beyond the imaginary. And in that sense it is also a hyperreality, because such intensification is equivalent to a sort of absolutisation. Basically, as soon as it is accepted as a process (for that is what a mobile state would be), it becomes something that passes into radical objectivity—not objectivity in the scientific sense, but, as the *other*[3] would say, radical '*objectity*'.

That may well be a sort of revenge. We have placed the object in the position of object: the subject has devoted itself to it as object, but with all the safeguards, etc. And the object escapes this kind of trap, this strategy which belongs to the subject, by entering into radical objectivity. At this moment it actually escapes the systems of decoding and interpretation. The problem is a bit like knowing if this thing that interests me is a modern detour or vicissitude, or if it is ultimately a question of metaphysics. I believe it is both. For me, there is an increasingly metaphysical dimension, or an anti-metaphysical one — which amounts to the same thing. Yet my interest lies in the actual modern conjunction: not a banal fatality, nor even the object of metaphysics or philosophy. Basically I'm not a philosopher, in the sense of being interested in arguments or terminology. Such things don't escape me, but I don't start out from that. It's not what I try to do. That's the way it goes! What interests me is to set out from contemporary nuclear situations: from object-situations, or even from strategies of the masses. They are the vicissitudes of modernity — or postmodernity, I have no idea — but those which are our lot. Even at the beginning, the 'system of objects' was nevertheless something that had never. been produced within other cultures. Here we might have a specific destiny.

Would you still call yourself a sociologist in this sense?

But of course! Sociology was born with modernity, with the investigation of modernity. Yes, I would be a sociologist in this sense.

Would you still place yourself in the framework of modernity or, as we like to say, in postmodernity? How would you situate yourself in relation to this play of temporality?

I don't know . . . Certainly, my work does not pursue history in the generic sense of the term, with a continuity, an evolution, the search for a succession, an origin for causes and effects. But all the same, it has a dimension that is not purely anecdotal; it is not a simple catalogue of modernity. It's quite different. Then perhaps I analyse this modernity in order to move beyond it — but then it's the same thing. It is the very effect of spiralling or doubling that I look for in modernity that ultimately brings me back to metaphysics. But then it is a question of a metaphysics resulting from this doubling of modernity, rather than from a history of metaphysics or Western millenarian thought. And we must put aside references if we want to describe this modernity in its effects of rupture and denial of the past. We must do the same with analysis: give the reference away, drop it! Not out of contempt, but in order to find, as Nietzsche would say, a radical *pathos*, a pure distance — not that distance of the critical gaze, not a negative distance, but a kind of pure distance. Only then does modernity appear in a different, more lively, more violent, and more radical light. It becomes more interesting. This is why I find it more easily in the United States than in the history of European philosophy. I find the American situation more challenging, more exciting. But once this radical break is made, there is no reason why modernity in all its permutations and self-reflexivity couldn't refer to a metaphysical dimension, rather than a sociological one. Moreover, this metaphysics is part of the same process. It doesn't come from somewhere else.

When you suggest that the object's mode of disappearance has replaced its mode of production, it seems to me that you are really setting Nietzsche against Marx. It sounds to me a bit like the question of Nietzsche's eternal return. Do you see it in this way?

There is certainly an echo of Nietzsche here, if not a direct reference to him. I once read him avidly, but that was a long time ago. I haven't read him since. Suddenly I lost almost all interest in him. Sure, the theme of the eternal return was undoubtedly quite influential in a sense. But Nietzsche's influence on me could also be found, for example, in the use of *metamorphosis*: in the possibility of linking forms without cause or effect . . . or again, this possibility at the level of disappearance. Something that disappears without a trace, that erases its origin and its end, that is no longer caught up in linearity. Fundamentally, this passage to a state of disappearance is disappearance of the linear order, of the order of cause and effect. So when things disappear beneath the horizon of other things, they have the possibility of reappearing. A curvature indeed exists here that didn't exist in the previous order, and this certainly implies something like the *eternal return* in the Nietzschean sense. But there is ultimately a very powerful conjunction here, but linked to a rise in power. A rise in power operates within this cycle: it precisely occurs when it is able to transfigure values, which is to say when it has the power of disappearance, the power to make things disappear, and not simply the power to transform them. Yes, that's different. Here was an order truly opposed to the rest of modernity (historical, ideological, etc.), which was to come later. But that isn't a return to anything. In any event, perhaps it would be much more Hölderlin than Nietzsche . . .

Somewhere you oppose the attitude of Baudelaire to that of Benjamin, the 19th-century attitude to the nostalgia of the 20th-century.

But it's not at all an opposition that favours one over the other. Benjamin is someone whom I admire deeply. In addition, there is a striking similarity between the tonalities of both periods — a very original combination, in Benjamin as well as Adorno, of a sort of dialectics with a presentiment of what is no longer dialectical: the system and its catastrophe. There is both dialectical nostalgia and something not at all dialectical, a profound melancholy. There is indeed a sort of testimony to the fatality of systems . . . I think that Baudelaire already saw modernity in somewhat the same terms. Yet on this point, it seemed to me that Baudelaire was less radical in an odd sort of way — the problem didn't present itself like that then — but that he perhaps already saw modernity with a fresher eye than Benjamin's, just as Benjamin saw it with a fresher eye than we do today! That is to say, the closer you are to the moment of rupture —

To the beginning?

Yes — the clearer you see things. I profoundly believe this. In practice, it is always true. The images are strong, either positive or negative, when things change. It is later on that they become blurred. This is quite evident at a psychological level. The same thing also happens in the analytic realm. Of course, Hegel had already foreshadowed this problem of art, of modern art, of the modernity of art, as well as the whole history of 'absolute merchandise' and all such practices . . . He was clearly aware of art as disappearance, as the magic of disappearance.

Perhaps this explains your interest in art. Somewhere you say that the practice of art is entirely taken up today with the magic of its disappearance.

Yes.

Is this the reason for your interest in art, however long-standing it may be?

Yes, but it's no longer my foremost interest. It's true that I haven't had much to do with it . . . I know many people, and I have experienced something here. But it would be correct to say that I am extremely interested in certain aspects of aesthetics in the true sense of the term, and particularly in the disappearance of the aesthetic dimension of the world. There is still an enormous stake in aesthetics: not aesthetics in the artistic sense, but as a mode of perception, which is precisely the art of appearance, the art of making things appear. Not creating them, but making them appear.

It is true that I have always been fascinated by this. But I'm not fascinated by the convolutions of modern art and all its competing movements. At one time I had a strong interest in Pop, and later in hyperrealism. But it was simply for analytical purposes, since art was only one of many fields that allowed me to clearly illustrate a number of things. I was also fascinated by trompe l'oeil, particularly in relation to seduction. But the history of art as such doesn't interest me. My interest in art extends to its forms, its outpourings, and nothing more. As for this stake in aesthetics, it is really quite a tedious term. I rarely use it myself. And I think I actually avoid it, since it sounds so —

Aestheticising?

Yes, you can't escape it. If only the word could sound as it literally means.

As opposed to ethics or morality, perhaps? Then it would become more interesting. It is possible to interpret the negative reactions of the audience to your lecture in precisely this way . . .

Yes, I heard echoes of this. What do you think?

Indeed, I thought that the response of the audience was somewhat moralistic, whereas your discourse actually had more to do with aesthetics . . .

. . . aesthetics, of course. The first question was quite revealing on this point: 'OK, but isn't all this disappearance just so much fiction?' Because when the analytic disappears, wherever that may finally be, when it seeks its own disappearance by trying to give rise to an object that would have things to tell us, but without in any way being related to a subjective system of interpretation, then what else could it be if not narrative? Then we enter into aesthetics, in the purest sense of the term. I really think that narrative is where fatality can operate. Narrative retains a fatal character, ultimately . . . a (hi)story.

Then again, you say that perhaps theory would be the only fatal strategy.

Yes, theory, but as narrative, as spiral, as concatenation. It's true that the concepts I use are not exactly concepts. I wouldn't insist on their conceptual rigour: that would be far too constricting . . . You can play around with them. But that isn't frivolous or mundane; it is very serious in my opinion. It is the only possible way to account for the movement of things. Theory — and this is a rather paradoxical statement — then becomes fatal. It becomes an object.

When I say narrative, this doesn't necessarily imply a return to a form of fiction, although at times I would really love to. Besides, there are passages in the book . . .

In other words, you seems to be saying that theory ultimately has the right not to be true.

Absolutely, the right to play or to be radical. Thus theory can be narrative, but in a double sense of 'departures' from history. In the books I write there are always little stories, little digressions, but things which are often sites of emergence — events, pointed remarks, dream-like flashes of wit, or *witz* . . . I like the German term better, *trait d'esprit* is a bit of a mouthful. Finally, the trace [*trait*] if you like: not a meta-language organised around signs, but rather a sort of tracking shot along the line of traces. When this occurs there is no continuity as a rule, and everything begins to move quite quickly. There is no discursivity.

So I think that narrative can be valuable as form of theory. But here the aim is not exactly fiction as such. It was a good comment the other day, but a little tendentious because it ultimately came down to a question of literature. But that's not what I try to do. We need to have many ways of expressing theory — including philosophy, provided that philosophy can at the same time dismantle its own apparatus of words, concepts, etc. It could even be poetry, but not 'poetry-poetry' . . . not anymore.

Would it perhaps be something like a 'communicational aesthetic'? In the sense that you would propose, in contrast to Habermas' 'communicational ethic' based on a *rational consensus*, an aesthetic based on *conflict* and *seduction*?

Yes, the challenge and the duel . . . But I've always had a prejudice against the very word 'communication'. It's always seemed to me to be precisely something like an exchange, a dialogue, a system . . . I don't know . . . of contacts, and all the linguistic and metalinguistic functions therein implied. If that is communication, I don't want to know about it.

There was already something different involved in *L'Échange symbolique et la Mort* (1976). But this category of the symbolic became unworkable: there was too much confusion about the term. So I dropped it. In my opinion, the really interesting relations between people don't occur in the form of communication. Something else happens: a form of challenge, seduction, or play, which brings more intense things into being. By definition, communication simply brings about a relationship between things already in existence. It doesn't make things appear. And what is more, it tries to establish an equilibrium — the message and all that. Yet it seems to me that there is a more exciting way of making things appear: not exactly communication, but something more of the order of challenge. I'm not sure that this would involve an aesthetic of communication strictly speaking.

What I meant by a 'communicational aesthetic' is not an aesthetic of communication, but rather a means of recuperating the communicational via the aesthetic . . . or of rekindling it.

Yes, but the communicational process has always seemed to me a little too functional, a little too functionalist, as if the only true purpose of things was to —

Persuade?

Yes, that's right — as if things always exist in a relation of content, be it pedagogical or moral. I don't believe that the really important stakes exist at the level of communication.

On this topic, the 'reversibility of signs' which you oppose as a sort of strategy to the 'transgression of the Law' seems quite fundamental. I would like you to explain what you mean by it, because this is where criticism has seemed the most intense. People have seen much perversity in it.

Yes, perhaps because it sounds slightly immoral to them, because this reversibility seems to be associated with an ironic superiority. Still, reversibility is a very important theme in all mythologies — but not in modernity at all. We are the only ones who live in systems which don't operate according to reversibility and metamorphosis, but which are based instead on the irreversibility of time, of production, etc. So what really interests me is the fatal strategy somewhere behind this beautiful order of the irreversibility and finality of things, and which nonetheless undermines them.

I think what disturbs people is when reversibility is fixed as a kind of Law. But I don't see it that way. I see it as a rule of play, which is different. But wherever it is seen as a Law . . . yes, that fixes things. But it's not a law, since a law can be transgressed. I don't see how reversibility could be transgressed, which is tantamount to saying there is no transgression. The order of things is charged with reversibility — even though, of course, ethics and morality profoundly resist it sometimes, because there must always be progress. Such an irresponsible tone cannot be tolerated. Thus, in terms of the irreversibility of things, the fatal is always interpreted negatively.

This theme has become extremely important to me. A theory of reversibility was already present in *L'Échange symbolique et la Mort*: the idea that subject and object are not opposed to one another, that distinctive oppositions don't really exist — or rather, that they have no truly significant function — and that what has to be revealed is in fact the reversibility of subject and object. Then these terms disappear as such, and they have to be put into another form of relationship . . . I have always preferred a radical antagonism between things. Then subject and object become irreconcilable, and cease to be dialectical. This is what the Principle of Evil means in *Les Stratégies fatales*: total irreconcilability and total reversibility at the same time. There is nevertheless a tension here in the opposition of these two things to the linear and the dialectical.

Thus, on the one hand, there is a radical antagonism — as Freud came to discover with his principles of Eros and Thanatos, and the impossibility of reconciling them. The two are not directly opposed to one another, which means that the first principle would account for all reconciliation, including the eventual reconciliation of both terms, while the second principle says no, Thanatos says no: Eros will never reconcile the world, and nothing can ever change that.

While we're on this topic, what do you think of the current interest in psychoanalysis?

Well, I've never really tackled the subject of psychoanalysis head on. At one time, I wanted to write a sort of 'mirror of desire' similar to *The Mirror of Production* (1973), to do a really critical job on it. But then I realised that it wasn't worth it. The situation had changed and a number of books had already been written — Deleuze et al. So I lost interest in that. Perhaps I felt it was too late, or that it didn't matter. Actually, there is something like a critique of this in *De la séduction* (1979), but without being directly critical or negative. You get nowhere by doing a critique of something, because this simply reinforces it. The book was immediately just a means of moving away from psycho-analysis.

So psychoanalysis became marginal to my interests, impractical, almost useless. But this would indeed amount to a radical critique, something of increasing importance for me.

Among other things, you accuse it of denying a second birth, initiation.

I know that seems simplistic to psychoanalysts. First, they see it as an attack, an aggression, which it isn't; and then they say, on rather super-ficial grounds, that 'psychoanalysis can easily do these kinds of things too'. And this is true, relatively speaking. In fact, I think that psycho-analysis is a quite enigmatic system of interpretation, and that in its better moments it manages to preserve something of this enigmatic character. But it is also a production machine, not at all a desiring machine — a machine which is entirely terrorising and terrorist. Yes, in this respect, the more it disappears the better. I have to thank Lacan for this. I have always admired him: certainly not as the builder of psycho-analysis, but as its destroyer, while precisely appearing to do the opposite. It's a fine example of seduction, of diversion through excess. That gave me a lot of pleasure. But psychoanalysts are not very happy when they are confronted with such things. No, it doesn't go down well with them at all.

I'm not sure about the situation today. I don't know how it is here, but psychoanalytic discourse in France has almost completely lost its impact. It no longer has that omnipotent authority it once had.

Just like Marxism, and almost at the same time. There is a sort of correlation between Marxist and Freudian thought. There was even a period when attempts were made to couple the two types of thought.

Ah yes, the grand epoch leading up to the 1970s, when all of this came to a head . . . It was undoubtedly a sign that both had buggered off, and that it was only through their desperate copulation that the knack could be saved, each becoming the other's nagging child. It didn't last long, but here we return to something perhaps much more interesting, because that really represented the ideological apogee of both of them.

At a given moment, you oppose art to obscenity. You present art as being in a sense the antithesis of obscenity. You say that the false that shines with all the power of the true is art, and on the contrary that the true that shines with all the power of the false is obscenity. So I would like you to briefly explain what you mean by obscenity, as well as its relation to the game of art.

Perhaps it would all hinge on illusion. The attempt at that time was precisely to render the artistic enterprise as a form of illusion: not in the sense of trickery, but in the sense of bringing something into play, of creating a scene, a space, a game, and a rule of play. Ultimately, it is about inventing ways of making things appear and about surrounding them with a void, thus annihilating the whole process of cause and effect, because this process is decidedly anti-artistic. Illusion tries to uncover the linkages between forms, at the place where they come into connection on their own. Art starts at this point where forms connect themselves according to an internal rule of play, a rule which one is unaware of most of the time, which the artist senses, but which to my mind remains secret. For once this rule can become a kind of style or method, we know that the game is over, and generally very quickly.

Thus in my opinion art is about the power of illusion, whereas obscenity is about the power of dis-illusion and objectivity. Obscenity is objectivity, in the sense of making visible. It is the bias of realism to make things visible as they are, to attempt to expose them, and ultimately to destroy all their illusory and playful overtones — as if to say: 'Here they are, they exist, they are incontestable!' Finally, all one is left with is the terror of the visible. That's obscenity. On the other hand, the only thing that enables play is art . . . even though this term is a bit vague, but it's all we've got. We are caught in a desperate system, be it the social or whatever, where people no longer know how to play, or don't even want to play. This is exactly why everyone is now busily reinventing communication.

But to my mind, art isn't about communication. It is really about seduction, about provocation. In other words, aesthetic pleasure has nothing to do with the pleasure of contemplation, or even with spectacle. Indeed, art is something of a gamble, in answer to a sort of challenge. Things change instantaneously with a sort of immanence of forms. The subject gets drawn into this game as well. Of course, art is always illusion, but illusion as the power to overcome the subject's defenses, its systems of causality. And then all of a sudden it shines with the power of . . . I did say the true, but while this formula is OK, even here we shouldn't be too quick to —

Fix things?

In other words there is a general rule here, which art understands, contrary to, shall we say, 'obscene' processes. Of course, it may very well involve entirely material processes of production, interpretation, explication, etc. But when I say that the false shines with the power of the true, I mean that the true, since we seem to imbue it with a kind of halo, can never be found by seeking it. The only strategy is to do the reverse! You can only attain the true or the beautiful — if they are to be the criteria of accomplishment — by going precisely in the opposite direction. All these things are very important in Eastern philosophies. One shouldn't make too much of that, but it nonetheless remains true. It is really quite misguided to hope to find the truth by seeking it . . . such is our morality. Fortunately, art is not so misguided. It knows full well that illusion is the only way to find anything, for if something is to be found — but 'found' without being sought — this can only really occur by the alternate route of something else. That's absolutely essential.

This was the direction I took in regard to the social, because the way we envisage it is terribly misguided — as is the case with *socialism*, which proposes (if not perversely, then unintelligently) that the social can be realised straightforwardly. But things never present themselves in a straight line, leading from beginning to end. Fortunately, things are much more subtle. Here again, it is the revenge of the object. Art is certainly one of the processes capable of taking this alternate route . . . of course, when it succeeds.

Throughout this discussion of art and obscenity, you specifically refer to a phenomenon which you identify as the disappearance of the scene of representation. What exactly is this according to you?

There's no mystery here — perhaps a secret somewhere, but no mystery. The scene is about the possibility of creating a space where things have the capacity to transform themselves, to perform in a different way, and not in terms of their objective purpose. It all comes down to this: altering space so as to turn it, as opposed to that other space without limits, into a space with limits, with a rule of play, an arbitrariness. Basically, the scene is about the arbitrary, which makes no sense in terms of normal space. This notion of the scene does not exist in certain cultures: the scene is unrepresentable. It was necessary to create this sort of minor miracle, this particular, quite specific, and to my mind, highly initiatory space. There is a secret in this, in the very existence of the scene; and I think a large part of its pleasure derives from this fact, from this perfectly arbitrary redirection. As with all games, pleasure is of the moment: a kind of territory is quite arbitrarily carved out, where there is the possibility of acting in any way whatsoever, in different ways, and where one is outside the real, outside the narrow constraints of conventional realist space.

So the scene was an invention. I don't know how it first occurred. Was it first conceptual, then theatrical, before it became the scene of the social? All the systems of representation, including that of the body, have secreted their scene. And perhaps what is lost today is the very possibility of inventing this kind of enchanted space, but also space as distance, and of playing upon this distance. But with the irruption of obscenity, the scene is lost. Obscenity doesn't have this arbitrary character: on the contrary, it always gives reasons for everything. It gives too many of them. It destroys that distance. It is the monstrous proximity of things: it loses that distance of the gaze, that play of distance. Obscenity no longer recognises rules, it conflates everything — it's the total promiscuity of things, the confusion of orders. It puts an end to those careful distinctions that all systems of ritual have maintained in order to avoid this obscenity of things, this total mental disorder, this shortcircuiting of the human into the inhuman. But here too, obscenity is more a qualifier than a concept, a sort of tonality if you like. More significantly, it actually corresponds to something that is difficult to analyse other than in terms of the loss of the scene. And it's true that one has the impression of something being lost here. All the same, one shouldn't go too far in this direction. Obscenity is another dimension. Perhaps we'll have to face up to this hypervisible dimension, and then that might open up other possibilities for play. I don't know. At a certain moment, representation became one of these possibilities for play — though it has never been played in the same way. This is quite evident in the art of the Renaissance, in its use of figurative space. When art was invented as representation, its treatment in the beginning was quite ecstatic, not at all representational or economical, which is what happened later on.

But then, I could be wrong. Every change of rules ought to bring about other possibilities for play, other ways of playing in these interstitial spaces. It will be interesting to see what happens in years to come, in response to the expansion of this cybernetic, telematic world and all its gadgets. Are people going to discover scenes or fragments of scenes in totally unexpected places? We should not assume that this system is fatal in the negative sense of the term, such as 'nothing can be done about it', etc. Of course, here we're dealing with a very powerful force that destroys illusion, that ensures this is a world without illusion in two senses: namely, that it has become disillusioned as well as having lost the ability to create illusions or a kind of secret — whereas in fact this power of illusion, this violent denial of the real existed in all ancient religions, cultures or mythologies, or even in the traditional order. This power was crucial for early religions. The religious experience has always been about a denial of the real, something like a radical doubt — the idea that what is essential happens elsewhere. And this is undoubtedly now being lost, is slowly disappearing, released from the workings of the world: the idea that the world is real and that all we have to do is operate it. Our world is no longer even utopian. There is no utopia anywhere. The scene for Utopia no longer exists. This was also a scene. So Utopia has now entered the real, and here we are.

Is this why theory should be radical rather than true?

Yes, certainly. Radicality is not a truth truer than what has been said before. It is about displacement, something that precisely brings into question our old objectives of revolution in the subversive sense. But radicality has changed, it no longer means that. It doesn't have to be the subversion of a system through negativity. Perhaps it really involves illusion, or rediscovering the sovereignty of illusion, of distance.

At the conference you remarked that you have now shifted from a logic of distinction to a logic of seduction. Distinction is a bit like what Bourdieu does, and what he's done for a very long time . . .

Yes, nothing has changed in fifteen years.

But you've done it yourself . . .

Indeed I have. I started out doing that. I was a good sociologist, no doubt about it. And after all, sociology has always had the virtue of being a way of reading things. But it became a kind of stereotype, an analysis for which you have to produce facts. Then, what's the use of producing facts? I found Bourdieu's work to be very strong at one time, but that was long ago. And then after a certain point, I didn't! This sort of conformity to facts, this compliance with truth is clearly never going to contest anything because all it does is constantly verify itself — a tautology which moreover can be found in the very form of Bourdieu's discourse. It would be true to say that I have completely moved away from this logic of differentiation or distinction, which in any case only interested me at an anthropological level.

And maybe at the level of irony? Because it seems that right from the start this type of sociology contained something truly ironic.

Yes, in relation to Marxism and all that. This sociology had an impact during the period of ideological upheaval. But then it turned sour. All of a sudden, this talk about culture and differentiation was met with: 'But then, what about class? Whatever became of class logic?' So there was a great clash. But all of this happened before 1968. When Bourdieu brought out his *La Reproduction* in 1970, it was almost too late to enter into this discussion again. The book was already an auto-reproduction of itself, which meant that what he described immediately undermined his own position. But ultimately you can't really criticise him for that. What is curious is that such things come back into fashion. They were actually taken up again very seriously in a revised form (and here we again find a type of simulation), because they'd had their hour of truth, so to speak, in the 1960s, and because what happened after 1968 largely diminished their importance. And behold!, after this great coup the same conjuring tricks return, without having budged an inch. This type of 'rewriting' doesn't interest me. But that's sociology: a kind of permanent recurrence. And behold!, at the low point of this intellectual stagnation, at the ebbtide of this historical moment, such systems of thought come back as convenient platforms, as last resorts.

Your relation to fashion seems highly ambiguous: it is not critical, but nor is it collusive. But it is ultimately difficult to know what your position is.

There is a problem about my position in general. My treatment of fashion is an ideal measure of this, because in so-called radical or leftist thought there is a denial or critique of fashion as immoral, as counter-revolutionary. I have lived with this for a long time. In fact, when I described objects my denegation of them was almost a moral one, based on the idea of an ideal alternative. It was a widely-held belief at the time. But things have changed, and it is no longer tenable. There is the feeling today that negation or critique is no longer an effective optic for analysing fashion, advertising, or television. This raises a very general problem, the same one that the present socialist regime raises for us. Where can one now situate oneself in relation to these things? Is it that one has lost all possibility of speaking out against them in a credible manner? In a certain sense, a margin of credibility no longer exists. There has been an absorption of things. How is one able to envisage such things, as you said, without entering into total collusion with them? Thus one would have to develop a new perception that is not a capitulation such as: 'But of course, fashion is resistant to that, because a part of it really has something to say. Everybody watches television, and even we watch it ourselves: you learn to live with it.' You have to draw a line at some point, because we all live in the same world! And some of the new generation approach things with this frame of mind. They get on with it, and formulate a new morality for social action. I don't happen to go that far myself, nor have I a desire to do so. But on the other hand, it's true that the whole leftist, revolutionary and moral-istic position of the 1970s is finished. Speaking for myself, at the moment I don't see any new, original, or credible position. It's a real problem.

At the political level?

Exactly. For me, it is not a question of expediency, of denial, passivity, or a disillusioned retreat. It's just that I don't know what type of dis-tance to adopt right now. That all came to an end with the journals, the first being a small radical review of the situationist type called *Utopie*. Then we knew what had to be done: the Other, Society and Power, they were on the other side. We knew that somewhere there existed, if not exactly a public, then at least a movement to be addressed. Everything was relatively straightforward. But with the appearance of the Gis-cardian type of liberalism in 1975-76, it suddenly became evident that these small journals were doomed because they no longer had anything to say that mattered. As far as I can remember, *Traverses* appeared at this time: it was no longer about transgression, but a sort of transversality, with the aim of discovering a different, more interstitial, more fluid type of negativity, both inside and outside the institution. Of course, in a very real sense, *Traverses* is both Beaubourg and anti-Beaubourg, or culturally different from Beaubourg. So there was a trade-off between collusion and something that still preserved a sort of scene, a public, etc. But to my mind, even the position of *Traverses* is untenable today. It's finished as well.

In what sense?

In the sense that a political ultimatum was delivered to the journal, via Beaubourg, to socialise itself, to become a 'social' review, to take the demands of the people into account, and to stop being a kind of intellectual review. It was a very difficult situation. The journal was almost forced to disappear by order of the socialists themselves. It was a good opportunity for them to turn it into a socialist review, as if to say: 'Intelligence and Power, you are ours!' It was an attempt to synergise things, even though this happens of its own accord. We tried to make them understand. But they didn't want to understand. The matter was put aside because they had other fish to fry. That time we survived, but in the knowledge that we no longer had any margin of autonomy, not even a liberal one.

So *Utopie* is finished; and in my opinion, *Traverses* is virtually finished. Of course, it will keep going for a little while yet. But things always outlive their usefulness. So what else can be done now? What other distance can be maintained in relation to this new society which has absorbed these margins, but which in other respects couldn't give a damn about marginal or heretical products? It doesn't want them but screws them all the same. It is impossible now to find a subversive position. It no longer means anything. All this is a very general problem. The same thing applies to fashion. Everything about it is fascinating, but can't be evaluated because we no longer have any criteria for this. It exists, it is immanent, but nevertheless engages many things. It is even a passion. It is not frivolous or meaningless. But analysis no longer has a privileged position in relation to fashion. Faced with the loss of this privileged position for analysis and the critical gaze, what can be substituted for it now? That's the problem.

You first analysed fashion as a system of social differentiation, as a means for people to distinguish among themselves. But do you now want to see it as a fatal power, as a

power of distinction in relation to nature, or really as a game with nature, as an affirmation of the ability of humans to distinguish themselves from nature . . . to produce their culture?

Yes, to produce artifice, or to give credence to it as a sort of truth. When things become indistinguishable from nature or the real, they are simply obscene. Everything consists of artifice, of the potential to become artificial — but in the Baudelairian, and not moral or pejorative, sense. I need to know that artifice exists. That is what is at stake. And fashion is an extremely powerful way of turning the body into a denial of its sexual, physiological, and functional reality. It is ultimately a sublime game of the body, for without it the body would clearly be pornographic: fashion is the absolute antithesis of pornography. Fashion ceases to exist as soon as a glimmer of — I would say truth — arises from the depths of the body. When the body is turned into a kind of obscenity, into the pure demand for sex, it's finished. Fashion has to continually play around this, but it should never overstep the bounds. It is entitled to be erotic, but never obscene.

What is inherently interesting about fashion is its extreme ambiguity. So it can epitomise, or illustrate, a more general condition. Not only does it continually adjust itself to reality, but it always remains an enigma. This is why it is extremely interesting.

Does your interest in fashion indicate perhaps a displacement from the nature of the political . . . towards culture?

Yes, my interest in things is not so much geared towards banal scenes. The scenes of the political and the social have become banal. Basically, we can only take part in the extension of this banality, in the adaptation and general redeployment of all these sorts of things. It seems that the whole paralysing effect of the political apparatus, as a form of revolution now as in the future, has totally lost its edge, has been eroded, and that the centres of interest can easily slide over things no longer at the front of the stage. For political ideology, of the right or the left, will still continue to occupy the front of the stage, but a false stage — this would be a system of simulation. A critique of the political is no longer worth the effort today. Let's move on, let's see what happens elsewhere.

NOTES

1. Jean Baudrillard, *Les Stratégies fatales*, Paris, Grasset, 1983, p. 12. [Marie Dorval was a famous stage actress in France during the early 19th-century.]
2. ibid., p. 263.
3. Of course, the reference is to Jacques Lacan.

Subjective Discourse or The Non-Functional System of Objects

I. THE MARGINAL OBJECT—THE BYGONE OBJECT

A whole category of objects seems to fall outside the [functional] system we have just analysed: rare, quaint, folkloric, exotic or antique objects. They seem inconsistent with the calculus of functional demands in conforming to a different order of longing: testimony, remembrance, nostalgia, escapism. One might be tempted to see them as relics of the traditional and symbolic order. Yet, for all their difference, these objects also form part of modernity, and this is the source of their double meaning.

Its Ambient Value: Historicity

In fact, they are not incidental to the system: *the functionality of modern objects can refer to the historicity of the bygone object* (or the marginality of the quaint object, or the exoticism of the primitive object) *without in any way losing its systematic function as a sign*. It is the 'natural' or 'naturalistic' connotation that really culminates in the signs of earlier cultural systems. We already saw that the cigarette lighter was mythological in its reference to the sea,[1] while still serving a purpose—the bygone object, however, is purely mythological in its reference to the past. It no longer has any practical importance, but exists solely in order to signify. It is astructural, it denies structure, and it epitomises the disavowal of primary functions. Yet it is not afunctional, nor is it simply 'decorative'. It has a quite specific function within the framework of the system: it signifies time.[2]

The ambient system is one of extensivity — but if it wants to become total, then it has to cover the whole of existence, and thus the fundamental dimension of time as well. Of course, what the bygone object encapsulates is not real time,[3] but the signs or cultural indices of time. Their allegorical presence is thus not inconsistent with the general organisation [of objects]: nothing escapes it, not even nature and time, since everything ends up as signs. However, if nature readily lends itself to abstraction and systematisation, this is not the case with time. It embodies a living contradiction that is hard to integrate into the logic of a system. It is this 'chronic' shortcoming that we interpret as the spectacular connotation of the bygone object. Whereas the natural connotation manages to be subtle, the 'historical' connotation always looks out of place. The bygone object always gives the appearance of being a wallflower. Beautiful though it may be, it remains 'eccentric'. Authentic though it may be, it always looks slightly bogus. And it is bogus to the extent that *it presents itself as authentic in a system whose rationale is not at all authenticity, but the calculated relations and abstraction of the sign.*

Its Symbolic Value: The Myth of Origin

So there is a particular status of the bygone object. Insofar as it exists to conjure time in the ambient system, and insofar as it is experienced as a sign, it is indistinguishable from and relative to all other elements.[4] But, on the other hand, insofar as it exhibits the least relativity to other objects and presents itself as totality, as authentic presence, it has a special psychological status. It is experienced differently. This is where, in serving no purpose, it serves a profound purpose. What motivates this craving for the antique (old furniture), the authentic ('period' pieces), the rustic, the artisanal, the handmade (indigenous pottery), folklore, etc.? What is this sort of phenomenon of acculturation which compels the civilised to seek out signs spatially and temporally remote from their own cultural system, signs which are forever anterior — the reverse phenomenon of that which compels the 'underdeveloped' to seek out the technical products and signs of industrial societies?

The need that bygone objects fulfil[5] is that of a definitive being, a complete being. The time of the mythological object is the perfect tense: it is that which occurs in the present as having previously occurred, and which by this very fact is based on an 'authentic' self. The bygone object is always, in the full sense of the term, a 'family portrait'.

It immemorialises a prior being in the form of a concrete object — a process equivalent, in the imaginary order, to the elision of time. This is what functional objects clearly lack: they only exist in the present, in the indicative, in the practical imperative, disappearing along with their use value without ever having previously existed — since, if they fix the environment more or less securely in space, they do not fix it in time. The functional object is effectual, while the mythological object is complete. This complete event that it signifies is birth. I am not the one who is here right now, as this is anguishing — I am the one who has always been, according to an inverse link with my birth for which this object is a sign, a regression plunging me from the present into time.[6] Thus does the bygone object present itself as a myth of origin.

'Authenticity'

This cannot but lead us to compare the taste for the antique with the passion for collecting[7] — since, in their narcissistic regression, in their systematic elision of time, and in their imaginary command over birth and death, there is a deep affinity between the two. Yet we need to distinguish two features in the mythology of bygone objects: a nostalgia for origins and an obsession with authenticity. Both these features seem to me to stem from that mythical reminder of birth constituted by the temporal closure of bygone objects — to be born implies the prior existence of a father and a mother. This degeneration to origins is effectively a regression to the mother: the older are the objects, the closer do they bring us to an earlier time, to an original 'divinity', nature, wisdom, etc. This sort of mystique, according to Maurice Rheims, already existed in the High Middle Ages: in the eyes of 9th-century Christians, a Greek bronze or intaglio covered with pagan signs took on magical qualities. The demand for authenticity is, strictly speaking, quite different, since it expresses an obsession with certitude — about the origin of a work, its date, author or signature. Value is conferred on a particular object by the simple fact that it once belonged to some famous or powerful person. The fascination with artisanal objects derives from their having passed through someone's hands, and whose labour is still inscribed on them: it is the fascination with that which has been *created* (and which is therefore unique, since the *moment* of creation is irreversible). But the search for *the creator's mark*, from actual impressions to the signature, is also the search for filiation and paternal transcendence. Authenticity always stems from the Father: he is the source of value. What the bygone object evokes in the imagination is this sublime filiation at the same time as the degeneration to the mother's womb.

The Neo-Cultural Syndrome: Restoration

This search for *authenticity* (a being-self-founded) is therefore identical to the search for an *alibi* (a being-elsewhere). Let us clarify these two notions with a well-known contemporary example of nostalgic restoration: 'How to assemble your own ruins.'

Here is how an architect dealt with an old farm in the 'Île-de-France': 'The walls, crumbling for lack of foundations, were torn down. Part of the rudimentary barn near the southern face was removed to make way for a terrace . . . The three main walls were rebuilt in a natural style. Ventilation was secured by digging a cavity 0.70 meters deep beneath the tar-sealed earthen floor . . . No stairs or mantelpieces existed in the old construction . . . window panes were brought in from Marseille, paving-stones from Clamart, tiles from Bourgogne, a garage was erected in the garden, large French-windows were installed . . . The kitchen is 100% modern, as are the bathrooms, etc.' BUT: 'The woodwork still in good condition was incorporated into the new building'; AND 'the masonry in the entranceway was carefully protected during demolition: the tiles and stones were used again' (*La Maison Française*, May 1963). Photographs show what actually remains of the old farm after being 'sounded out by the architect and his unequivocal discernment' — three wooden beams and two stones. As if to say, on this stone I will build my house in the country; as if the value of the entire edifice rests on these few, symbolically inaugural portal stones; as if they could exonerate the whole project of all the compromises that modernity strikes with nature in its intention, however innocent, of making life more comfortable. The architect, having become lord of the farm, has in reality built himself the modern house of his dreams: but modernity is not sufficient to lend value to this house, to turn it into a 'dwelling' — it needs more being. Just as a church is not truly sacred until it has been sanctified with a few bones or relics, so the architect cannot feel at home (in the true sense of not having dispelled something like anguish) until he can discern, deep within his new walls, the minute but sublime presence of a stone testifying to past generations. Without these stones, the oil heating and the garage (surmounted by an alpine garden) would — alas! — be simply what they are: the sad necessities of comfort. Not only are the functional amenities exonerated by the authenticity of these stones, but to some extent so too are the culturally exotic furnishings (despite their 'excellent taste and totally unrustic appearance'): opaline lamps, reproduction wicker chairs, an armchair covered with a Dalmatian rug 'once thrown over the back of a donkey', an antique mirror, etc. The ruses of this cultural bad conscience even lead to a strange paradox: whereas the garage is concealed beneath a fake alpine garden, a real rustic accessory like the warming-pan is said 'to be there not simply as decoration, but to serve a purpose!' 'It is used in winter!' In the first instance the material function is disguised, and in the second the essential function is reinstated by an acrobatic feat: in a house with oil heating, a warming-pan is perfectly useless. Then, it is no longer a real one, but simply a cultural sign; this unwarranted and cultural warming-pan becomes an all too faithful image of the whole vanity of this house and its attempt to retrieve a state of nature — it also becomes an all too faithful image of the architect himself, who basically has no business being there, whose real social existence is elsewhere, whose *being* is elsewhere, and for whom nature is nothing but a cultural indulgence. While this is quite acceptable when one treats it like that, such was not his intention. As this warming-pan serves no purpose, it is merely a sign of wealth: it belongs to the order of having and of prestige, not to the order of being. This is why it is said to serve a purpose, while those truly useful objects like the oil heater or garage are carefully camouflaged, as though indelible stains in the bosom of this nature. Hence the warming-pan is strictly mythological, as is the entire house for that matter (although on a totally different functional or real level, since it quite precisely fulfils a desire for comfort and clean air). If the architect, instead of entirely demolishing the old dwelling and replacing it with something more comfortable, chose to preserve its stones and wooden beams, it is because the refined and impeccable functionalism of his country home would have been an inauthentic and profoundly dissatisfying experience for him.

Man is not 'at home' in the functional milieu. He needs, in order to make it livable, something like that splinter of the True Cross which sanctified a church, something like a talisman, like a fragment of absolute reality which would be at the heart of the real, and enshrined in the real. Such is the bygone object, which always assumes, in the womb of the environment, the value of an embryo or mother cell. Through it, a splintered being identifies with that original and ideal condition of an embryo, degenerating to the centered and microcosmic condition of being before birth. These fetishised objects are thus not accessories, nor are they simply cultural signs among others: they symbolise internal transcendence — that phantasmic core of reality upon which all mythological and individual consciousness feeds; that phantasmic projection of a fragment which would be equivalent to the ego, around which the rest of the world revolves; that sublime phantasm of authenticity which always ends up just short of reality (*sub limina*). The bygone object, like the relic[8] whose function it secularises, reorganises the world into a form of constellation, as opposed to the extensive functional organisation, endeavouring to preserve against it the profound and undoubtedly essential unreality of one's innermost being.

Symbolising a scheme for inscribing value in a closed circle and in the perfect tense, the mythological object is no longer a discourse with others, but indeed with oneself. Like islands or legends, these objects transport man from the here and now back to his infancy, and even earlier still — to a time before birth where ambience stood as a direct metaphor for pure subjectivity, and where this ambience was nothing but a perfect discourse of being with itself.

The Synchronic, The Diachronic, The Anachronic

In private surroundings, these objects constitute an even more private sphere: they are less objects of possession than those of symbolic intercession, like ancestors — for ancestors are *privatissime*. They offer an escape from everyday life, since no escape is so absolute as that into time,[9] and no escape is so profound as that into one's own childhood. Perhaps this metaphorical escape occurs in every aesthetic sensibility — but whereas the work of art as such requires a rational process of reading, the bygone object needs no reading: it is 'legendary', since it is defined first and foremost by its quotient of myth and authenticity. Whatever its epoch, style, model or series, whether valuable or not, genuine or fake, none of this changes its lived specificity. It is neither true nor false: it is 'perfect'. It is neither interior nor exterior: it is an 'alibi'. It is neither synchronic nor diachronic (it can neither be inserted into an ambient structure, nor into a temporal one): it is *anachronic*. In relation to whoever possesses it, it is neither an attribute of the verb 'to be' nor an object of the verb 'to have', but belongs instead to the grammatical category of the internal object, which inflects almost tautologically the substance of a verb.

The functional object is absent being. Reality precludes it from regressing to that 'perfect' dimension from which one has only to proceed in order to be. And if it appears so impoverished, it is because, whatever its worth, qualities or prestige, it conforms and will always conform to the loss of the image of the Father and the Mother. Highly functional but low in meaning, it is referred to the latest trend, dissipating itself in everyday life; whereas the mythological object, low in function and highly meaningful, is referred to ancestry, or even to the absolute anteriority of nature. At the level of lived reality, these contradictory devotions coexist within the same system as complementarities — this is why the architect can have in his possession oil heating as well as a rustic warming-pan; or, elsewhere, why a paperback book can coexist with its rare or old edition, an electric washing machine with an old clothes mangle, a functional built-in cupboard with a conspicuous Spanish sideboard.[10] This complementarity is epitomised by the now standard dual property: an apartment in town and a house in the country.[11]

This duel of objects is fundamentally a battle within consciousness: it indicates a shortcoming and the attempt to overcome this shortcoming by way of regression. In a civilisation where the the real tends to be controlled exclusively and systematically through its *synchronic* and *diachronic* organisation, there appears (at the level of objects as much as at the level of social behaviour and structures) a third, *anachronic* dimension. Testifying to the relative failure of the system, this regressive dimension nonetheless takes refuge in the system, by which it paradoxically permits it to function.

The Inverse Projection: Technical Objects Among The Primitive

This equivocal coexistence of the modern with the antique, of the functional with the 'decorative' only really occurs at a certain stage of economic development — that of industrial production and its concrete saturation of the surrounding world. Those less privileged, 'primitive' social sectors (farm workers and labourers) want nothing to do with the antiquated and aspire to the functional. Yet the two alternatives exist in a certain relationship: when a 'savage' pounces on a watch or fountain pen, simply because it is a 'Western' object, here we encounter a kind of comic absurdity — he doesn't attribute to the object its meaning, but voraciously appropriates it in an infantile relation and as a phantasm of power. The object no longer has a function but a virtue: it is a sign. But isn't this process of impulsive acculturation and magical appropriation identical to the compulsion of the 'civilised' for 16th-century woodcuts or icons? What both 'savage' and 'civilised' seek to obtain, in the form of an object, is 'virtue' — the former as a guarantee of technical modernity, the latter as a guarantee of ancestry. Yet this 'virtue' is not identical in each case. With the 'underdeveloped', the image of the Father invoked is one of *Power* (namely, colonial power[12]); whereas, with the 'civilised' and their nostalgia, it is one of *Heredity* and worth. It is a mythic projection in the first instance, and a mythic degeneration in the second. A myth of power versus a myth of origin: what man lacks is always invested in the object — while power is fetishised by the 'underdeveloped' in technical objects, heredity and authenticity are fetishised by the 'civilised' in mythological objects.

Even so, it is the same fetishism: at the very limit, every bygone object is desirable *simply because it has survived and thus becomes a sign of prior existence*. It is this anguished curiosity about our origins that causes us to juxtapose functional objects as signs of our present mastery with mythological objects as signs of an earlier dominion. For we want at one and the same time to be only *of* ourselves and to be *from* someone: to succeed the Father and to proceed from the Father. Perhaps man will never be able to choose between the Promethean ambition of reorganising the world and of taking the place of the Father, and that of descending by grace of filiation from an original being. Objects themselves testify to this unresolved ambiguity. Some mediate the present, while others mediate the past—and the value of the latter concerns incompletion. It is as if bygone objects were prefixed by a nobiliary particle, and as if their inherited nobility compensated for the premature obsolescence of modern objects. Formerly the elderly were revered because they were 'closer to God', richer in experience. Today our technical civilisation has renounced the wisdom of the aged, deferring instead to the solidity of old things, since they alone have a fixed and secure value.

The Market for Antiques

This is nothing more than an indulgence in cultural snobbery and prestige, as in the example given by Vance Packard (*The Status Seekers*, Harmondsworth, 1961) where chic Bostonians adorn their windows with old blue-tinted glass: 'the defectiveness of those panes is highly cherished. The panes were part of a shipment of inferior glass foisted off on Americans by English glaziers more than three centuries ago' (p. 68). Or else: 'When the suburbanite aspires to move up into the "lower upper class, he will buy antiques—symbols of old social position bought with new money"' (p. 67). Because, finally: social prestige can be expressed in myriad ways (cars, modern houses, etc.). But then why does it choose to signify itself with the past?[13] All acquired value tends to transform itself into inherited value, into a mark of grace. But once blood, birth and titles lose their ideological value, superiority comes to be represented by material signs: furniture, articles, jewelry and art from all periods and all countries. A whole forest of signs and idols 'with documentation' (no matter whether they are authentic or not), a whole magical thicket of genuine or fake furniture, manuscripts and icons swamps the market in service of the well-to-do. The entire past enters the cycle of consumption; it even forms a kind of black market. The whole of the New Hebrides, Romanic Spain and flea markets combined are no longer capable of feeding the voracious appetite of Western bourgeois interiors for primitivism and nostalgia. An increasing number of paintings and statues of the Virgin or the saints disappear from museums and churches. They are bought illegally by wealthy owners of residences too new to give them profound satisfaction. And finally, there is this cultural paradox, but economic truth: that only the counterfeit can now quench this thirst for 'authenticity'.

Cultural Neo-Imperialism

The same basic imperialism exists in the subjugation of nature through technical and domestic objects as in the subjugation of cultures through bygone objects. The same private imperialism exists in the accumulation of a functionally domesticated milieu as in the accumulation of domesticated signs of the past — those essentially sacred, but desacralised, ancestral objects required to lend a glow of sacredness (or historicity) to a domesticity devoid of history.

Thus does the entire past, as a repository of consumer forms added to the repository of present forms, come to constitute a transcendent sphere of fashion.

II. THE MARGINAL SYSTEM: THE COLLECTION

Among other things, Littré defines the object as: 'Anything that is the cause or subject of a passion. Figuratively and in the broadest sense: the object of affection.'

Let us admit that our everyday objects are indeed the objects of a passion, the one for private ownership — a quotidian passion whose investment of affect is in no way inferior to that of human passions, since it often prevails over all other passions, and sometimes to their exclusion. We are only dimly aware of the fundamental role that this tempered and diffuse passion plays in regulating the equilibrium of subjective and group life, in the very decisions of life. Objects are in this sense, beyond the use to which they are put, and at a given moment, something else profoundly relative to the subject: not only as a material body that resists me, but as a mental enclosure over which I rule, a thing for which I am the meaning, a property, a passion.

The Object Abstracted of Its Function

If I use a refrigerator for cooling purposes, then the mediation is a practical one: it is not an object, but a refrigerator. To this extent, I don't possess it. Possession never applies to a tool, since the latter relates me to the world — possession always applies to the object *abstracted of its function and thus made relative to the subject*. At this level, all objects of possession participate in the same *abstraction* and relate to one another insofar as they relate only to the subject. It is thanks to the subject's attempt to constitute them into a world or private totality that they thus constitute themselves into a system.

Thus every object has two functions: one of being practical, the other of being possessed. The former belongs to the domain of the subject's practical totalisation of the world, whereas the latter belongs to subject's attempt at abstract totalisation of himself outside the world. These two functions are inversely proportional to one another. At one extreme, the strictly practical object takes on the social status of a machine. At the other extreme, the pure object — devoid of function, or abstracted of its use — has a strictly subjective status: it becomes the object of collection. It ceases to be a rug, table, compass or curio to become an 'object'; a collector would say a 'beautiful object', not a beautiful figurine. When the object is no longer specified by its function, it becomes subjectively qualified; but then, all objects are equal in possession, in this passionate abstraction. A single object is not enough: there always has to be a succession of objects, with the ultimate aim of having a complete set. This is why the possession of any particular object is at once always so satisfying and so frustrating: a whole series enhances and disturbs its possession. Something similar to this happens at the sexual level: if the aim of amorous relations is singularity, then amorous possession as such can only be satisfied by a succession of objects, by the repetition of the same object, or by the presumption of all of them. Only a more or less complex organisation of objects related one to another gives any one of them sufficient abstraction to enable it to be incorporated by the subject in the abstract experience that is the sensation of possession.

The collection is this organisation. The normal environment itself betrays an ambiguous status: here the functional unceasingly breaks down into the subjective, and possession becomes confused with use, in a forever frustrated attempt at total integration. On the other hand, the collection provides us with a model: this is where the passionate enterprise of possession triumphs, and where the quotidian prose of objects turns into poetry, into an unconscious and victorious discourse.

The Object-Passion

'The taste for collecting,' according to Maurice Rheims, 'is a kind of passionate game' (*La Vie étrange des objets*, 1959, p. 36). For the child, arranging, ordering and manipulating is the most rudimentary form of mastering the external world. The active phase of collecting seems to occur between the ages of seven and twelve, in that period of latency between prepubescence and puberty. The taste for collecting tends to disappear with the onset of puberty, sometimes reappearing soon after.

Those who manifest this passion later on are most frequently men over forty. In brief, a relation to the sexual conjuncture is everywhere visible; the collection emerges as a powerful compensation during the crucial phases of sexual development. It always precludes active genital sexuality, but it is not simply a substitute for it. It constitutes in relation to it a regression to the anal phase, which is expressed by conduct of accumulation, orderliness, aggressive retention, etc. Collecting behaviour is not equivalent to sexual activity; its aim is not the satisfaction of a drive (like fetishism), but it can nonetheless achieve a reactive satisfaction that is as intense. Here the object entirely assumes the meaning of an object of affection. 'The passion for an object encourages the belief that it is something created by God . . . [T]he collector of porcelain eggs . . . believes that God never created a form as beautiful or more unique, and that He conceived it for the sole pleasure of collectors . . .' (M. Rheims, p. 39). '"I'm crazy about this object," they declare. And all of them without exception, even when a fetishist perversion is not involved, surround their collections with an air of clandestinity, protectiveness, secrecy and mendacity, exhibiting all the characteristics of a guilty relationship. It is this passionate game that makes such regressive behaviour sublime, justifying the belief that any person who does not collect something is simply a cretin and a poor excuse for a human being.'[14]

So this sublime state is not attained by the collector through the nature of the objects he collects (which vary according to age, profession, and social class), but through his own fanaticism — a fanaticism identical in both the wealthy lover of Persian miniatures and the collector of matchboxes. For this reason, the distinction made between the two — that the amateur loves objects for their diverse singular charms and that the collector loves them as a function of their succession in a series — is not relevant. Pleasure for both of them comes from what profit possession derives, on the one hand, from the absolute singularity of each element, which makes it the equivalent of a being, and fundamentally of the subject himself; and, on the other, from the possibility of a series, and thus of an indefinite play of substitutions — a qualitative quintessence and a quantitative manipulation. If possession is the product of a confusion of the senses (touch and sight), of an intimacy with the preferred object, then it is just as much the product of searching, ordering, manipulating, and combining. In other words, it has about it the fragrance of the harem, whose whole charm is that of a series of intimacies (always with a preferred object) and of intimacy with a series.

Man surrounded by his objects is *par excellence* master of a secret seraglio. In the field of human relations, which are unique and conflictual, this fusion of absolute singularity and an indefinite series is not permitted, which is why they are a source of continual anguish. Whereas the field of objects, made up of successive and homologous terms, is comforting—of course at the cost of an illusory reality, of abstraction and regression: but that hardly matters. 'The object,' according to Maurice Rheims, 'is for man a sort of impassive dog which receives and returns caresses after a fashion, or rather reflects them like a mirror faithful not to real images, but desired images' (p. 59).

The Most Beautiful Domestic Animal

This image of a dog is apt: pets are a species intermediary between beings and objects. The pathetic existence of dogs, cats, birds, tortoises or canaries indicates the failure of human relations and the recourse to a narcissistic domestic universe, where subjectivity can be fulfilled in complete tranquility. Let us observe in passing that these animals are sexless (they are sometimes neutered for domestic purposes), being as devoid of a sex, though living beings, as objects; it is at this cost that they can be emotionally reassuring, it is at the cost of a real or symbolic castration that they can play, at the side of their owners, the role of regulators for the anguish of castration—a role eminently played by all the objects that surround us, for the object is itself the perfect domestic animal. It is the only 'being' whose qualities exalt rather than delimit my identity. Objects are, in the plural, the only existing beings with whom coexistence is truly possible, since their differences do not set them one against the other as happens with living beings, but obediently converge around me, to be added together without difficulty in consciousness. The object is that which is most easily both 'personalised' and rendered into account. Nothing is excluded from this subjective accountancy, since everything in it can be possessed, invested, or, as with the game of collecting, ranked, sorted, and classified. The object is indeed a mirror in the strict sense: the images it reflects cannot but form a non-contradictory succession. And it is a perfect mirror, since it reflects not real images, but desired images. In brief, it is a dog for whom faithfulness is all that remains—for I can look at it without it looking at me. *This is why everything incapable of being invested in human relations is invested in objects*. It is in order to 're-collect' himself in them that man so willingly regresses. But let us not be deceived by this re-collection and by the whole emotional literature on inanimate objects. This re-collection is a regression, and this passion is a passionate escape. Objects undoubtedly play the role of regulators in everyday life, abolishing in themselves many neuroses, and gathering up into themselves much of the tension and energy of mourning. This is what gives them a 'soul', and what makes them 'ours'. But it is also what turns them into the setting for a persistent mythology, the ideal setting for a balancing of neuroses.

A Serial Game

Yet this is a poor mediation: how can consciousness be taken in by it? This is where the cunning of subjectivity operates. The possessed object is never a poor mediation, but always one of absolute singularity: not really because possession of the 'rare' or 'unique' object is the ideal aim of appropriation, but because, on the one hand, the test of a particular object's uniqueness is not carried out in the real world, and because, on the other, subjectivity can quite easily get along without it. The object's specific quality or exchange value is related to the cultural and social domain. What makes it absolutely singular is on the contrary my possession of it, since it permits me to recognise myself in it as an absolutely singular being — a majestic tautology, but it nevertheless constitutes the whole complexity of the relation to objects, its derisory complaisance, its illusory but intense gratification.[15] Better still: this closed circle can also govern human relations (however less easily), but what is impossible at the inter-subjective level is possible here. A particular object can never oppose the multiplication of the very process of narcissistic projection onto an indefinite number of objects; on the contrary, it prescribes it, thus lending itself to a total environment, to a totalisation of images of self, which is the precise miracle of the collection. For one always collects oneself.

We can now better understand the structure of the possessive system: the collection is the product of a succession of terms, but whose final term is the person of the collector. Conversely, the latter is only constituted as such by successively substituting himself for each term of the collection. At the sociological level, a homologous structure can be found in the system of the model and the series. In both cases, we can see that the series or the collection are constituents in the possession of the object, which is to say in the reciprocal integration of the object and the person.[16]

From Quantity to Quality: The Unique Object

One could argue that this hypothesis does not apply to the amateur's passion for some particular object. But it is evident that the unique object is precisely nothing other than the final term which sums up the entire genre, or the privileged term of a whole paradigm (no matter whether virtual, obscure or inferred); in a word, the emblem of the series.

La Bruyère, in those portraits where curiosity is depicted as a passion, describes for us a collector of engravings: 'I suffer,' says the latter, 'from an acute affliction, which will eventually force me to give up engravings. I have all of Callot, except for one, which in truth is not one of his better works. On the contrary, it is one of his worst, but it would complete the Callot collection. I have laboured for twenty years to uncover this engraving, and I am finally beginning to despair of ever finding it. Life is cruel!' In this arithmetic logic we can discern an actual equivalence between the whole series minus one and the final term absent from the series. [17] This term, without which the series is nothing, symbolically sums it up: hence it assumes a strange quality, quintessential for the whole quantitive alignment. It is specified as a unique object due to its terminal position, thus giving the illusion of a particular finality. It might indeed amount to this; but we can see that it is ceaselessly led from quantity to quality, and that the value concentrated on this solitary signifier actually extends across the whole chain of intermediary signifiers in the paradigm. This is what one might call the symbolism of the object, in the etymological sense (of *symbolein*) in which a chain of significations can be summed up in a single one of its terms. The object is a symbol: not of some external agency or value, but above all, of the whole series of objects of which it is a term (as well as of the person for whom it is an object).

La Bruyère's example discloses a further rule, which is that the object only achieves exceptional value in its absence. It is not simply a question of covetousness. *It must be asked whether the collection is meant to be completed*, and whether its incompletion doesn't play an essential and even positive role, since it is through this incompletion that the subject objectively regains possession of himself: whereas the presence of the final object would in a profound sense signify the death of the subject, the absence of this term allows him merely to play out his own death by representing it in an object, which is to say to conjure it. This incompletion is experienced as suffering; but it is also the rupture enabling him to avoid completing the collection, which would signify the definitive elision of reality. Let us therefore compliment La Bruyère's amateur on having failed to find the last Callot, for had he done so he would have ceased to be a man still in the fullness and passion of life. And let us say that delirium sets in once the collection reaches its conclusion and is no longer organised around this absent term.

Another anecdote (as told by Maurice Rheims) may help to corroborate this phenomenon. A bibliophile who owned the only extant copies of books learnt one day that a bookshop in New York was selling a volume identical to one already in his possession. He immediately rushed to the shop and bought it, summoned a bailiff to witness the burning of the second copy and draw up an affidavit of its destruction, then attached it to his own copy which had again become unique, and slept peacefully. So is this a negation of the series? Only in appearance: in reality, the only extant copy was invested with the value of all potential copies, since, by destroying the second copy, the bibliophile did no more than restore the perfection of a compromised symbol. Whether denied, ignored, destroyed or virtual, the series is always there. In the lowliest of everyday objects as in the grandest of rare objects, it provides impetus for the passionate game of ownership. Without it, no play would be possible, thus no possession either, and, strictly speaking, no object. A truly and absolutely unique object, one without antecedent, without dispersal in any series whatsoever, is unthinkable. It can no more exist than a pure sound. For just as harmonic series provide sounds with their perceptual quality, so do more or less complex paradigmatic series, in the sphere of human relations of mastery as well as playfulness, provide objects with their symbolic quality.

Objects and Habits: The Watch

Every object is situated halfway between a specific use or function, which is something like its manifest discourse, and its absorption into a collection or series, where it becomes the term of a latent and repetitive discourse — the most elementary and tenacious of discourses. This discursive system of objects is homologous with that of habits. [18]

Habit is discontinuity and repetition (and not, as common usage suggests, continuity). It is by dividing up time into 'habitual' patterns that we resolve the anguish which its continuity and the absolute singularity of events can cause us. Similarly, it is by their discontinuous integration into series that we put objects at our disposal, that we possess them. This is the very discourse of subjectivity and its privileged register of objects — interposing, between ourselves and the irreversible movement of the world, a barrier of discontinuity that is classifiable, reversible, and repeatable at will, our own little private corner of the world manipulable by hand and mind, dispelling anguish. Objects not only help us to master the world, by their insertion into instrumental series; they also help us, *by their insertion into mental series*, to master time, making it discontinuous and organising it in the same way as habits, submitting it to the very constraints of association which govern the arrangement of space.

The watch is a good example of this discontinual and 'habitual' function.[19] It typifies the twofold way in which we experience objects. On the one hand, it informs us about objective time — for chronometric exactitude is the very dimension of practical constraints, social exteriority, and death. But at the same time as it subjects us to an irreducible temporality, the watch as object also helps us to have time to ourselves. Just as a car 'eats up' the miles, so does the watch-object consume time.[20] By concretising and dividing up time, it turns it into an object of consumption. Time is no longer that hazardous dimension of praxis: it is a domesticated quantity. Not only has knowing the time become a staple diet or reassurance for civilised people, but also 'having' the time in an object of one's own, having it continually registered before one's eyes. Time is no longer in the home, in the ticking heart of a clock, but is always registered, in the watch, with the same physical satisfaction as intestinal regularity. Time reveals itself, through the watch, to be the very dimension of my objectification, and altogether to be a domestic product. Any object whatsoever would for that matter support this analysis of the recuperation of the very dimension of objective constraints: the watch, by its direct relation to time, is simply the clearest example of this.

The Object and Time: The Planned Cycle

The problematic of time is essential to the collection. 'A phenomenon often accompanying the passion for collecting,' according to Maurice Rheims, 'is the loss of a sense of present time' (p. 42). But is this simply a matter of nostalgic escapism? Someone who identifies with Louis XVI down to the legs of his armchairs or who has a passion for 16th-century snuff-boxes clearly isolates himself from the present through a historical reference. But this reference is secondary compared with the systematic experience of the collection. The underlying power of collected objects does not actually stem from their singularity or distinct historicity; it is not for this reason that the time of the collection is not real time, *but that the organisation of the collection is itself a substitute for time*. This is undoubtedly the basic function of the collection: to resolve real time into a systematic dimension. The collection can lead to wider relations of taste, curiosity, prestige and social discourse (always restricted to a group of initiates), but in any case it remains first and foremost a 'pass-time' in the true sense. It quite simply abolishes time. Or rather: the collection, by itemising time into immutable terms which it can mobilise in reverse, represents the perpetual recurrence of a planned cycle, where man, departing from any of its terms in the certainty of returning to it, plays with infallibility the ceaseless game of birth and death.

This is why the environment of private objects and their possession — whose epitome is the collection — is a dimension of our lives as essential as it is imaginary, as essential as dreams. It has been said that if someone were experimentally prevented from dreaming, then a severe psychic disturbance would rapidly ensue. It is certain that disorientation would be as immediate if someone were deprived of that regression or escapism in the game of possession, if he were prevented from upholding his own planned discourse, from inflecting his self through objects outside of time. We cannot live in absolute singularity, in an irreversibility whose sign is the moment of birth. It is this irreversible movement from birth to death that objects help us to resolve.

This equilibrium is understandably neurotic, as is this remedy against anguish regressive, since time is objectively irreversible and since even objects, whose function is to preserve us from time, are swept away by it; the defence mechanism of discontinuity at the level of objects is understandably always thrown into question, since the world of men is continuity. But is it possible to talk about normality or abnormality? The refuge in synchronic closure might be viewed as a denial of the real and as an escape when one considers that in the object is invested what 'should' be invested in human relations — but such is the cost of the immense power of objects as regulators. Objects today are fast becoming, with the disappearance of all religious and ideological authority, the consolation of consolations, a quotidian mythology absorbing the anguish of time and death.

Let us brush aside here the spontaneous mythology which would have it that man prolongs and perpetuates himself in his objects. This refuge process is not one of immortality, perpetuity or survival through a *reflection in objects* (in which man has never fundamentally believed), but the far more complex game of 'recycling' birth and death through *a system of objects*. What man seeks through objects is not the guarantee of his own perpetuation, *but that of every moment continuously living out the process of his existence in a controlled and cyclical form, and thus of symbolically transcending that real existence whose irreversible event eludes him.*

Here we are not far from that reel (in Freud's analysis) by which a child, in making it disappear and reappear, alternatively lives out the absence and presence of his mother — *fort-da, fort-da* — and responds to the anguish of absence by the reel's endlessly cyclic reappearance. The symbolic significance of this game for the series is readily apparent, from which one could therefore conclude that the object is *that by which we mourn ourselves* — in the sense that it represents our own death, but

transcended (symbolically) because we possess it, because it is by intro-
jecting it in the work of mourning, which is to say by integrating it into
a series which 'works' at constantly re-enacting this cycle of absence and
re-emergence from absence, that we resolve the agonising event of real
absence and death. We apply this work of mourning to ourselves at
every moment of everyday life with the aid of objects, and this enables
us to live a life, regressively of course, but a life nonetheless. The man
who collects is dead, but he literally perpetuates himself through a
collection which, even in this life, repeats him indefinitely in the hereafter, *by integrating death itself into a series or cycle*. Here we could again
make an analogy with dreams: if each object is, through its function
(practical, cultural, social), the mediation of a *wish*, then it is also, as
one term among others of that systematic game just described, the
manifestation of a *desire*—the latter setting in motion, across an indefinite chain of signifiers, the indefinite repetition or substitution of
oneself through death and beyond it. And if the function of dreams is to
preserve the continuity of sleep, then it is through a similar sort of
compromise that objects preserve the continuity of life.[21]

The Sequestered Object: Jealousy

At the end of this regressive movement, the passion for objects ter-
minates in pure jealousy. The most profound satisfaction of possession
thus derives from the value the object may have for others and from
depriving them of it. This jealousy complex characteristic of fanatical
collecting also dominates, all things considered, the common reflex of
ownership. It is a strongly anal-sadistic scheme that leads to the seques-
tering of beauty for one's sole pleasure: this perverse sexual behaviour
filters through to most relations with objects.

What does the sequestered object represent? (Its objective value is
secondary, since its seclusion comprises its whole charm.) If one doesn't
lend one's car, fountain pen or wife, it is because jealousy turns these
objects into narcissistic equivalents of one's ego: if any of these objects
are lost or damaged, it is castration. More to the point, one doesn't lend
one's phallus. What the jealous lock away and keep to themselves in the
image of an object is their own libido, which they attempt to conjure
through a system of seclusion—the same system according to which the
collection resolves the anguish of death. They become castrated
through the anguish of their own sexuality, or rather they forestall by
symbolic castration— sequestration—the anguish of real castration.[22]
This desperate enterprise forms the horrible pleasure of jealousy. One
is always jealous of one's self. It is one's self that one watches over and
protects. It is in one's self that one takes pleasure.

This jealous pleasure clearly takes place in a context of absolute frustration, since systematic regression never totally effaces consciousness of the real world and of the bankruptcy of such behaviour. It is the same with the collection: its sovereignty is fragile, since the sovereignty of the real world lingers behind it and continually menaces it. But this frustration itself forms part of the system. It is frustration as much as satisfaction that mobilises it — a frustration never referring to the world, but to some ulterior term, with frustration and satisfaction succeeding one another in a cycle. The neurotic snowballing of the system is due to this component of frustration. The series gathers ever greater momentum, the differences wear down and the machinery of substitution accelerates. The system can go on like this to the point of destruction, which is the subject's self-destruction. Maurice Rheims cites examples where such collections are violently 'put to death', in a kind of suicide brought about by the impossibility of ever circumscribing death. In the system of jealousy, it is not unusual for the subject to end up destroying the sequestered object or being, due to a sense of the impossibility of completely averting the misfortunes of the world and of his own sexuality. Here passion reaches its logical and illogical end.[23]

The Fragmented Object: Perversion

The efficacy of this possessive system is directly linked to its regressive character — for this regression is linked to the very mode of perversion. If perversion in matters of objects reveals itself most clearly as a form of fetishist fixation, then nothing prevents us from seeing throughout the whole system how, in organising itself according to similar ends and modes, the possession/passion of the object is, let us say, *a tempered form of sexual perversion*. Just as possession operates in fact through the discontinuity of a series (whether real or virtual) and through the selection of a privileged term, so is sexual perversion the result of an inability to grasp the other, except discontinuously, as the object of desire in its total individual singularity: the other is transformed into a paradigm of various erotic parts of the body, objectively fixing on one of them. This woman is no longer a woman, but a sexual organ, breasts, belly, thighs, voice or face — whatever the preference.[24] From that point onwards she becomes an 'object', constituting a series whose different terms are ranked by desire, whose real signified is no longer at all the person loved, but the subject himself in his narcissistic subjectivity, collecting-eroticising himself and turning amorous relations into a discourse with himself.

This is amply demonstrated by the opening sequence of Jean Luc

Godard's *Contempt*, where the dialogue of this 'nude' scene unfolds as follows:

'Do you love my feet?' she asks. (Note that throughout this scene she examines herself in a mirror, which is not insignificant: she evaluates herself as seen through her own image, and thus as already discontinuous in space.)

'Yes, I love them.'

'Do you love my legs?'

'Yes.'

'And my thighs?'

'Yes,' he again replies, 'I love them.' (And so it continues, all the way up to her hair.)

'So you love everything about me.'

'Yes, I love everything about you.'

'Me too, Paul,' she says, summing up the situation.

It may be that the filmmakers have glimpsed here the lucid algebra of love demystified. It nonetheless remains that this absurd reconstitution of desire is inhumanity itself. Disintegrated into a series composed of her body, this woman become pure object is then incorporated into a series of all women-objects, in which she is only one term among others. The only activity possible within the logic of this system is the game of substitution. It is what we have identified as the very stimulus for satisfaction in the collection.

This fragmentation of the object into discontinuous details in an autoerotic system of perversion is halted in amorous relations by the other's living integrity;[25] whereas it is the rule where material objects are concerned, particularly those manufactured objects which are sufficiently complex, to lend themselves to mental deconstruction. As regards the automobile, for example, one says: *MY* brakes, *MY* mudguard, *MY* steering wheel. Or: *I* am braking, *I* am turning, *I* am driving off. All these organs or functions can be ascribed in isolation to the person by the use of the possessive case. This does not involve personalisation at the social level, but a process belonging to the order of projection — not the order of having, but of being. The same confusion was not possible with the horse, even though it provided man with an instrument of remarkable power and transcendence. This is because the horse is not made up of components; first and foremost, it has a sex. One can say: my horse, my wife, but that is where the possessive pronoun ends. Whatever has a sex is resistant to projection as fragments, and thus to the form of appropriation we have identified as an autoerotic passion, and ultimately as a perversion.[26] Confronted by a living being, one can say *MY* but not *I*, as happens with the symbolic appropriation of the car's functions and organs. Such regression is impossible. The horse can be strongly invested as a symbol (that of the sexual straddle, but also of the wisdom of the Centaur, its head being a terrifying phantasm linked to the image of the father, but its composure also representing the protective power of Chiron the pedagogue) — but it is never invested like that reductive, narcissistic, weaker, and more infantile type of ego projection into the structural detail of a car (according to an almost identical analogy with the disassociated elements and functions of the human body). If the horse has a symbolic dynamism, then it is precisely to the extent that identification with its functional and organic detail is impossible, as is the exhaustion of its relations through an autoerotic 'discourse' on its disparate terms.

This compartmentalisation and this regression presupposes a technical process, but one autonomised at the level of the partial object. Thus the woman resolved into a syntagm of different erogenous zones is doomed to a merely functional gratification, thus one that corresponds to an erotic technique — an objectifying, ritualising technique which masks the anguish of personal relations, and which also serves as a real (gestural, effectual) alibi at the very core of the phantasmatic system of perversion. Indeed, every mental system needs 'credibility', a reference to the real, a technical 'reason', an alibi. Thus, the accelerator in 'I am accelerating', or the headlight in 'my headlight', or the entire automobile in 'my car' are real technical supports for a whole narcissistic recuperation that falls short of the real. The same goes for the deployment of erotic technique as such: at this level, we are no longer in the genital order of emergence into the real and into pleasure, but in the anal and regressive order of a systematic series, whose sole alibi is the erotic gesture.

We can see how the technical process is far from being always 'objective'. It is objective when socialised, taken up by technology, and informing new structures. In the everyday domain, on the other hand, it presents a field always conducive to regressive phantasms, because the possibility of fragmentation always surfaces there. Assembled and mounted, the elements of a technical object are implicitly coherent. But this structure is always unstable before the mind: it is linked to the external world through its function, whereas it is formal for the *psyche*. At any moment, this hierarchy of structural elements can break down, becoming equivalent to one another in a paradigmatic system where the subject inflects himself. The object is always potentially discontinuous, and is easily made discontinuous by thought — and all the more so since the object (especially the technical object) is no longer, as it once was, put together by some human agency or force. If the car constitutes, as opposed to the horse, such a perfect object for narcissistic manipulation, it is because the mastery of a horse requires muscular strength, coordination, and a sense of balance — whereas the mastery of a car is simplified, functional, and abstract.

From A Serial Motivation to A Real Motivation

Throughout this whole analysis, we have disregarded the precise nature of the objects collected: we have concentrated on their systematic aspects, without taking into account their thematic ones. But collecting old masters is clearly not the same as collecting cigar bands. At the outset, we should recognise that the concept of collection (*colligere*: to select and assemble) is distinguishable from that of accumulation. Its basic phase is the accumulation of materials: hoarding paper, stockpiling provisions — activities situated halfway between oral introjection and anal retention — and then the serial accumulation of identical objects. The collection, however, is directed toward culture: its aim is differentiated objects, often with exchange value, which are either 'objects' of conservation, barter, social ritual, or exhibition — perhaps even a source of advantage. These objects have a variety of purposes. Without ceasing to lose their internal relations, this game with objects includes external, social and human, ones.

Yet, even when there is a strong external motivation, the collection never escapes from internal systematisation, and at best forms a compromise between the two: even if the collection develops into a discourse with others, it is always primarily a discourse with oneself. A serial motivation is everywhere visible. Studies show that buyers of book collections (*10/18*, *Que sais-je?*), once hooked on a collection, continue to purchase titles of no interest to them: variation in the series suffices to create a formal interest in place of a real one. The constraints of association are the only motivation in this purchase. It is not unlike the behaviour of readers who find it difficult to read unless surrounded by all their books: reading as a specific activity thus tends to disappear. Further still, what matters is less the book than the moment of placing it among others on the library shelf. Conversely, having 'lost the thread' of a collection, the buyer can only pick it up again with great difficulty: he will no longer even purchase titles of real interest to him. These observations suffice to clearly distinguish the two motivations, which are mutually exclusive, and which can only coexist as a form of compromise — with a definite tendency to favour, through inertia, the serial motivation over the dialectical motivation of interest.[27]

But the pure collection can also lead to real interests. The person who began by systematically purchasing the whole of *Que sais-je?* often ends up organising his collection around a single theme, like music or sociology. Once he has crossed a certain quantitative threshold in their accumulation, he is able to become more selective. But there is no absolute rule here. One can collect with equal regressive fanaticism old masters and camembert labels; whereas stamp collecting among children is a continual source of exchange. One cannot infer a collection's link to the real world from its thematic complexity. At the very most, this complexity can provide a clue or guide.

What distinguishes the collection from pure accumulation is as much its cultural complexity as its deficiency or incompletion. Incompletion, or the absence of a particular object, is indeed always an absolute requirement. And this requirement, expressing itself as a search, passion, or message to others,[28] suffices to break the mortal spell of the collection, where the subject is plunged into an abyss of pure fascination. This was amply demonstrated by a television program: each time a collector presented his collection to the audience, he mentioned a quite specific 'object' that still eluded him, inviting everyone to obtain it for him. Thus was he able to usher the object into social discourse. But by the same token we must bow to the facts: *it is rarely its presence, and more often its absence, which ushers it in.*

A Discourse With Oneself

A characteristic feature of the collection remains, at a given moment, that division separating it from its degenerative system and assigning it an agenda or demand (for prestige — no matter whether cultural or commercial, so long as the object ends up bringing man into contact with another: it then becomes a message). Yet, whatever external link the collection may have, it still contains an element of irreducible unrelatedness to the world. It is because he feels alienated and volatilised in a social discourse whose rules elude him that the collector attempts to constitute a discourse which would be transparent to him, since he can possess its signifiers, and since its final signified is fundamentally himself. But he is doomed to failure: believing himself to be beyond discourse, he does not see that he quite simply replaces an open and objective discontinuity with a closed and subjective discontinuity, where the very language he employs loses all general value. This totalisation through objects thus always bears the mark of solitude: it fails to communicate, and communication is missing from it. The question can be posed another way: can objects constitute themselves into any other kind of language? Can man institute through them any other language than a discourse with oneself?

If the collector is never a hopeless maniac, precisely because he collects objects which always prevent him in a way from regressing to the point of total abstraction (delirium), then it is for the same reason that the discourse to which he clings can never go beyond a certain destitution or infantilism. The collection is always a limited, recurrent process, since its very material — objects — is too concrete, too discontinuous to enable it to be articulated in a real dialectical structure.[29] If 'the one who collects nothing is a cretin', then the one who collects is always somewhat impoverished and inhuman as well.

NOTES

1. [See *Le Système des objets*, Paris, Gallimard, 1968, pp. 82-83.]
2. Our analysis here is limited to 'bygone objects', because they offer the clearest example of 'non-systematic' objects. But the same sort of analysis could just as easily be applied to other sub-categories of the marginal object.
3. Just as naturalism is fundamentally the disavowal of nature, so too is historicity itself, behind the exaltation of its signs, the refusal of history — the disavowed presence of history.
4. In fact, the bygone object is entirely integrated into the structures of ambience, since, wherever they are present, they are indiscriminately experienced as 'hot' in opposition to the the whole modern environment, which is 'cold'.
5. And once again, by extension, exotic objects: for modern man, the removal from familiar surroundings or a change in latitude is in every way equivalent to being plunged into the past (cf. tourism). The fascination with handmade or indigenous objects, with trinkets from around the world, is not so much due to their picturesque diversity, but to the earlier forms and modes of their manufacture, to their allusion to a former world, one always relayed by the world of childhood and its toys.
6. There are two opposing movements here: insofar as bygone objects have become integrated into the *present* cultural system, they signify, from the depths of the past, *the present as an empty dimension in time*. On the other hand, insofar as individual regression is a movement from the present into the past, it projects there an empty dimension in being.
7. See below, 'The Collection'.
8. The relic thus signifies the possibility of containing the person of God or the soul of the dead within an object — since there is no relic without its shrine. Value 'migrates' from the relic to the shrine, which, made of gold, clearly contributes to its authenticity, thus enabling it to become symbolically more effective.
9. Thus tourist travel is always accompanied by the search for lost time.
10. Let us not seek a direct correlation between these terms: modern objects differ from bygone objects in the division of their functional fields. However, the sole function of bygone objects in this instance is the absence of function.

11. This splitting of the old single dwelling into primary and secondary residences, into functional and 'naturalistic' habitats undoubtedly offers the clearest example of the systematic process: the system splits into two in order to counterbalance formally contradictory but inherently complementary terms. And this occurs throughout everyday life, as in the leisure-work structure for example, where leisure is not at all a distancing, nor even a release from working life, but is the result of the same splitting of everyday life that enables it to establish itself, beyond its real contradictions, as a coherent and definitive system. To be sure, this process is less visible at the level of objects taken in isolation, but it nonetheless remains true that each object-function is capable of being split into two, *and thus of being formally opposed within itself so as to be better integrated into the general system.*

12. With the child, ambient objects also proceed from the Father (and from the phallic mother during the first few months). The appropriation of objects is the appropriation of the power of the Father (Roland Barthes notes this in relation to the car; see *Réalités*, October 1963). This usage follows a process of paternal identification, with all the conflicts that this entails: it is always ambiguous and tinged with aggressivity.

13. To be sure, the higher up one is on the social scale, the more this is true; but in any event, it happens very quickly once a certain standing and a minimal 'urban acculturation' are achieved.

14. M. Fauron, President of the Society of Cigar-Band Collectors (in *Liens*, Club Français du Livre, May 1964).

15. But also its frustration, linked to the tautological character of the system.

16. The series is almost always a kind of game permitting one of its terms to be privileged and to be constituted as a model. A child tosses bottle tops: which one will come out in front? It is no accident that it is always finally the same one — his favourite. This invented model or hierarchy is himself: he identifies, not with one of the tops, but with the fact that it wins in each toss. But he is also actually present in each of the tops as an unmarked term of the contest. To toss them one by one is to play at constituting oneself into a series in order to constitute oneself as a model: the one who wins. This sheds light on the psychology of the collector: by collecting privileged objects, it is once again himself the object who always comes out in front.

17. Any term in the series is able to become this ultimate term: any Callot can be the one which 'would complete the Callot collection'.

18. The object indeed becomes the immediate support for a network of habits, the point of fixation for repetitive behaviour. Conversely, there is perhaps no habit which doesn't revolve around an object. One is inextricably bound up with the other in everyday life.

19. On the other hand, when one considers the disappearance of the clock, the watch is significant in terms of an irreversible tendency of modern objects: miniaturisation and individualisation.

In addition, the watch is the oldest, smallest, most precious, and most familiar of personal machines. It is an intimate and highly charged mechanical talisman, an object of everyday complicity, of fascination (for the child), and of jealousy.

20. Exactitude is equivalent here to velocity in space: it is necessary to consume time to the nearest point.

21. That the collection is a game with death (a passion), and in this sense symbolically stronger than death itself, is amusingly illustrated by a story of Tristan Bernard: a man had built up a collection of children, ones who were legitimate, illegitimate, from first and second marriages, adopted, found, bastards, etc. One day he gave a reunion party for them all. A cynical friend remarked: 'There is one missing.' The disturbed collector inquired: 'Which one?' 'The posthumous child,' replied the friend. Thereupon this passionate man got his wife with child and committed suicide.

The same system can be found in its pure state, relieved of thematic elements, in the game of chance. Whence the even more intense fascination that this exerts. What is indicated here is the pure hereafter, a pure subjectivity investing the pure series with an imaginary mastery — in the certainty, within the very vicissitudes of the game, that no one has the power to reintroduce into them the real conditions of life and death.

22. Of course, this is also true for 'pets', and, by extension, for the 'object' of sexual relations, whose manipulation through jealousy belongs to the same order.

23. We must not confuse this frustration, as the internal stimulus for the regressive system of the series, with the incompletion that we spoke about earlier, which on the contrary is a factor whose source is external to the system. Through frustration, the subject is drawn ever deeper into the system; through incompletion, he moves (relatively speaking) towards the world.

24. And ultimately, hair, feet and, following this regression down to its most impersonal details, to the point where fetishism ultimately fixes on the opposite pole of the living being, to the garter or bra: here we again discover the material object, whose possession takes on the character of a perfect elision of the other's presence.

25. This is why passion in this instance is transferred to the fetish, which radically reduces the living sexual object into something equivalent to the penis, and invests it as such.

26. Possessive identification can also operate to the extent that a living being can be felt to have no sex (the baby): 'So, "I" have a pain in "my" head?' one says to a baby. Or else: 'So, "we" have a pain in "our" head?' This conflationary identification is brought to a halt before the sexed being by the anguish of castration.

27. This distinction between serial satisfaction and true pleasure is an essential one. In the latter case, there is something like a pleasure in pleasure, by which satisfaction is exceeded as such, being based in relations; whereas, in serial satisfaction, this second term of pleasure, this dimension which qualifies it as pleasure disappears, is missing, or frustrated. This satisfaction is reflected in succession, projecting by extension and compensating by repetition an unachievable totality. So do we see people, once they cease to read the books they buy, buying more and more of them. So do we see the repeated sexual act, or

the multiplication of partners, indefinitely gratifying the aim of amorous investigation to the full. A pleasure in pleasure is no longer there. Only satisfaction remains. The two are mutually exclusive.

28. Nevertheless, even in this instance, the collector tends to require others simply to act as witnesses to his collection, and tends to integrate them simply as third parties into pre-existing relations between subject and object.

29. As opposed, for example, to science and memory, which are also collections, but collections of facts, of knowledges.

Mass Media Culture

THE NEO — OR ANACHRONISTIC RESURRECTION

As Marx said of Napoleon III, sometimes the same events occur twice in history: the first time they have a real historical impact, whereas the second time they are no more than its farcical evocation and its grotesque avatar — nourished by a *legendary reference*. Cultural consumption can thus be defined as the time and place of the farcical resurrection and parodic evocation of that which is already no more — of that which is 'consumed' in the original sense of the word (consummated and terminated). Consumers are like those tourists who journey by coach to the Far North to retrace the steps of the gold rush, and who hire prospecting equipment and Eskimo costumes to lend a touch of local colour: they consume in ritual form what was once a historical event, necessarily re-enacted as legend. Historically, this process is called restoration: it is the denial of history and the fixist resurrection of earlier models. Consumption, too, is completely saturated with this anachronistic substance. Take a typical example: in winter, ESSO sells firewood and barbecue kits at its service stations — here are the champions of petrol, the 'historical liquidators' of firewood and its whole symbolic value, who serve it up to you again as the neo-firewood ESSO. What is being consumed here at the same time as the pleasure in the automobile is the mixed and complicit pleasure in the defunct charms of everything killed off by the automobile — and those resurrected in the automobile! This should not be seen as simple nostalgia for the past: throughout this 'lived' dimension, consumption can be historically and structurally defined as *the exaltation of signs based on the denial of the reality of things*.

We have already seen how the news in mass communications pathetically and hypocritically exalts the tranquility of everyday life with all the signs of catastrophe (deaths, murders, rapes, revolution, etc.).[1] But this same pathetic overabundance of signs is legible everywhere — in the exaltation of all youth and extreme age, in the thrill of blue-blood marriages on the front page, in the mass media hymn to the body and sexuality. Everywhere we witness the historical disintegration of certain structures which in a sense celebrate, under the sign of consumption, their real disappearance as well as their farcical resurrection. The family is breaking down? We exalt it. Children are no longer children? We make childhood sacred. The elderly are lonely, left by the wayside? Old age moves all of us to tears. And more clearly still: we glorify the body in direct proportion to the atrophy of its real possibilities, and to its increasing harrassment by the system of inspection with all its urban, professional and bureaucratic constraints.

CULTURAL RECYCLING[2]

One of the characteristic features of our society in relation to professional knowledge, social position and personal advancement is *recycling*. For those who do not want to be left behind, held back or excluded, it implies the necessity of 'parading' their skills, their knowledge, and all told their 'practical experience' on the labour market. Today this notion applies particularly to management trainees and, to a lesser extent, teachers. It thus professes to be scientific and based on the continual advancement of skills (in the exact sciences, in marketing techniques, in teaching, etc.), which normally everyone must take into account in order to keep up 'with the pack'. In fact, the term 'recycling' can prompt certain remarks: it inevitably evokes the 'cycle' of fashion — here everyone also feels compelled to be *'au courant'*, and to update themselves annually, monthly or seasonally in their clothes, possessions and cars. If they don't do this, they can't be true citizens of the consumer society. But here it is clearly not a question of continual progress, since fashion is arbitrary, changeable or cyclical, and adds nothing to an individual's intrinsic worth. It nonetheless has a deeply constraining character, sanctioning either social success or failure. We might enquire whether the supposedly scientific 'updating of skills' does not actually conceal the same type of accelerated, obligatory and arbitrary recycling as occurs in fashion; and whether it does not bring into operation, at the level of knowledge and individuals, the same 'planned obsolescence' imposed on material goods by the cycles of production and fashion. If this were the case, then what we have before us is not a rational process of scientific accumulation, but a social and non-rational process of consumption consistent with all its other forms.

Take the medical 'check up', or the upgrading of one's body, muscles, and fitness — health clubs for men, diets and beauty treatments for women, holidays for everyone. But this notion can (and *must*) be extended to phenomena on an even wider scale. The very 'rediscovery' of the body is a recycling of the body, just as the 'rediscovery' of Nature — in the form of a countryside trimmed down to sample specimens framed against an immense urban sprawl, partitioned and 'domesticated' as green belts, nature reserves, or as a backdrop for weekend cottages — is actually a recycling of Nature. In other words, Nature is no longer at all a primeval and original presence symbolically opposed to culture, but a *simulation model*, a 'consommé' of the recirculated signs of nature; in short, it is nature *recycled*. If this is not yet the situation everywhere, it is nonetheless the current tendency. And whether it is called the management or preservation of nature reserves and the environment, it always involves the recycling of a nature condemned by its very existence. Nature as event, and as knowledge, is governed in this system by the *principle of the latest trend*. Functionally, it *has* to change like fashion. It has the value of *ambience*, and therefore is subject to a cycle of renewal. Today the same principle encroaches upon the professional domain, where the scientific and technical values of education and competence yield to a process of recycling; in other words, to the pressures of mobility, status, and a career *profile*.[3]

This organising principle dominates the whole of 'mass' culture today. That to which all the acculturated have a right is not culture, but *cultural recycling* (and ultimately not even the 'cultured' can or will escape it). It is to be 'in the know', to be 'in the swing of things', to parade one's cultural baggage at monthly or annual intervals. It is to suffer the constraint of the short-term, to perpetually change like fashion, and this is the *total opposite* of culture conceived as:

1. The inherited characteristics of works, thoughts, and traditions;

2. The continuity of theoretical reflection and its transcendent critical and symbolic function.

Both of these are repudiated by this cyclical subculture composed of obsolescent cultural ingredients and signs, by this culture of *the latest trend* running from kinetic art to weekly encyclopaedias. It is culture recycled.

It is clear that the problem of the consumption of culture is not strictly linked to its content, nor to a 'discerning public' (this is the eternally false problem of the 'vulgarisation' of art and culture, to which practitioners of 'elitist' culture and champions of mass culture both fall victim). The decisive factor is not how many thousands or millions partake of a specific work, but that this work, like the car of the year, or nature in green belts, is condemned to be nothing more than an ephemeral sign — condemned because produced, intentionally or not, in a dimension of production which is universal today, that of the cycle and of recycling. Culture is no longer produced to last. Of course, it remains a universal authority, an ideal reference, and all the more so when it loses its essential meaning (just as Nature is never more exalted than when it is universally destroyed); but in its reality, as much as in its mode of production, culture is subject to the same demand to be 'up to date' as are material goods. Once again, this does not concern the *industrial diffusion* of culture. It is quite beside the point whether Van Gogh is exhibited in major department stores or Kierkegaard sells 200,000 copies. The *meaning* circulated by these works is that *all signification has become cyclical*: in other words, it is precisely through the system of communication that the same mode of succession, alternation, and combinatorial modulation is imposed upon them as is imposed upon the length of skirts or television broadcasts (cf. 'The Medium is the Message'); and thus that culture, as a pseudo-event in 'current affairs', as a pseudo-object in advertising, can also be produced (or potentially so) *from within the medium itself* and its referential code. Here we again link up with the logical mechanism of 'simulation models'[4] or that which can be seen operating in gadgets, which are no more than *the manipulation of technological forms*. At the very limit, there is no difference between 'cultural creativity' (in kinetic art, etc.) and this technical and ludic combinatory, just as there is no difference between 'avant-garde creations' and 'mass culture'. The latter simply combines stereotyped themes as its content (ideological, populist, sentimental, moral or historical), whereas the former combines modes of expression as its form. But above all, both manipulate a code through a calculus of amplitude and longevity. It is furthermore curious how the system of literary awards, currently scorned for its academic decrepitude (it is indeed stupid to award a prize to *one book per year*, covering everything), has remarkably managed to survive by adapting itself to the functional cycle of modern culture. But the regularity of such awards — an absurdity at any other time — is again compatible with the current tendency to recycle cultural fashions. Formerly, these awards singled out a book for posterity, which was comical. Today, they single out a book for the latest trend, and this is effectual. It is in this way that they have found their second wind.

TIRLIPOT[5] AND *COMPUTER*[6], OR
THE LOWEST COMMON CULTURE (L.C.C.)

The mechanism of *Tirlipot*: theoretically, it is the exploration through question and answer of the definition of a verb (*tirlipoter* is equivalent to the 'thingummybob' [*machin*], a floating signifier for which a specific signifier is substituted by a random process of selection) — thus theoretically a kind of intellectual instruction. But, in reality, contestants are for the most part incapable of posing genuine questions: questioning, probing, and analysing bothers them. They begin by guessing the answer (any verb that comes into their head), and try to deduce the question by putting its dictionary definition into an interrogative form. (For example, a contestant might ask: 'Is "to *tirlipot*" to put an end to something?' If the compere says, 'Yes, in a certain sense', or even simply, 'Perhaps . . . what do you think it is?', the automatic response is 'to finish' or 'to complete'). It is like the approach of a handyman who tries one screw after another to find one that fits, a rudimentary exploratory technique of assembly by trial and error without rational investigation.

Computer works on the same principle: no instruction necessary. A mini-computer asks you questions, and for each question presents a list of five answers. You select the right response. The time counts: if you respond immediately, you get maximum points — you are the 'champion'. Hence it is not the time of reflection, but reaction time. The device doesn't set in motion intellectual processes, but mechanisms of instant reflex. You shouldn't weigh up or deliberate over the suggested responses; you have to *see* the right answer, to register it as a stimulus, like the motor-optic system of a photoelectric cell. To know is to see (cf. David Riesman's 'radar', which is a means of instantly identifying positive and negative responses in one's dealings with others, and thus of making or breaking contact with them). Above all, there is no analytical reflection: this is penalised by a low score proportional to the amount of time wasted.

So if the function of these games is not one of instruction (which is always advanced by the comperes themselves and the ideologues of mass media), then what is it? In *Tirlipot*, it is clearly participation: its content is of no importance. For contestants, it is the thrill of occupying the air waves for the twenty seconds it takes to get their voice across, to blend in with the compere's voice, to hold his attention while engaging in a brief dialogue with him, and to establish through him a magical contact with that benign and anonymous multitude which is the public. Most contestants are clearly not at all disappointed by their failure to answer correctly. They've got what they wanted, which is a sort of *communion*; in other words, that modern, technical, and aseptic form of 'contact' which is *communication*. Consumer society is not in fact characterised by its lamented absence of ceremony: radio game shows are just as ceremonial as the religious mass or sacrifices in primitive society—except it is no longer a ceremonial communion consecrated by bread and wine, said to be flesh and blood, but by the mass media (which are composed not only of messages, but of transmitters, networks, stations, receivers, and, of course, programmers and the public). In other words, *communion is no longer achieved through a symbolic medium, but a technical one*: this is what makes it communication.

What is shared, then, is no longer 'culture': a living body, the actual presence of a collectivity (all those things which once comprised the symbolic and metabolic function of a ceremony or feast); nor is it even knowledge in the strict sense, but that strange corpus of signs, references, school reminiscences and signals of intellectual fashion called 'mass culture', but which could be named the L.C.C. (Lowest Common Culture)—akin to the lowest common denominator in arithmetic, or else [Riesman's] 'Standard Package', a term designating the lowest common collection of objects that the average consumer must possess in order to gain a certificate of citizenship in this consumer society. Thus the L.C.C. defines the lowest common collection of 'correct answers' that the average individual must possess in order to gain a certificate of cultural citizenship.

Mass communication precludes culture and knowledge. There is no question of genuine symbolic or didactic processes coming into play, since it would only compromise the meaning of this ceremony, which is collective participation—a participation that can only occur in the form of a *liturgy*, or as a formalised code of signs meticulously emptied of every drop of meaning.

We can see that the term 'culture' is laden with misunderstanding. As a cultural 'consommé', 'digest', or repertoire of codified questions and answers, this L.C.C. is to culture what life insurance is to life: it is designed to conjure the risks of life and to exalt, by means of a denial of living culture, the ritualised signs of *culturalisation*.

Fuelled by a mechanical process of question and answer, this L.C.C. nonetheless has many affinities with school 'culture'. Indeed, all these game shows are inspired by the model of the EXAM. And this is no accident. The exam is the preferred means of social advancement. Everyone wants to pass exams, even in such bastardised forms as radio, because to be examined is a matter of prestige today. A powerful mechanism of social integration thus exists in the endless proliferation of these game shows: one can ultimately imagine the integration of the whole of society into these mass media contests, all social organisation becoming dependent on their sanction. History has already seen one society where there was a total system of selection and organisation based on exams: China under the Mandarins. But that system only extended to a privileged few. With our society, it would be the entire masses mobilised in a endless game of double or nothing, where everyone would ensure or put at risk their own social destiny. Thus would the archaic machinery of social control come to comprise an economy, since the best system of social integration has always been ritualised competition. But we haven't reached that point yet. For the time being, let us simply note a powerful longing for the process of examination — a twofold process since everyone can be examined in it, but also integrated into it as examiner or judge (insofar as everyone is a member of that collective authority called the public). As with splitting in dreams, this desire to be both one and the other is truly fantasmatic. But it also involves a tactical process of integration through the delegation of power. *Mass* communication can thus be defined as its technical supports in combination with the L.C.C. (and *not the total number of the mass participating*). *Computer* is also a mass medium, even if it seems to be an individualised game. Your choices are still programmed by a collective agency in this slot machine — an admirable synthesis of knowledge and household electrical appliances — where mental dexterity registers as blips and beeps. The medium of *Computer* is simply a technical materialisation of the collective medium, of that system of 'lowest-common-cultural' signals which prescribes to each the participation of all, and to everyone the same participation.

Once again, it is useless and even absurd to compare and contrast the merits of High Culture and Mass-Mediated Culture. The former has a 'complex' syntax, while the latter is a combinatory of elements always dissociable in terms of stimulus/response and question/answer. This schema is most vividly illustrated by radio games shows. But, apart from governing the ritual of these spectacles, it also governs the behaviour of consumers in their every transaction and in their general conduct, organising all tastes, preferences, needs and choices as a series of responses to various stimuli. With regard to objects as with relations, consumers are constantly solicited, 'quizzed', and summoned to respond. In this context, a purchase is comparable to the radio game show: it is today less the personal transaction of an individual with the view to satisfying a concrete need, than first and foremost *the response to a question* — a response that engages the individual in the collective ritual of consumption. A purchase is a game to the extent that each object is always presented within a range of options, from which the individual is required to choose: the act of purchasing is a choice, the determination of a preference — exactly as one chooses from among the various answers presented in *Computer*. This is how the purchaser plays, by responding to a question with no direct bearing on the object's utility, but with an indirect bearing on the 'play' of variation in the object. This 'game' and the choices it sanctions characterise the purchaser/consumer as the complete opposite of the traditional user.

THE LOWEST COMMON MULTIPLES (L.C.M.)

The L.C.C. (Lowest Common Culture) of media broadcasts or mass-circulation weeklies has branched out into art today. It is the miraculous multiplication of artworks, whose prototype can be found in the Bible and the famous miracle of the loaves and fishes on the shores of Lake Tiberias — the very same Bible that is now multiplied and delivered to the masses in weekly instalments.

A great democratic wind has blown across the celestial Jerusalem of culture and art. 'Contemporary art', from Picasso to Rauschenberg, from Chagall to Vasarely and the younger generation, is now on preview at Printemps department stores (admittedly on the top floor, so as not to compromise the 'Interior Decoration' section on the second floor, with its seaports and sunsets). The work of art as a unique object and privileged moment has escaped the solitude to which it was confined for centuries. Museums, as everybody knows, were once sanctuaries. But now the masses have taken over from the private owner or enlightened amateur. What delights the masses is not only the industrial reproduction of a work of art, but that it is simultaneously unique and collective: the Multiple Edition. 'A bold initiative! Jacques Putman, in collaboration with Prisunic department stores, has just published a collection of original engravings at a very affordable price (100F) . . . No one will think it strange in the future to acquire a lithograph or etching *along with a pair of stockings or garden chair*. A second "Prisunic Collection" has just been exhibited at the Galerie L'Oeil, and can now be purchased at its stores. This is not a promotion, nor a revolution [!]. The multiplication of images is a response to the growing public demand for them, which fatally [!] leads to the demand for new venues. Experimental research no longer indicates the enslavement to money and power: the amateur/benefactor has given way to *the customer/participant* . . . Each engraving, numbered and signed, is printed in editions of 300 copies . . . The victory of the consumer society? Perhaps. But what does it matter so long as quality is preserved . . . Those who don't want to understand contemporary art really have to try hard today.'

Art speculation based on the rarity of the product is finished. With the 'Unlimited Edition', art moves into the industrial age (it just so happens that these editions, which in reality are limited in number, very quickly become almost everywhere the object of parallel speculation on the black market — such is the cunning naivety of those who conceive and produce them). Works of art find their way into delicatessens, and abstract canvases into factories . . . Don't say: 'Art, what's that?' Don't say: 'Art, it's too expensive.' Don't say: 'Art, it's not for me.' Read *Les Muses*.

It would be facile to say that a Picasso canvas on a factory wall will never abolish the division of labour, and that the multiplication of multiple editions, were this to be realised, will never abolish social division and the transcendence of Culture. There is nonetheless something quite revealing in this illusion shared by the ideologues of multiple editions and those who generally believe in the dissemination or promotion of culture (without mentioning those dealers and artists who, as conscious or subconscious speculators, are by far the most numerous in the affair). Like those designers who would like 'to create beautiful objects accessible to all', their noble effort to democratise culture is blatantly at odds with the failure to achieve this goal — or, which amounts to the same, has been so commercially successful that culture becomes suspect. But this is only an apparent contradiction: culture survives because these good souls persist in *treating it as a universal, all the while attempting to distribute it in the form of finished objects* (whether unique, or multiplied in their thousands). But they do no more than submit to the logic of consumption (or to the manipulation of signs) certain contents or symbolic activities formerly not subject to it. The multiplication of these works does not in itself imply any 'vulgarisation' or 'loss of quality': what happens when works are multiplied as serial objects is that they indeed become commensurate with 'a pair of stockings or garden chair', and assume meaning in relation to them. They no longer exist as *works of art*, as materials with meaning, and as *open* significations in opposition to all other *finished* objects, but have become finished objects themselves, entering into the constellation of those displayed accessories by which the 'socio-cultural' standing of the average citizen is determined — at least, in the ideal circumstances where everyone would have real access to them. For the time being, while these pseudo-works may have ceased to be works of art, they nonetheless remain rare objects, economically or 'psychologically' inaccessible for most people, because as distinctive objects they cater to a parallel and somewhat larger market for Culture.

It is perhaps more interesting — even though the problem remains the same — to see what is consumed in weekly encyclopaedias like *La Bible*, *Les Muses*, *Alpha*, *Le Million*, or in mass-circulation music and art publications like *Grand peintres* and *Grand musiciens*. The potential public they reach is clearly enormous: all those office workers, juniors, and secretarial staff with an average secondary or technical education (or with children so educated).

To these recent mass publications we should add those, like *Science et Vie*, *Historia*, etc., which have long catered to the demand for culture among the 'rising classes'. What do they seek in familiarising themselves with esoteric scientific, historical, and musical knowledge? In other words, what do they seek in these established and recognised disciplines whose content, unlike that disseminated by the mass media, has a specific function? Do they seek instruction and a real cultural education, or a sign of increased standing? Do they seek in culture a training or a commodity to appropriate, knowledge or status? Don't we discover here that 'display effect' which we have already seen to designate — as one sign among other signs — the object of consumption?

In the case of *Science et Vie* (here we refer to a survey of its readership carried out by the Centre de Sociologie Européenne), this demand is ambiguous: there is, in the accession to technical culture, a camouflaged and clandestine aspiration to 'literate' culture. To read *Science et Vie* is the result of a compromise: the aspiration to elite culture, but with a defensive counter-motivation in the form of a refusal of elitism (which is to say, an aspiration to the upper classes and at the same time a reaffirmation of class position). More precisely, this reading operates *as a sign of acceptance* — but into what? Into the abstract community, into the potential collectivity of all those driven by the same ambiguous requirement, and who also read *Science et Vie* (or *Les Muses*, etc.). It is an act of allegiance of a mythological order: the reader dreams of a group whose presence he consumes *in abstracto* in his reading — an unreal, *mass-scale* relation whose effect is literally *'mass' communication*, an undifferentiated complicity which nonetheless constitutes the profoundly real substance of this reading, with all its mythical qualities of recognition, acceptance and participation (a process also readily detected among the readers of *Nouvel Observateur*, since to read this periodical is to *associate oneself* with its readers, and to engage in 'cultural' activity as a class emblem).

Of course, most readers (we should say 'adherents') of these mass publications, of these vehicles for 'undercultured' culture will argue, in all good faith, that they are interested in their actual content, and that their aim is knowledge. But the objective finality of this cultural 'use value' is largely overdetermined by its sociological 'exchange value'. It is this demand, indexed to a statutory and increasingly lively competitiveness, that the huge quantity of 'culturalised' material in reviews, encyclopaedias, and pocket editions fulfils. All this cultural material is 'consumed' to the extent that its content does not cater to autonomous practice, but to the rhetoric of social mobility — a demand which aims at an object *other* than culture, or rather which aims at culture insofar as it is *a codified element of social status*. There is thus an inversion, and the strictly cultural content no longer appears here except as a connotation, as a secondary function. We could therefore say that it is consumed, just as a washing machine is the object of consumption, once it ceases to be a tool and becomes an aspect of well-being or prestige. We know that it then ceases to have a specific purpose, and that many other objects could be substituted for it — among them, precisely culture. Culture is an object of consumption to the extent that, gravitating towards this other discourse, it becomes substitutable for and commensurate with other objects (even if hierarchically superior). And this is not only true of *Science et Vie*, but also of 'high' culture, 'great' painting, classical music, etc. All these can be sold together in drugstores or newsagents. But it is not strictly a question of where they are sold, the size of their editions, or the 'cultural level' of their public. If they are all sold together, and consumed in this way, it is because culture is subject to the same demand for competitive signs as any other category of objects, and because it is *produced as a function of this demand*.

At this point, culture is reduced to the same form of appropriation as those other messages, objects, and images responsible for the 'ambience' of our daily life: it is reduced to a form of *curiosity* — not necessarily a casual or indifferent curiosity, since it can be particularly passionate for those sectors in the process of acculturation, but a curiosity subject to the constantly changing cycles and dictates of fashion, thus one replacing the elitist practice of culture as a system of symbolic meaning with a ludic and combinatory system of signs. 'Beethoven, what a groove!'

At the very limit, what individuals undergo in this process of 'culture' — from which the autodidact, that marginal hero of traditional culture, is just as much excluded as the cultured man, that fragrant garland of a humanism now rapidly beginning to decay — is 'cultural' recycling, an aesthetic recycling which forms part of their overall 'personalisation', of their cultural grooming in a competitive society, which generally speaking is not unlike dressing up the object through packaging. The industrial aesthetic, or design, has no other goal than to imbue mass-produced objects, deeply scored by the division of labour and marked by their function, with a second function: that 'aesthetic' homogeneity, formal unity, or ludic character which binds them all together into a kind of 'environment' or 'ambience'. This is the work of 'cultural designers' everywhere today: they attempt, in a society where individuals are deeply scored by the division of labour and their fragmented tasks, to 'redesign' them through a process of 'culture', to integrate them with the same outward appearance, to promote exchange under the sign of cultural advancement, and to 'acclimatise' people like design refashions objects. But we should not lose sight of the fact that, just like the 'beauty' packed into objects by the industrial aesthetic, this cultural packaging or recycling is, as Jacques Michel has said, 'incontestably a commercial argument'. 'It is a recognised fact today that a pleasant environment, created by the harmony of shapes and colours, and of course by the quality of materials [!], has a ben-eficial effect on productivity' (*Le Monde*, 28 September 1969). And he is right: people acculturated in the same way as designed objects are socially and professionally better integrated, better 'synchronised', more 'compatible'. This functionalisation of human relations finds in cultural advancement one of its most fertile fields — here 'human design' links up with 'human engineering'.

We need a term which would be to culture what 'Aesthetics' (in the sense of an industrial aesthetic, a functional rationalisation of forms, a game of signs) is to beauty as a symbolic system. We have no word to designate this functionalised material of messages, texts, images, classi-cal masterpieces or comic strips, this codified 'creativity' and 'recep-tivity' which have replaced inspiration and sensibility, this *planned* collective labour on significations and communication, this 'industrial culturality' haunted by cultures of every description and from every epoch, which, at the risk of total misunderstanding, and for want of a better word, we continue to call 'culture'— forever dreaming, in this hyperfunctionalist cultural consumption, of the universal, of the myths enabling our epoch to be deciphered without being at the same time mythological overproductions, and of an art enabling modernity to be deciphered without causing it to disappear.

KITSCH

Kitsch, along with the gadget, is one of the major categories of the modern object. Knick-knacks, rustic odds-and-ends, souvenirs, lamp-shades, and African masks: the kitsch-object is collectively this whole plethora of 'trashy', sham or faked objects, this whole museum of junk which proliferates everywhere, with a decided preference for holiday and tourist spots. Kitsch is equivalent to the 'cliché' in discourse. And this should help us to understand that kitsch, just like the gadget, concerns a *category* — one which, while difficult to define, should not be confused with any *real* objects. Kitsch can be found anywhere: in the detail of an object as in the general design of a matching set, in an artificial flower as in a photo-novel. It can best be defined as a *pseudo-object*, which is to say as a simulation, copy, facsimile, or stereotype; as the paucity of true signification and as the overabundance of signs, allegorical references, or disparate connotations; as the exaltation of detail, and as the saturation by detail. Furthermore, there is a direct relationship between its internal organisation (a disconnected overabundance of signs) and its appearance in the market (a heaped mass of assorted objects). Kitsch is a *cultural category*.

This proliferation of kitsch — which results from industrial multiplication, from the vulgarisation, at the level of the object, of distinctive signs borrowed from every register (the bygone, the neo, the exotic, the folkloric, the futuristic), and from the disordered escalation of 'readymade' signs — has its basis, like 'mass culture', in the *sociological* reality of the consumer society. The latter is a mobile society: large sectors of the population move up the social ladder, attaining a higher status at the same time as complying with a cultural demand, which is nothing but the necessity of demonstrating this status through signs. At all levels of society, generations of 'parvenus' need their displays. Thus, blaming the 'vulgarity' of the public or the 'cynical' tactics of manufacturers wanting to peddle their shoddy goods is pointless. Even if this were an important factor, it cannot *explain* this cancerous excrescence in the population of 'pseudo-objects'. Demand for them still has to exist, and this demand is a function of social mobility. There is no kitsch in a society without social mobility: a limited quantity of luxury goods would suffice to lend distinction to the privileged elite. Even the copy of a work of art still had, in the classical age, 'authentic' value; whereas the grand epochs of social mobility saw the object flower as different species. With the rising bourgeoisie of the Renaissance and the 17th-century, there emerged 'preciosity' and the baroque — which, though not the direct ancestors of kitsch, already testify to the explosive surge of distinctive material in a conjuncture of social tension and the relatively mixed character of the upper classes. But it was above all with Louis-Philippe, and with the *Gründerjahre* in Germany (1870-1890), and, in all Western societies, since the end of the 19th-century and the era of the great department stores, that the ubiquitous knick-knack becomes one of the major manifestations of the object, and one of the most fertile branches of commerce. This era is without end, since our societies are now virtually in a state of perpetual mobility.

In fact, kitsch reaffirms the value of rare, precious, or unique objects (whose production can also be industrial). Kitsch and the 'authentic' object thus combine together to organise the world of consumption, according to the logic of distinctive material forever changing and expanding today. Kitsch has a minimal value of distinction, but this minimal value is linked to a maximum statistical profitability, since kitsch appeals to whole classes. This can be contrasted with the maximum distinctive quality of rare objects, linked to their limited supply. What is in question here is not their 'beauty', but their power of distinction, which is a *sociological* function. In this sense, all objects arrange themselves into a hierarchy of values determined by their statistical availability and their relative supply. At any moment, and for any condition of the social structure, this function makes it possible for a given social group to distinguish itself and to designate its status through a particular category of objects or signs. But when groups with the greatest number appropriate a particular category of signs, the upper classes are obliged to distance themselves through other signs which are restricted in number (either because of their pedigree, like genuine antiques and paintings, or because they are artificially limited, like deluxe editions and custom-made cars). Kitsch adds nothing new to this logic of distinction, since it is characterised by its derivative and minimal value. In return, this weak valency is one of the reasons for its limitless multiplication. Kitsch *increases itself in quantity*, while, at the top of the scale, 'high-class' goods *restrict themselves to quality*, rejuvenating themselves by becoming rarer.

This derivative function is also linked here to its 'aesthetic' or anti-aesthetic function. What kitsch opposes to the aesthetic of beauty and originality is the *aesthetic of simulation*: everywhere it reproduces objects on an unnaturally small or large scale, it imitates materials (paste, plastic, etc.), it mimics forms and combines them discordantly, it *repeats fashion* without belonging to its process. All things considered, kitsch is homologous to the gadget at a technical level: the gadget is also this technological parody, this functionally useless excrescence, this constant *simulation* of function with no real practical referent. This aesthetic of simulation is profoundly linked to kitsch's socially assigned function of expressing high-class aspirations and social expectations, as well as a magical affiliation with culture, with the forms, manners and signs of the upper classes[7], an aesthetic of acculturation leading to a subculture of the object.

THE GADGET AND THE LUDIC

The machine was once the emblem of industrial society, whereas the gadget is the emblem of post-industrial society. There is no rigorous definition of the gadget. But if we can agree that the object of consumption is defined by the relative disappearance of its objective function (as a tool) to the benefit of its function as a sign, and if we can agree that the object of consumption is characterised by a kind of *functional uselessness* (since what is consumed is precisely something other than the 'useful'), then *the gadget is indeed the truth of the object in consumer society*. In this sense, *anything can become a gadget*; and everything is one, potentially. The definition of the gadget would be its potential uselessness and its ludic combinatory value.[8] Thus gadgets are just as much like badges which have had their moment of glory, as they are like 'Venusik', a 'pure' cylinder of polished metal which is perfectly useless (or perhaps useful only as a paper-weight, but such is the function ascribed to every object that is good for nothing!). 'For all you lovers of formal beauty and potential uselessness, the fabulous "Venusik" has arrived!'

But they are just as much like — for where does 'objective' uselessness begin and end? — that typewriter which can type in thirteen different character registers, 'depending on whether you are writing to your banker, your notary, a very important client, or an old friend'. It is like cheap imitation jewelry, or even the I.B.M. dictaphone: 'Imagine a small device (12 x 15 cm) that can accompany you everywhere, on trips, to the office, over the weekend. You hold it in one hand, push a button, and whisper your decisions, dictate your instructions, and proclaim your victories to it. Everything you say is committed to its memory . . . Whether you are in Rome, Tokyo, or New York, your secretary will not miss a single word you utter . . .' Nothing could be more useful, and nothing more useless: when the technical process is given over to a magical type of mental practice or a fashionable social practice, then the technical object itself becomes a gadget.

Are gadgets those chrome fittings, two-speed windshield wipers and power-operated windows of a car? Yes and no: they do have some usefulness in terms of social prestige. The negative connotations associated with the term 'gadget' are quite simply the result of a moral perspective on the utility of objects: some are thought to have a purpose, while others none — but on the basis of what criteria? There is no object, neither the most marginal nor decorative one, that is without purpose, because, even if this purpose is to serve no purpose at all, it still becomes a distinctive sign.[9] Conversely, there is no object that does not in a sense serve no purpose (which is to say a purpose other than its designated one). There's no getting away from it, at least from defining the gadget as something explicitly devoted to secondary functions. Thus, once they become part of the logic of fashion and prestige, or of a fetishistic logic, not only do the chrome fittings become a gadget, but so do the steering column and the entire car. For the systematic character of objects today drives them all in this direction.

The world of the pseudo-environment and the pseudo-object is a source of constant delight for all 'creators' of 'functional objects'. Witness the work of André Faye, 'technician in the art of living', who creates Louis XVI cabinets whose doors open to reveal the smooth and dazzling surface of the turntable or speakers of a hi-fi system . . . 'His objects stir, like Calder mobiles: in their construction they serve as ordinary objects as much as genuine works of art, whose alternation coordinated with chromophonic projections brings them ever closer to the *total spectacle* to which he aspires . . . There is cybernetic furniture, revolving and adjustable desks, a calligraphic teleprinter . . . A telephone finally become an integral part of man, making it possible to ring up New York or to take calls from Honolulu alongside the pool or deep within the estate.' For Faye, all this represents the 'subservience of technology to the art of living' — irresistibly evoking the Lépine competition. Is there any difference between an office videophone and a cold-water heating system dreamt up by some eccentric inventor? But there is a difference. Whereas the good old invention of the artisan grew out of curiosity and the somewhat delirious poetry of heroic technical skills, the gadget itself forms part of a systematic logic grasping all of everyday life as a form of spectacle, with the result that the whole environment of objects and, by extension, all its concomitant human and social relations, becomes suspiciously artificial, bogus, or useless. In its widest sense, the gadget attempts to supersede this general crisis of the *finality* and utility of things *through a form of game*. But it doesn't achieve, nor can it achieve, the symbolic freedom of a plaything for the child. It is limited to being an effect of fashion, a kind of artificial booster for other objects; it is caught in a vicious circle where the useful and the symbolic end up merging, as in those 'total' visual spectacles, into a sort of useless combinatory, where the festival itself is a gadget, which is to say a social pseudo-event or game without players. No doubt the pejorative tone conveyed by the term today ('It's so much gadgetry!') reflects both a moral judgment and an anxiety produced by the general disappearance of use value and the function of the symbolic.

But the reverse is also true: which is to say the 'new look' combinatory of gadgetry can oppose — and this applies to any object at all, even the gadget itself — *the exaltation of novelty*. Novelty represents in a sense the sublime phase of the object, and in certain instances can even acquire, if not the quality, then the intensity of the emotion of love. This phase is the one of symbolic discourse, which involves neither fashion nor any reference to others. The child experiences his objects or toys as this form of intense relationship. And what later attracts us to a new car, book, article of clothing, or gadget is nothing less than the charm of immersing ourselves in perpetual childhood. This logic is the inverse of that of consumption.

It is in fact neither its utilitarian nor its symbolic function that defines a gadget, but its LUDIC function. Our relationship to objects, people, culture, leisure, sometimes work, and even politics is increasingly governed by the ludic. The dominant tonality of our daily activities is becoming ludic, precisely to the degree that all objects, goods, relations and services become gadgets. The ludic corresponds to a very specific type of investment: not economic (since objects are useless), nor symbolic (since the object-gadget has no 'soul'), it comprises a game with combinations or a combinatory modulation — a speculation in the varieties or technical potentialities of the object, *a game with the rules of the game* through innovation, and a game with the ultimate combination of life and death through destruction. Here, our domestic gadgets link up with slot machines, *Tirlipot* and the other cultural game shows on radio, the drugstore *Computer*, automobile dashboards, and the whole range of 'serious' equipment from telephones to computers which comprise the modern 'ambience' of work — everything with which we more or less consciously *play*, through our fascination for the way it functions, through our childlike discovery and manipulation of things, through our vague or passionate curiosity in the mechanical 'workings' of things, in the play of colours and changing patterns. Its soul is the very passion for play, but a diffuse and generalised passion, thus one that is all the more barren, devoid of pathos and reduced to *curiosity* — something between indifference and fascination, which could be described as the opposite of *passion*, since passion may be understood as a concrete relation to the *whole person*, or to some object that stands for the person. Passion implies a total investment and assumes an intense symbolic value; whereas ludic curiosity is only interested, however violently, in the *play of elements*.

For example: the pinball player becomes engrossed in the sounds, jolts and flashes of the machine. He plays with electricity. By manipulating the controls, he sees himself as releasing impulses and currents across a network of multicoloured filaments, as complex as a nervous system. This manipulation creates the illusion of a magical participation in science. To prove this you only need to go to a café and observe the crowd gathering around a repairman when he opens up a pinball machine. No one comprehends its network of wires, but they all accept this foreign world as an absolute and indisputable given. Their relationship to the machine has nothing in common with that of a knight to his horse, worker to his tool, or amateur to a work of art. Here the relationship of man to his object is truly magical, which is to say hypnotic and manipulatory.

This ludic activity can give the appearance of being a passion. But it never is. It is consumption — here, the abstract manipulation of blips, flippers, and electrical reaction times; elsewhere, the abstract manipulation of signs of prestige through changes in fashion. Consumption is always a combinatorial investment: it precludes passion.

POP: AN ART OF CONSUMPTION?

As we have seen, the logic of consumption can be defined as the manipulation of signs. The symbolic values of creation, and the symbolic relations of interiority are absent here: it is pure exteriority. The object loses its objective finality and its function to become a term in a much wider combinatory or series of objects, in which its value is purely relational. In another sense, it loses its symbolic meaning, its millennial anthropomorphic status, and tends to disappear in a discourse of connotations, which are also relative to one another in the framework of a totalitarian cultural system, which is to say one capable of integrating all significations whatever their origin.

We have based our analysis on *everyday* objects. But there is another discourse on the object: the discourse of art. A history of the changing status of objects and their representation in art and literature would be revealing on its own. Having played a minor symbolic and decorative role in all traditional art, objects in the 20th-century ceased to be tied to moral or psychological values, ceased to live in the shadow of man as his proxy, and began to take on extraordinary importance as autonomous elements in an analysis of space (Cubism, etc.). By the same token, they became fragmented to the point of abstraction. Having celebrated their parodic resurrection in Dada and Surrealism, and their decomposition and volatilisation through Abstraction, we now find them in Neo-Figuration and Pop apparently reconciled with their image. This raises the question of their contemporary status; in any event, it is forced upon us by this sudden elevation of objects to the pinnacle of artistic figuration.

In a word: Is Pop an art form contemporaneous with this logic of signs and of consumption under discussion? Or rather, is it not simply an effect of fashion, and thus a pure object of consumption itself? The two are not mutually exclusive. It could be argued that, whereas Pop Art turns this object-world upside down, it still ends up (according to its own logic) in objects pure and simple. Advertising shares the same ambiguity.

Let us pose the problem another way: the logic of consumption eliminates the traditionally sublime status of artistic representation. Strictly speaking, the object is no longer privileged over the image in terms of essence or signification. One is no longer the truth of the other: they coexist in the same physical and logical space, where they 'operate' equally as signs[10] (in their differential, reversible, and combinatorial relations). Whereas all art before Pop was based on a vision of the world 'as depth'[11], Pop claims to be at one with that *immanent order of signs*, with their industrial and serial production, and thus with the artificial or manufactured character of the whole environment, with the physical saturation as well as culturalised abstraction of this new order of things.

Does it succeed in 'rendering' this systematic securalisation of objects, in 'rendering' this new environment of signs in its total exteriority — in such a way that nothing remains of that 'inner light' which once constituted the mystique of all earlier painting? Is it an *art of the non-sacred*, which is to say an art of pure manipulation? Or is it itself a non-sacred art, which is to say productive of objects and thus non-creative?

Certain people will say (including Pop artists themselves) that things are much simpler, that they make their art because they feel like it, that they're basically having a good time, that they simply look around, paint what they see, and that it's a spontaneous form of realism, etc. But this is mistaken: Pop signifies the end of perspective, the end of evocation, the end of testimony, the end of the expressive gesture, and, last but not least, the end of the subversion and malediction of the world through art. It not only aims at the immanence of the 'civilised' world, but at its total integration into this world. It reveals an insane ambition: to abolish the annals (and foundations) of an entire culture of transcendence. Perhaps it is also simply an ideology. Let us dispense with two objections: 'It is American art', in its subject matter (including the obsession with 'stars and stripes'), in its optimistic and pragmatic empirical practice, in the incontestably chauvinistic infatuation of certain patrons and collectors who 'identify' with it, etc. Even though this objection is tendentious, let us reply objectively: if all this is *Americanism*, then Pop artists, according to their own logic, cannot but adopt it. If manufactured objects 'speak American', it is because they have no other truth than the mythology that inundates them — so it is only logical to integrate this mythological discourse, and to be integrated into it oneself. If consumer society is engulfed by its own mythology, if it has no critical perspective on itself, and if *this is its exact definition*[12], then there can be no contemporary art that is not, in its very existence and practice, a compromise with and an accomplice of this manifest opacity. Indeed, this is why Pop artists paint objects according to their real appearance, since *it is how they function mythologically — as readymade signs, 'fresh from the assembly line'*. It is why they prefer to paint the logos, trademarks, or slogans transported by these objects, and why they can only finally paint these things (like Robert Indiana). This is not due to chance, nor to 'realism', but to the recognition of an obvious fact about consumer society — namely, that the truth of objects and products is their *trademark*. If this is 'Americanism', then such is the very logic of contemporary culture, and Pop artists can hardly be reproached for bringing it to light.

No more than they can be reproached for their commercial success, and for accepting it without shame. The worst thing would be to damn them, and thus to reinvest them with a sacred function. It is logical for an art that does not contradict the world of objects, but explores its system, to become itself part of the system. It is even the end of hypocrisy and total illogicality. Unlike the early painting of the 20th-century, whose inventive and transcendent spirit did not prevent it becoming a *signed* object and being commercialised in terms of its signature (Abstract Expressionists carried this triumphant inventiveness and shameful opportunism to new heights), Pop artists reconcile the object of painting with the painting as object. Is this coherent or paradoxical? Pop, as much in its commercial success as in its predilection for objects, in its infinite figuration of 'trademarks' and consumables, is the first movement to explore the very status of art as a 'signed' and 'consumed' object.

Yet this logical enterprise — whose extreme consequences, were they to contravene our traditional *moral* aesthetic, could not but meet with our approval — is coupled with an ideology into which it is in danger of sinking: the ideology of Nature, Revelation ('Wake Up!') and authenticity, which evokes the better moments of bourgeois spontaneity.

This 'radical empiricism', 'uncompromising positivism' and 'anti-teleologism' (Mario Amaya, *Pop as Art*) sometimes begins to look suspiciously like a form of *initiation*. Oldenburg: 'I drove around the city one day with Jimmy Dine. By chance we drove along Orchard Street, which is crowded with small stores on both sides. As we drove I remember having a vision of *The Store*. In my mind's eye I saw a complete environment based on this theme. It seemed to me that I had discovered a new world. Everywhere I went I began wandering through the different stores *as if they were museums*. I saw the objects displayed in windows as precious works of art.' Rosenquist: 'Then suddenly the ideas seemed to flow toward me through the window. All I had to do was seize them in mid-air and start painting. Everything spontaneously fell into place, the idea, the composition, the images, the colours — everything began to happen of its own accord.' On the theme of 'Inspiration', we can see that Pop artists are in no way inferior to early generations. What this theme implies, since Werther, is an idealised *Nature* to which one only needs to be faithful in order to be true. All you have to do is awaken or reveal it. In the words of musician and theorist John Cage, who inspired Rauschenberg and Jasper Johns: '. . . art should be an affirmation of life — not an attempt to bring order . . . but simply a way of *waking up* to the very life we are living, which is so excellent, once one gets one's mind and one's desires out of the way and lets it act of its own accord.' This affirmation of a revealed order — of an underlying *nature* shining through the universe of images and manufactured objects — leads to mystico-realist professions of faith: 'A flag was just a flag, a number was simply a number' (Jasper Johns). Or again John Cage: 'We must set about discovering a means to let sounds be themselves'. All this presupposes an essence of the object, a level of absolute reality which never belongs to the everyday environment, but which plainly constitutes a surreality with respect to it. Wesselman thus speaks of the 'superrealism' of a common kitchen.

In brief, we are confronted with a bewildering sort of behaviourism produced by the juxtaposition of things as they appear (something resembling an impressionism of consumer society) coupled with a vaguely Zen or Buddhist mysticism stripping the Ego and Superego down to the 'Id' of the surrounding world, with a dash of Americanism thrown in for good measure!

But there is above all a grave equivocation and inconsistency. For, by manifesting the surrounding environment not as it is, which is to say first and foremost as an artificial field of manipulable signs, a total cultural artifact where neither sensation nor vision comes into play, but differential perception and the tactical game of significations; by manifesting it as a revealed nature and essence, Pop takes on a double connotation: on the one hand, the ideology of an integrated society (contemporary society = nature = an ideal society; but we have seen how this collusion forms part of its logic), and, on the other, the restoration of the whole *sacred process of art*, a process destroying its basic objective.

Pop claims to be an art of the commonplace (it is for this very reason that it is called Popular Art). But what is the commonplace if not a metaphysical category, a modern version of the category of the sublime? The object is only commonplace in its use, at the moment of its use (as with the 'working' radio in Wesselman's installations). But the object ceases to be commonplace once it begins to signify: as we have seen, the 'truth' of the contemporary object is to serve no purpose other than to signify, to be manipulated not as an instrument but as a sign. And the success of Pop in its better examples is that it demonstrates this to us.

Andy Warhol, whose approach is the most radical, is also the one who best epitomises the theoretical contradictions in this artistic practice, and the difficulties it encounters when it tries to envisage its real object. He says: 'The canvas is an absolutely everyday object, like this chair or that poster.' (Always this will to absorb and reabsorb art, where we find both American pragmatism — terrorism of the useful, blackmail of integration — and something like an echo of the mysticism of sacrifice.) He adds: 'Reality needs no intermediary, all you have to do is isolate it from the environment and put it on canvas'. But this is the whole problem: since the everydayness of this chair (or hamburger, tailfin, celebrity pin-up) is precisely its context, and specifically the serial context of all similar or slightly dissimilar chairs, etc. Everydayness is *difference in repetition*. By isolating a chair on canvas, I remove it from all everydayness, and at the same time I remove from the canvas all its character as an everyday object (which should, according to Warhol, make it absolutely resemble a chair). This is a familiar impasse: art can no more be absorbed by the everyday (the canvas = the chair) than it can capture the everyday as such (the chair isolated on canvas = the real chair). Immanence and transcendence are equally impossible: they are two sides of the same dream.

In brief, there is no essence of the everyday or the commonplace, and thus no art of the everyday: this is a mystical aporia. If Warhol (and the others) believe that, it is because they delude themselves about the very status of art and the artistic act, and this is not at all uncommon among artists. Furthermore, this mystical nostalgia can even be found in the productive act or gesture: 'I'd like to be a machine,' says Andy Warhol, who indeed paints with stencils and silkscreens, etc. There is no worse arrogance for art than the pretence of being machinic, and there is no worse conceit for someone who enjoys the status of creator, whether he wants it or not, than being dedicated to serial automatism. However, it is not possible to accuse Warhol and the other Pop artists of bad faith, since their rigorous logic runs up against the sociological and cultural status of art, about which they can do nothing. Their ideology reflects this powerlessness. When they try to desacralise their practice, society sacralises them all the more. And from this one can conclude that even their most radical attempt to securalise the themes and practice of their art ends up as an precedented exaltation and manifestation of the sacred in art. Quite simply, Pop artists fail to see that if a picture is to avoid being a sacred super-sign (a unique object, a signature, a noble and magical object of commerce), then content or the intentions of the author are not enough; it is the structures of cultural production that decide this. Ultimately, only the rationalisation of the market for paintings, as with any other manufacturing enterprise, could desacralise them and turn them into everyday objects. [13] Perhaps this is neither thinkable, nor possible, nor even desirable — who knows? In any case, it is the point of no return: either you stop painting, or else you continue at the cost of regressing to the traditional mythology of artistic creation. And this downhill slide leads to the recuperation of classical pictorial values: Oldenburg's 'Expressionist' treatment, Wesselmann's Fauvism à la Matisse, Lichtenstein's art nouveau and Japanese calligraphy, etc. What are we to make of these 'legendary' resonances? What are we to make of these techniques that seem to say: 'It's all painting just the same'? The logic of Pop is not to be found in an aesthetic of multiplication or in a metaphysic of the object — its logic is elsewhere.

Pop could be defined as a *game* of manipulating different levels of mental perception — a kind of mental Cubism which would seek to diffract objects not in terms of spatial analysis, but according to the modalities of perception elaborated across the centuries by an entire culture through its intellectual and technical apparatuses: objective reality, image as reflection, drawn figuration, technical figuration (the photo), abstract schematisation, discursive utterance, etc. On the other hand, the use of the phonetic alphabet and industrial techniques have imposed schemas of division, doubling, abstraction, and repetition (ethnographers have described the bewilderment experienced by 'primitives' upon being shown *absolutely* identical books: their whole view of the world is turned upside down). We can see in these various modes the countless figures of a *rhetoric of designation* and recognition. This is where Pop comes into its own: it works on the differences between these diverse levels or modes, and on the perception of these differences. Thus the silkscreen of a lynching is not an evocation, because it presupposes the transmutation of this lynching into a news item, into a journalistic sign by virtue of mass communications, a sign taken one step further by silkscreening. The repetition of the same photo presupposes the unique photo, and beyond that the real being of whom it is a reflection; furthermore, this real being could figure in the work without disrupting it — it would be only one more combination.

Just as there is no order of reality in Pop, but levels of signification, so is there no real space: the only space is that of the canvas, that of the juxtaposition of different sign-elements and their relations. Nor is there any real time: the only time is that of reading, that of the differential perception of the object and its image, of a particular image and the same repeated, etc. It is the time necessary for a *mental correction*, for an *accommodation* to the image or artifact in its relation to the real object (it doesn't involve reminiscence, but the perception of an *immediate* and *logical* difference). Nor can this reading ever be a search for articulation or coherence, but always an extended scan, a verification of succession.

We can see that the activity Pop prescribes (once again in its ambition to be rigorous) has little to do with our 'aesthetic sensibility'. Pop is a 'cool' art: it demands neither aesthetic ecstasy nor affective or symbolic participation ('deep involvement'), but a kind of 'abstract involvement', an *instrumental curiosity* — one preserving something of childhood curiosity or the naive enchantment of discovery (and why not?, Pop can also be seen as popular illustration, or as a Book of Hours for consumers), but above all one triggering those intellectual reflexes of decoding, deciphering, etc., which we described before.

In a word, Pop is not popular art. For the ethos of popular culture (if it exists at all) is based precisely on unambiguous realism, on linear narration (and not repetition or the diffraction of levels), on allegory and the decorative (that is not Pop Art, since these two categories refer to something essentially 'other'), and on emotional participation associated with moral vicissitudes.[14] It is only on a quite rudimentary level that Pop can be mistaken for 'figurative' art, colourful imagery, a naive chronicle of consumer society, etc. It is true that Pop artists take pleasure in this pretence. Their candour is immense, as is their ambiguity. As for their humour, or the humour they are credited with, once again we are on tricky ground. In this regard, it would be instructive to observe public reactions. For many, the works provoke a laugh (at least the inclination to laugh) which is both moral and obscene (these canvases are obscene from the classical point of view). Then, a smile of derision, such that one cannot tell if they are judging the objects painted or the painting itself — a smile that turns willing accomplice, all more or less contorted in the shameful desolation of not knowing what angle to take on it: 'That can't really be serious, but we're not going to be scandalised by it, because perhaps deep down . . .' Even so, Pop is both full of humour and humourless. By all logic it has nothing to do with subversive or aggressive humour, with a surrealistic telescoping of objects. What is precisely involved is no longer the shortcircuiting of objects in their function, but the juxtaposition of them in order to analyse their relations. This approach is not terroristic,[15] but at best entails effects more like cultural estrangement. In fact, something entirely different is involved. Let us not forget, to return to the system being described, that a 'certain smile' belongs to the *obligatory signs* of consumption — a smile no longer comprised of humour, of critical distance, except as a reminder of that transcendence of critical value manifested today in a knowing wink. This false distance is present everywhere, in spy films, in Godard, in modern advertising which continually uses it as a cultural allusion, etc. At the very limit, one can no longer distinguish in this 'cool' smile between the smile of humour and that of commercial complicity. This is also what happens in Pop, whose smile sums up its whole ambiguity: it is not the smile of critical distance, but the smile of *collusion*.

THE ORCHESTRATION OF MESSAGES

TV, radio, the press and advertising comprise a heterogeneous mass of signs and messages where all orders are equivalent. Here is a selection taken at random from radio:

— an ad for Remington razors,
— a summary of social unrest over the past fortnight,
— an ad for Dunlop SP-Sport tyres,
— a debate on the death penalty,
— an ad for Lip watches,
— a report on the war in Biafra,
— and an ad for new blue Crio laundry detergent.

In this litany alternating between the story of the world and portraits of objects (altogether forming a kind of poem in the style of Prévert, with alternate gloomy and rose-coloured passages — the latter of course being advertising), the accent apparently falls on information. But it also falls, paradoxically, on neutrality and impartiality: the discourse on the world tries to be detached. Its 'bland' tone directly clashes with the valedictory discourse on objects, with its shrill note of rapturous cheer — the whole pathos of real vicissitudes, of real persuasion, is transferred to the object and its discourse. In this careful blend of discourse on 'world affairs' and discourse on 'consumption' to the exclusive emotional advantage of the latter, advertising tends to function as backdrop, as a reassuring litany of interwoven signs, into which the vicissitudes of the world are inscribed as a diversion. These latter, neutralised by cutting, immediately fall victim to consumption themselves. The newscast is not the hodgepodge it seems: its systematic alternation dictates a single form of reception, that of consumption.

It is not just because the valedictory tone of advertising suggests that the story of the world is fundamentally unimportant, and that the only things worthy of consideration are consumer goods. This is secondary. Its real efficacy is more subtle: it prescribes through the systematic succession of messages an *equivalence* between story and news item, between event and spectacle, between news and advertising *at the level of the sign.* This is where the true effect of consumption lies, and not in the express discourse of advertising. It consists, thanks to the technical supports, the technical media of TV and radio, of cutting up events of the world into discontinuous, successive, and non-contradictory messages, into signs which can be juxtaposed and combined with other signs in the abstract realm of broadcasting. What we consume, then, is not a particular spectacle or image as such; it is the potential succession of all possible spectacles — and the certainty that this law of succession and division of programs will ensure that nothing will emerge from them which is not a spectacle or sign of one kind or another.

'THE MEDIUM IS THE MESSAGE'

Here we need to accept, in this sense at least, McLuhan's formula 'the medium is the message' as fundamental to the analisis of consumption. It indicates that the true message delivered by the media of radio and TV, one decoded and 'consumed' at a deep unconscious level, is not the manifest content of sounds and images, but a coercive system, linked to the very technical nature of these media, for disarticulating the real into successive and equivalent signs — the *normalised*, programmed, and miraculous transition from Vietnam to the variety show through their total mutual abstraction.

And there is something like a law of technological inertia which says that the closer you get to 'live' documentary reportage, and the more finely attuned to reality is the colour and resolution, the wider becomes the gulf between perfection in technical perfection and the real world; and the 'truer' becomes the assertion that, for TV and radio, the primary function of each message is to refer to another message, as Vietnam does to advertising, and advertising does to the newscast, etc. — their systematic juxtaposition being the discursive mode of the medium, its message, its meaning. But in thus uttering itself as the message, we can easily see how it imposes a whole divisible system of interpretation on the world.

This technological process of mass communication delivers a highly imperative sort of message: *the message of message consumption*, of fragmentation and spectacularisation, of misrecognition of the world and the valorisation of information as commodity, the exaltation of content as sign. In brief, its function is one of packaging (in the publicity sense of the word — in the sense that advertising is the 'mass' medium par excellence, one whose devices permeate all the others) and of misrecognition.

This is true of all the media, and even of the medium of books or 'literacy', which McLuhan made into a major demonstration of his theory. He maintains that the appearance of the printed book was a fundamental turning point for our civilisation — not so much through the content (ideological, informational, scientific, etc.) passed from one generation to the next, but through *the profound constraint of systematisation exerted by its technical nature*. He maintains that the book is first a *technical* model, and that the order of communication which governs it (the visible fragmentation into letters, words, pages, etc.) is ultimately a more fruitful and far-reaching model than any symbol, idea, or phantasm constituting its manifest discourse: 'The effects of technology do not occur at the level of opinions and concepts, but alter sense ratios or patterns of perception steadily and without any resistance.'

It is obvious that the content mostly conceals from us the real function of the medium. It presents itself as message, whereas its real message (compared to which the manifest discourse is perhaps only a connotation) is the profound structural change brought about in human relations in terms of scale, models, and habits. Put crudely, the 'message' of a railway is not the coal or passengers it transports, but a new vision of the world, a new state of conurbation, etc. The 'message' of TV is not the images it transmits, but the new modes of perception and relations imposed by it, the alteration of traditional family or group structures. Further still, in the case of TV and modern mass media, what is received, assimilated and 'consumed' is less a particular spectacle than potentially all spectacles.

So the truth of mass media is that they function to neutralise the unique character of actual world events by replacing them with a multiple universe of mutually reinforcing and self-referential media. At the very limit, they become each other's reciprocal content — and this constitutes *the totalitarian 'message' of the consumer society*.

What the medium of TV circulates through its technical organisation is the idea (or ideology) of a world visualisable and divisible at will, one that is readable as images. It circulates the ideology of *the total dominance of a system of reading over a world now become a system of signs*. The images on TV aspire to the metalanguage of an absent world. Just as the most minor technical object or gadget promises the universal assumption of technology, so are these image-signs the presumption of an imagination exhausting the world, and a total assumption of the mode of reality to images which would be something like its memory cell, that of universal reading. Behind the 'consumption of images' is outlined an imperialistic system of reading: what will increasingly tend to exist is only that which can be read (or *must* be read: the 'legendary'). And then the truth of the world and its history will no longer be in question, but simply the internal coherence of a system of reading. It is on this chaotic, conflictual, and contradictory world that each medium thus imposes its most abstract and coherent logic; or imposes itself, according to McLuhan's formula, as the message. And it is the substance of a world fragmented, filtered, and reinterpreted according to this technical but 'legendary' code that we 'consume'. All actual cultural or political value has vanished from the whole materiality of the world, from a whole culture industrially converted into finished products and the material of signs.

If we consider the sign as an articulation of signifier and signified, then it is possible to specify two types of confusion. For the child, or for the 'primitive', the signifier can disappear in favour of the signified (like the child who mistakes his own image for a living being, or those African television viewers who wonder what becomes of the man that disappears from the screen). Conversely, in the image centered on itself, or in the message centered on the code, the signifier becomes its own signified; there is a confused circularity of the two in favour of the signifier, an abolition of the signified and *a tautology of the signifier*. This is what defines consumption, or the systematic *effect of consumption*, at the level of mass media. Instead of arriving at the world via the mediation of the image, it is the image which turns round on itself via the detour of the world (it is the signifier which designates itself behind the alibi of the signified).

One passes from the message centered on the signified (the transitive message) to the message centered on the signifier — in the case of TV, for example, from the events signified by the image to the consumption of the image as such (which is to say as something precisely different from those events, or as Brecht would say, as a spectacular and 'culinary' substance, devouring itself in the very course of its absorption, and never referring beyond it). Also different in the sense that the image presents them neither to be perceived nor comprehended in their historical, social, or cultural specificity, but delivers all of them to indiscriminant reinterpretion according to the same code, whose structure is at once *technical* and *ideological* — in other words, in the case of TV, the ideological code of mass culture (the system of moral, social, or political values), and the mode of division and articulation of the medium itself, prescribe a certain type of discursivity which neutralises the multiple and fluctuating content of messages, for which it substitutes its own rigid constraints of meaning. This profound discursivity of the medium is, as opposed to the manifest discourse of images, decoded *unconsciously* by the spectator.

THE MEDIUM OF ADVERTISING

In this sense, advertising is perhaps the most remarkable mass medium of our epoch. Just as it potentially glorifies all objects when speaking of a particular one, and just as it actually refers, when speaking of a particular object or trademark, to a totality of objects and a universe entirely made up of objects and trademarks, so does it address all consumers through each of them, and each consumer through all of them, thus simulating a *totality of consumers*, and retribalising them in a McLuhanesque sense; in other words, through an immanent complicity or collusion at the direct level of the message, but above all at the level of the very code of the medium itself. Each advertising image prescribes a consensus among all those individuals potentially summoned to decipher it; which is to say, in decoding the message, to automatically conform to the code in which this image has been encoded.

Thus the function of advertising as mass communication is not related to its content, its modes of diffusion, its overtly economic or psychological objectives, or the actual size of its audience (even though all of this has its importance and serves as its support), but to its very logic as an autonomised medium: which is to say, a medium no longer referring to real objects, to a real reference in the world, but referring *one sign to another, one object to another, one consumer to another*. In a similar fashion, the book becomes a means of mass communication when it refers one of its readers to all the other readers (thus the substance of reading is no longer meaning, but quite simply the sign of cultural complicity), and when the book-object refers to others in the same collection, etc. One could analyse the way in which the symbolic system of language itself becomes a mass medium at the level of the trademark and the discourse of advertising.[16] Everywhere mass communication is defined by this systematisation at the level of the technical medium and its code, by this systematic production of messages — not about the world, but about the medium itself.[17]

THE PSEUDO-EVENT AND NEO-REALITY

Here we enter the world of the pseudo-event, of pseudo-history and of pseudo-culture described by Daniel Boorstin in *The Image*; in other words, a world of events, history, culture and ideas produced not from the fluctuating and contradictory nature of reality, but *produced as artifacts from the technical manipulation of the medium and its coded elements*. It is this, and nothing else, which defines all signification whatsoever as *consumable*. It is this generalised *substitution of the code for the reference* that defines mass media consumption.

The raw event is exchange, and not the material of exchange. It is not 'consumable' unless filtered, fragmented, and re-elaborated by a whole series of industrial procedures — by the mass media — into a finished product, into the material of finished and combined signs, analogous to the finished objects of industrial production. Makeup on the face undergoes the same operation: the systematic substitution of its real but imperfect features by a network of abstract and coherent messages made up of technical elements and a code of prescribed significations (the code of 'beauty').

We should be careful not to interpret this immense enterprise for producing artifacts, makeup, pseudo-objects and pseudo-events that invades our everyday existence as the denaturation or falsification of authentic 'content'. Given everything mentioned thus far, we can readily see that the misappropriation of meaning, depoliticisation of politics, deculturation of culture, and desexualisation of the body in mass media consumption is situated quite beyond the 'tendentious' reinterpretation of *content*. It is in *form* that everything has changed: everywhere there is, in lieu and in place of the real, its substitution by a 'neo-real' entirely produced from a combination of coded elements. An immense *process of simulation* has taken place throughout all of everday life, in the image of those 'simulation models' on which operational and computer sciences are based. One 'fabricates' a model by combining characteristics or elements of the real; and, by making them 'act out' a future event, structure or situation, tactical conclusions can be drawn and applied to reality. It can be used as an analytical tool under controlled scientific conditions. In mass communications, this procedure assumes *the force of reality*, abolishing and volatilising the latter in favour of that *neo-reality of a model* materialised by the medium itself.

But once again, let us be wary of language which automatically refers to the 'false', the 'pseudo' and the 'artifical'. And let us return with Boorstin to advertising in our attempt to grasp this new logic, which is also a new practice and a new 'mentality'.

a is event as object?

BEYOND THE TRUE AND THE FALSE

Advertising occupies a strategic position in this process, since it is the dominion of the pseudo-event par excellence. Advertising turns the object into an event. In fact, it constructs it as such by eliminating its objective characteristics. It constructs the object as a model, as a spectacular news item. 'Modern publicity was born when advertisements ceased to be spontaneous recommendations, becoming instead "fabricated news items"' (this is why advertising is commensurate with the 'news', both being subjected to the same 'mythic' labour: advertising and the 'news' thus constitute the same visual, graphic, acoustic and mythic substance, whose succession and alternation at the level of all the media appears *natural* to us — they give rise to the same 'curiosity', to the same spectacular and ludic absorption[18]). Journalists and publicists are *manipulators of myth*: they stage an object or event as fiction. They 'liberally interpret' it — at the very limit, they deliberately construct it. And thus it is necessary, if one wants to judge them objectively, to apply to them the categories of myth: the latter is neither true nor false, and the question is not believing or disbelieving it. Whence this endless debate on two false problems:

1. Do publicists believe in what they do? (for which they could be partly forgiven).

2. Don't consumers truly believe in advertising? (from which they could be partly saved).

Boorstin thus presents the idea that publicists should be exonerated — all this persuasiveness and mystification is much less due to their lack of scruples than to our desire to be deceived; it proceeds less from their desire to seduce than from our desire to be seduced. And he points to the example of Barnum, whose 'genius lay not in discovering how easy it is to fool the public, but rather in how much the public loved to be fooled'. It is a seductive hypothesis, but a false one: all of this does not rely on a certain reciprocal perversity, on a cynical manipulation or collective masochism revolving around the true and the false. The truth is that advertising (and the other mass media) doesn't fool us: *advertising is beyond the true and the false*, just as fashion is beyond the ugly and the beautiful, and just as the modern object, in its sign function, is beyond the useful and the useless.

The problem of the 'veracity' of advertising should be posed in the following manner: if publicists really 'lie', it would be easy to unmask them — but they don't do this. And if they don't, it's not because they are too intelligent for this, but because 'above all the art of advertising involves the invention of persuasive arguments which are neither true nor false' (Boorstin) — for the very good reason that, since things no longer find their origin or reference in reality, advertising has to find a different type of *verification*, as do all myths and magical speech, that of 'self-fulfilling prophecy' (a statement which becomes true by its very utterance). 'The successful publicity agent is master of a new art, that of rendering things true by asserting that they are true. He is well versed in the technique of self-fulfilling prophecies.'

Advertising is a spoken prophecy to the extent that it isn't meant to be comprehended or apprehended, but to be foretold. What it says doesn't presuppose a prior truth (like the object's use value), but a posterior confirmation through the reality of the prophetic sign it emits. This is its mode of efficacy. It turns the object into a pseudo-event which, through its incorporation into the consumer's discourse, becomes a real event in everyday life. One can see that the true and the false are indistinguishable here — just like electoral opinion polls, where one no longer knows if the voting simply confirms the polls (and thus is no longer a real event, but a mere substitute for these polls which, as *indexical* simulation models, have become *determinant* agents of reality), or if it is the polls that reflect public opinion. This relationship is impossible to untangle. Just as nature imitates art, so does everyday life end up as a replica of its model.

The mode of 'self-fulfilling prophecy' is tautological. Reality is nothing more than this model of self-utterance. So it is with magical speech, so it is with simulation models — and so it is with advertising which, among all those discourses available to it, prefers to operate through tautological discourse. Everything in it is a 'metaphor' for one and the same thing: the trademark. Phrases like 'A Better Beer' (but better than what?), and 'Lucky Strike, A Toasted Cigarette' (of course, they all are!), patently rely on a circular argument. As Hertz ('the world's number one in car rentals') concludes in a long advertisement: 'Let's be logical. If you didn't get that little bit more from us, we wouldn't have achieved the position we occupy . . . And perhaps someone else would be doing this advertisement.' What else is this but pure tautology, argument after the fact? It is thus repetition itself that everywhere ensures effective causality. Just as certain laboratories work on the artificial synthesis of molecules, so does advertising work on the 'artificial synthesis' of the true by means of efficacious speech. 'Persil Washes Whiter' is not a sentence, but Persil-speak. Like other advertising syntagms, it does not explain or offer meaning — they are neither true nor false, but precisely eliminate meaning and proof. They substitute for the latter indicatives without sentences, repetitive imperatives. And as with magical speech, this tautology in discourse attempts to induce tautological repetition *by an event*. Through his purchase, the consumer can do no more than consecrate *the event of myth*.

We could take this analysis of advertising discourse further in this direction, as well as extend it to the different modern media, in order to see that everywhere, according to a total inversion of the traditional logic of signification and interpretation based on the true and the false, it is this myth (or model) that finds its event, according to a production of speech now industrialised in direct proportion to the production of material goods.

NOTES

1. [See 'Le vertige consommé de la catastrophe', *La Société de consommation*, pp. 30-35.]
2. [Fr. *Recyclage*, also 'retraining', 'reprocessing' and 'upgrading'.] *recycle*
3. If beauty is in the 'line', then the career is in the 'profile'. The connivance of this lexicon is significant.
4. Cf. below, 'The Pseudo-Event and Neo-Reality'.
5. [Fr. *Tirlipot* is a reference to a famous quiz show on French radio during the 1960s.]
6. [Fr. *Computer* would appear to be the brand name of a specific type of slot machine that tests people's mental reflexes and grades them accordingly.]
7. In this sense, there is a certain relationship between kitsch and snobbery. But whereas snobbery is linked to a process of aristocratic or bourgeois acculturation, kitsch is essentially the product of the rising 'middle' classes in bourgeois industrial society.
8. But it is not a plaything, since for the child this serves a symbolic function. Yet, by this very fact, the 'new-look' or latest plaything can also become a gadget.
9. The *pure* gadget, defined by its total uselessness for anybody whatsoever, would be nonsensical.
10. Cf. Daniel Boorstin, *L'Image* [*The Image: A Guide to Pseudo-Events in America* (1961), New York, Atheneum, 1971].
11. Cubists still searched for the 'essence' of space, attempting to unveil its 'secret geometry', etc. With Dada, Duchamp and the Surrealists, objects were stripped of their (bourgeois) function and paraded in their subversive banality, as a reminder of lost essence and that order of authenticity evoked through the absurd. For Ponge, there was still an active poetic consciousness or perception in his attachment to naked and concrete objects. In brief, whether critical or poetic, all art, 'without which things would be no more than what they are', feeds (before Pop) on transcendence.
12. Cf. below, 'The Consumption of Consumption' [*La Société de consommation*, pp. 311-16].

13. In this sense, the truth of Pop would be the wage and the billboard, not the commission and the art gallery.

14. 'Popular' art is not attached to objects, but first and always to man and his exploits. It wouldn't depict a delicatessen or an American flag, but a-man-eating or a-man-saluting-the-American-flag.

15. In fact, we often read this 'terrorist' humour into it. But through critical nostalgia on our part.

16. It is easy to see how language [*langage*] can be 'consumed' in this sense. Language becomes an object of consumption or a fetish from the moment that, instead of being a vehicle for meaning, it takes on the connotations, vocabulary, and inflections of membership in a group, class, or caste (the intellectual jargon of the 'smart' set, or the political jargon of parties and cliques); from the moment that language, instead of being *the means of exchange*, becomes the *material of exchange* for the private use of a group or class (its real function being, behind the alibi of a message, one of collusion and recognition); and from the moment that, instead of bringing meaning into circulation, it circulates itself as a password or token of passage in a tautological group process (the group is what it speaks).

It is no longer language [*langue*] employed as a system of distinct denotative signs, but consumed as a system of connotation, as a distinctive code.

17. The same process applies to the 'consumption of medicine'. We are witnessing an extraordinary inflation of the demand for health, directly linked to raised standards of living. There is no longer any distinction between the demand for 'basic' health care (but on what definition of minimum health and bio-psychosomatic equilibrium could it be based?) and the compulsion of consumers for medical, surgical and dental services. The practice of medicine has changed into *the use of doctors themselves*; and this extravagent and ostentatious use of the doctor-object, of medication as an object, links up with the dual residence and the automobile for displaying one's social standing. Here again, medication, and above all doctors for the well-heeled classes (Balint: 'The medication most frequently dispensed in general medicine is the doctor himself'), have become an end in themselves, after having been a means to health considered as the ultimate good. They are thus consumed, according to the same systematic misappropriation of practical and objective functions for the purpose of mental manipulation, of a kind of fetishistic calculus of signs.

In all truth, we need to distinguish two levels of this 'consumption': the 'neurotic' need to receive medication and medical care for reducing anxiety. This demand is no less objective than the one relating to organic complaints, but it still involves an aspect of 'consumption' to the extent that the doctor no longer has a specific value: as someone who reduces anxiety, or as an agent of care, he is substitutable for any other mechanism of partial regression — alcohol, 'shopping', and collecting (the consumer 'collects' doctors and medicines). Here the doctor is consumed as one sign among others (in the same way that the washing machine is consumed as a sign of wealth and status — see above).

Thus, in a very real sense, what the 'consumption of medicine' institutes is, through this neurotic logic of individuals, a logic of social status that integrates the doctor — beyond all objective usefulness and on a par with any other *measure* of worth — into the general system as a sign. We can see that medical consumption is based on the abstraction (or reduction) of the medical function. Everywhere we discover this form of systematic misappropriation as the very principle of consumption.

18. This is why the whole resistance to the introduction of advertising on TV and elsewhere is simply a moralistic and archaic reaction. The problem really lies at the level of the system of signification.

The End of Production

We are at the end of production. Production coincides, in the West, with the formulation of the commodity law of value, or with the reign of political economy. Before that nothing was strictly *produced*: everything was *deduced*, through the grace (of God) or beneficence (of nature) of an agency that offers or refuses its wealth. Value emanated from the reign of divine or natural qualities (these have retrospectively become indistinguishable for us). This is how the Physiocrats still perceived the cycle of land and labour: the latter had no specific value. We can therefore enquire whether an actual *law* of value exists here, since value is *dispensed* without the possibility of rational expression. Value is not detachable from its form, since it is bound to an inexhaustible referential substance. If a law of value exists here, it would be a *natural* law, as opposed to a commodity law, of value.

But as soon as value is *produced*, as soon as its reference becomes labour, and its law becomes the general equivalence of all types of labour, a great change rocks this edifice of the natural distribution or dispensation of wealth. Value is now assigned to the specific and rational function of human labour (or social labour). It is measurable, and so all of a sudden is surplus value.

The critique of political economy begins at this point, taking social production and the mode of production as its references. The concept of production alone makes it possible to extract, through the analysis of this strange commodity which is labour power, a *surplus* (or surplus value) for regulating the rational dynamics of capital, as well as the equally rational dynamics of revolution.

Today everything has changed again. Gone for us is that quantitative, material and measurable configuration which defined production: the commodity form, labour power, equivalence, and surplus value.

Productive forces once defined a reference — inconsistent with the relations of production, but nonetheless a reference — of social wealth. An element of production still supported that social form called capital, and its internal critique called Marxism. And even the revolutionary demands were based on the abolition of the *commodity* law of value.

But we have now passed from the commodity law to the structural law of value, and this passage coincides with the disintegration of the social form called production. Are we consequently still in a capitalist mode? It is possible that we are in a hypercapitalist mode, or in an altogether different order. Is the form of capital linked to the law of value in general, or does it have a particular and determinate form of value? (Perhaps we are indeed already in a socialist mode? Perhaps this metamorphosis of capital, under the sign of the structural law of value, is simply the inevitable outcome of socialism? Ouch!) If the life and death of capital is contingent upon the *commodity* law of value, and if the revolution depends on the mode of production, then we are neither in capital, nor in the revolution. If revolution implies the liberation of the social and generic production of man, then there is no prospect of revolution any longer, because there is no more production. If, on the other hand, capital is a *mode of domination*, then we are well and truly still there, because the structural law of value is the purest and the most illegible form of social domination, like surplus value, but without reference anymore in a dominant class or relation of force, without violence, and entirely absorbed without a trace of blood into the signs that surround us, being everywhere operational in the code by which capital has finally attained its purest discourse, a discourse beyond the dialects of industry, commerce and finance, beyond the dialects of class which held sway in the 'productive' phase — a symbolic violence everywhere inscribed in signs, and even in signs of revolution.

The structural revolution of value destroys the foundations of the 'Revolution'. The first to be mortally affected by this referential loss are revolutionary references, which can no longer find the certainty of political change in any social material of production or in any truth of labour power. This is because labour is no longer a *force*. It has become a *sign* among other signs, produced and consumed like all the rest. It is interchangeable with non-labour, with leisure, according to an exact equivalence: it is commutable with every other sector of daily life. Labour is no longer 'alienated' to a greater or lesser degree; it is no longer the locus for a specific historical 'praxis' engendering specific social relations. It is, like most practices, nothing other than a set of sign operations. It enters into the general design of life, or into its framing by signs. Labour is not even that historical suffering or prostitution which once acted as the inverted promise of final emancipation (or, for Lyotard, as the locus of worker *gratification*, the fulfilment of desire in the abject and relentless pursuit of value according to the rules of capital). None of this is true anymore. The sign form has seized upon labour and emptied it of all its historical and libidinal signification, absorbing it in the process of its own reproduction: behind the empty allusion of what it designates, the function of the *sign* is to replicate itself. Labour was once able to designate the reality of social production, of the social objective of accumulating wealth, even while exploited by capital and surplus value — it is precisely here that it still maintained use value for the expanded reproduction of capital, and for its ultimate destruction. In any case, it was marked by a finality. Even if a worker is absorbed into the pure and simple reproduction of his own labour power, it does not follow that the process of production itself is experienced as senseless repetition. Labour, through its very abjection, revolutionises society in the form of a commodity whose potential always exceeds the pure and simple reproduction of value.

But such is not the case today. Labour is no longer productive, since it has become reproductive of the *assignment to labour*, as the general habit of a society no longer certain whether it wants to produce or not. No more myths of production, no more content of production: national balance sheets merely trace a numerical and statistical growth, devoid of meaning — as inflated signs of accountancy, they are even incapable of providing a fantasy for the collective will. The pathos of growth is now dead, as is the pathos of production which was its final, panicked and paranoid erection — presently detumescent according to the figures. No one believes them anymore. So it becomes all the more essential to reproduce labour as a social attribution, reflex, morality, consensus, regulation, and reality principle. But the reality principle of labour is that *of the code*. An immense *ritual of the signs of labour* extends across the whole of society — no matter whether it still produces or not, so long as it reproduces itself. Socialisation by ritual, and by signs, is much more effective than socialisation by energies bound to production. All that is asked of you is not that you produce, nor that you strive to excel yourself (this classical ethic has become rather suspect), but that you be socialised. All that is asked is that you take no part in value, according to the structural definition which here takes on its full *social* significance, except as one term in relation to others; that you function as a sign within the general scenario of production, just as labour and production now only function as signs or terms interchangeable with non-labour, consumption, communication, etc. As a multiple, incessant, and spiralling relation within the whole network of other signs, and thus emptied (and quite generally disinvested) of all its energy and its substance, labour re-emerges as the model of social simulation, bringing all other categories of political economy into the aleatory realm of the code.

There is a disquieting strangeness about this sudden plunge into a kind of second existence, separated from you with all the distance of a former life, since there was a familiarity or intimacy in the traditional process of labour. Even the concrete reality of exploitation, the violent sociality of labour is familiar. That is all gone today. And this is not so much due to the *operative* abstraction of the *process* of labour, which is so often blamed, as to the passage of all *signification* of labour into an *operational* field where it becomes a floating variable, bringing with it the whole imaginary of a former life.

Beyond the autonomisation of production as a *mode* (with all its internal convulsions, contradictions and revolutions), the *code* of production must be made apparent. This is the form it currently takes, after the period of 'materialist' history which succeeded in legitimating production as the true principle of social change. (For Marx, art, religion, the law, etc., have no history of their own — only production has a history, or better: production *is* history, it *grounds* history. What an incredible fiction of labour and production as historical reason and as the generic model of fulfilment!)

The end of this religious autonomisation of production allows us to imagine that it could easily have been entirely *produced* (this time in the sense of a theatrical or film production), and for completely different purposes than those internal finalities secreted by production (among them the revolution).

To analyse production as a code is to move beyond the material presence of machines, factories, labour time, products, wages and money, as well as the more formal but equally 'objective' presence of surplus value, the market and capital, in order to identify the rules of the game — to destroy the logical network of the instances of capital, including the critical network of its analysis by Marxist categories (for they are nothing other than the second-degree appearance of capital, its *critical* appearance), in order to identify the elementary signifiers of production, as well as the social relations it installs, forever buried under the historical illusion of the producers (and theoreticians).

LABOUR

Labour power is not a force. It is a definition or axiom, since its 'real' function in the labour process, its 'use value', is nothing but the replication of this definition in the operation of the code. It is at the level of the sign, never at the level of energy, that violence is fundamental. The *mechanism* of capital (and not its law) operates through surplus value — the non-equivalence of wages and labour power. Even if the two were equivalent, leading to the end of surplus value, and even if wages (the selling of labour power) were abolished, man would still be marked by this axiom, by this destiny of production, and by this sacrament of labour that sets him apart like a sex. No, the worker is no longer a man, neither man nor woman: he has a sex uniquely his own, which is this labour power that assigns him an end, and marks him just as a woman is marked by her sex (her sexual definition), or as blacks are marked by the colour of their skin — these are also signs, and nothing but signs.

We need to totally distinguish between what pertains to the *mode* of production and what pertains to the *code* of production. Before it becomes an element in the commodity law of value, labour power is first a status, or a structure of obedience to a code. Before it becomes exchange value and use value, it is already, like any other commodity, a *sign* of the extraction of value from nature, by which production can be defined, and which is the fundamental axiom of our culture, and no other. Far more fundamental than quantitative equivalence is this underlying message of commodities: the uprooting of nature (and mankind) from indeterminacy and its subjection to the determinacy of value. What one can sense in this furious construction by bulldozers, in this mania for freeways and 'infrastructures', in this civilising frenzy of the productive era and its rage to leave no plot of ground unturned, to countersign everything by production, but without even the prospect of increasing wealth — is producing for the sake of marking, producing for the sake of reproducing mankind as marked. What is production today if not this terrorism of the code? This is just as evident to us now as it was to the first industrial generations, who dealt with machines as though they were mortal enemies, bearers of total disintegration, before the lofty dream of the historical dialectic of production took hold. This emergence almost everywhere of Luddite practices, this savage attack on the tools of production (and above all on themselves as the force of production), this endemic sabotage and defection have a lot to say about the fragility of the productive order. Smashing machines is a deviant act if they are the *means* of production, or if there remains some ambiguity concerning their future use value. But if the *ends* of production collapse, the respect owed to the means also collapses; machines appear in their true light, as direct, unmediated, and operative signs of the social relations of death upon which capital thrives. Then nothing can oppose their immediate destruction. In this sense, the Luddites were much more lucid than Marx concerning the full impact of the industrial order. And so today, the *catastrophic* outcome of this industrial process, about which even Marx himself misled us in his *dialectical* euphoria of productive forces, is in a way the revenge of the Luddites.

To say that labour is a sign is not to invoke the prestige associated with specific kinds of work, nor the improved standard of living that wage labour signifies for the Algerian immigrant in relation to his tribal community, nor what it means for the Moroccan kid from the High Atlas Mountains whose only dream is to work for Simca, nor even what it means for women in our own society. In these instances, labour refers to a specific value—either an increase or change in status. But in the present scenario, labour is no longer a function of this referential definition of the sign. Any particular kind of labour, even labour in general, no longer has its specific meaning: it has now become a labour system of interchangeable positions. 'The right man in the right place', that old adage from the era of the scientific idealism of production, is finished. Nor are there any longer interchangeable yet indispensable individuals in a determinate labour process. The process of labour itself has become interchangeable: a mobile, polyvalent, intermittent system of job placement, indifferent to every objective, and even to labour in the classical sense of the term. Its only function is to locate each individual in a social nexus where nothing ever converges, except perhaps in the immanence of this functional matrix, an indifferent paradigm that inflects all individuals on the same radical, or a syntagm that associates them in the form of an indefinite combinatory.

Labour (in the form of leisure as well) invades all of life as a fundamental oppression, as a type of control, and as a permanent occupation in pre-determined places and times, according to an omni-present code. People must be *kept occupied* in all situations: at school, in the factory, on the beach, in front of the TV, or in job retraining. It is a permanent general mobilisation. But this form of labour is no longer productive in the original sense: it is no more than the mirror of society, its imaginary, its fantastic reality principle. Its death drive perhaps.

This is the tendency of every present strategy concerning labour: 'job enrichment', flexible hours, mobility, retraining, continual education, autonomy, worker-management, and the decentralisation of the labour process, including the Californian utopia of computerised work in the home. You are no longer brutally snatched away from your daily life to be surrendered to machines; you are integrated in the system, along with your childhood, your habits, your human relations, your unconscious drives, even your rejection of work. A position will be found for you somewhere, a personalised job, and if not, you will receive an amount of unemployment benefits adjusted to your personal equation. In any case, you will never be abandoned. The important thing is that everyone be a terminal in the network, a lowly terminal, but a term nevertheless — above all, not an inarticulate cry, but a linguistic term, and at the terminus of the whole structural network of language. The very choice of employment, the utopia of a job custom-made for everyone means that *the die is cast*, and that the system of job placement is complete. Labour power is no longer brutally bought and sold: it is 'designed', 'marketed' and 'merchandised', linking production with the consumerist system of signs.

The first stage of the analysis was to conceptualise consumption as an extension of the sphere of productive forces. But now we must do the reverse. We need to conceptualise the whole sphere of production, labour, and productive forces as tilted towards the sphere of 'consumption' — but here taken as a universal axiomatic, as a coded exchange of signs, and as a general design of life. So it is with knowledge, skills, and aptitudes (Verres: 'Why not consider the aptitudes of the staff as one of the resources to be managed by the boss?'[1]), but also with sexuality, the body, and imagination (Verres: 'Imagination is the only thing still connected to the pleasure principle, whereas the psychical apparatus is subordinated to the reality principle (Freud). We must stop this waste. Let imagination actualise itself as a productive force, let it invest itself. Power to imagination: the catchcry of technocracy'), and with the unconscious, the Revolution, etc. Yes, all these things are in the process of 'investment' and absorption within the sphere of value, but not so much market value as computable value; in other words, they are not mobilised for production, but rather indexed, assigned, and summoned to function as operational variables. They have become not so much productive forces, but chess pieces of the code, and checked by the same rules of the game. Whereas the axiom of production tends to reduce everything to *factors*, the axiom of the code reduces everything to *variables*. And whereas the former leads to equations and a balance sheet of forces, the latter leads to fluctuating and random combinations that neutralise by *connection*, not by *annexation*, whatever resists or escapes them.

All this is far removed from the Scientific Management of Labour (O.S.T), even though the appearance of the latter marks an important milestone in the investment by the code. Here we can distinguish two phases:

Succeeding the 'pre-scientific' phase of the industrial system, characterised by the maximum exploitation of labour power, is the phase of
machinery and the preponderance of fixed capital, where 'objectified
labour . . . appears not only in the form of a simple product, or of the
product employed as the means of labour, but in the form of the force of
production itself' (*Grundrisse*, p. 694[2]). This accumulation of objectified
labour that supplants living labour as the force of production is there-
after multiplied to infinity by the accumulation of knowledge: 'The
accumulation of knowledge and of skill, of the general productive forces
of the social brain, is thus absorbed into capital, as opposed to labour,
and hence appears as an attribute of capital, and more specifically of
fixed capital' (*Grundrisse*, p. 264).

This phase of machinery, the scientific apparatus, the collective
labourer, and the O.S.T. is one in which the 'production process has
ceased to be a labour process in the sense of a process dominated by
labour as its governing unity' (*Grundrisse*, p. 693). There is no longer
any 'original' force of production, but simply a general machinery that
transforms productive forces into capital — or rather, a machinery that
manufactures the force of production and labour power. The whole social apparatus of labour is drained of its force by this mechanism: it is the collective machinery that now directly produces all social finality, and that
produces production.

It is the supremacy of dead labour over living labour. Primitive
accumulation is nothing else: the accumulation of dead labour to the
point where it is capable of absorbing living labour — or better, to the
point where it can control its production, and for its own ends. This is
why the collapse of primitive accumulation marks a decisive turning
point for political economy: it is the passage to a preponderance of dead
labour, to a form of social relations crystallised and embodied in dead
labour, weighing on all of society as the very code of domination.
Marx's fantastic error was that he still believed in the innocence of
machines, the technical process, and science — all of which he thought
capable of becoming a sort of living social labour once the system of
capital was liquidated, even though they were the very basis of this
system. This pious hope came from having underestimated the death
in dead labour; and from thinking that the dead passes over into the
living, beyond a certain critical moment of history, by a sort of involun-
tary burst of production.

Nevertheless, Marx had sensed this when he notes that 'objectified
labour confronts living labour within the labour process itself as the
power which *rules* it; a power which, as the appropriation of living
labour, is the form of capital' (*Grundrisse*, p. 693). This is also apparent

in the formulation according to which, at a certain stage of capital, man *'steps to the side of the production process,* instead of being its chief actor' (*Grundrisse,* p. 705) — a formulation which goes far beyond political economy and its critique, since what it literally implies is no longer a process of production, but of exclusion and displacement.

Again we need to draw out all the consequences of this. When production attains this circularity and turns in on itself, it loses all objective determinacy. It incants itself as myth, its own terms having become signs. And when simultaneously this sphere of signs (including the media, information, etc.) loses its specificity as a representation of the unity of the global process of capital, then we need to say along with Marx not only that the 'production process has ceased to be a labour process', but that 'the process of capital itself has ceased to be a production process' (*Grundrisse,* p. 693 *et passim*).

The whole dialectic of production collapses with this supremacy of dead labour over living labour. But also neutralised here, and in the same manner, are use value/exchange value, as well as productive forces/relations of production — all those oppositions by which Marxism functions, and according to the same fundamental oppositions by which rationalist thought functions (the true and the false, appearance and reality, nature and culture). Everything in production and the economy becomes commutable, reversible, and exchangeable according to the same indeterminate specularity as exists in politics, fashion, or the media. Such is the indeterminate specularity of productive forces and the relations of production, of capital and labour, of use value and exchange value: the dissolution of production through the code. And today the law of value does not reside in the exchangeability of all commodities under the sign of the general equivalent, but in the far more profound exchangeability of all categories of political economy (and its critique) in accordance with the code. All the determinations of 'bourgeois' thought were neutralised and abolished by the materialist conception of production, which reduced everything to one great historical determination. But this conception is in turn neutralised and absorbed by a revolution in the terms of the system. And just as other generations could dream of a pre-capitalist society, we are beginning to dream of political economy as a lost object, and this discourse only assumes such referential force today because its object is lost.

Marx: 'On the whole, types of work that are consumed as services and not as products separable from the worker [*prestataires*] and hence not capable of existing as commodities independently of him . . . are of microscopic significance when compared with the mass of capitalist production. Thus they may be put aside for the moment, and will be dealt with in the chapter on wage-labour . . .' (*Capital*).[3] This chapter of *Capital* was never written: the problem posed by this distinction, one which overlaps with the distinction between productive and unproductive labour, is perfectly insoluble. Marxist definitions of labour are falling apart on every front, but this was so right from the very beginning. As Marx says in the *Grundrisse*: 'Labour becomes productive only by producing its own opposite [capital]' (p. 305). From this it can be logically concluded that when labour becomes self-reproductive, as is the case today throughout the whole process of the 'collective labourer', it ceases to be productive. This is the unforeseen consequence of a definition blind to the fact that capital might be grounded in something other than the 'productive', and perhaps precisely in a labour emptied of its productivity, in an 'unproductive' labour, a neutralised labour as it were, but one by means of which capital precisely frustrates the dangerous potential of a 'productive' labour, and can begin to establish its real domination, not only over labour, but over all of society. By misunderstanding this 'un'productive labour', Marx stepped to the side of the true *indefinition* of labour upon which the strategy of capital is based.

'Production for unproductive consumption is quite as productive as that for productive consumption; always assuming that it produces or reproduces capital' (*Grundrisse*, p. 306). The resulting paradox, according to Marx's own definition, is that human labour becomes increasingly unproductive, but without apparently preventing capital from extending its domination. In fact, all this is a parlour trick. There are not two or three types of labour:[4] capital itself prompted Marx to construct these elaborate distinctions. Capital has never been so stupid as to believe in them, for it has always 'naively' gone its own way. There is only one type of labour, and in fact one fundamental definition, which unfortunately is the one that Marx discarded. And today if all forms of labour take their cue from a single definition, then it is from this bastard, archaic, and unanalysed category of labour-service, and not from the classical and supposedly universal one of 'proletarian' wage-labour.

It is not labour-service in the feudal sense, since labour has lost that quality of obligation and reciprocity it once had, but in the sense indicated by Marx: in a service, the act of prestation is inseparable from the prestator — something which appears archaic from the productivist perspective of capital, but which becomes fundamental when capital is understood as a system of domination, as a system of 'enfeoffment' to a society of labour; in other words, to a certain type of political society for which labour is the rule of the game. This is where we are now (even if it was not already so in Marx's time): the reduction of all labour to a service, labour as pure and simple presence/occupation, as the consumption of time, the *prestation* of time. One performs an 'act' of labour, like one registers attendance or swears an oath of allegiance. This is indeed the sense in which the act of prestation is inseparable from the prestator. A service rendered is the commitment of one's body, time, space, and grey matter. Whether it is productive or not makes no difference with regard to this personal indexation. Surplus value is of course put to flight, and the meaning of the wage changes (we will return to this). It is not a 'regression' of capital to feudalism, but a movement toward *real* domination; in other words, toward the total solicitation and conscription of individuals. The tendency of all efforts to 'reconsolidate' labour is to make it into a total service, where the prestator becomes evermore present and personally implicated.

In this sense, labour can no longer be distinguished from other practices, and particularly from its opposite term, free time — which, because it implies the same mobilisation and investment as labour (or the same productive disinvestment), has for this reason become today *a service rendered*,[5] and so by rights should merit a wage (which in fact is not impossible[6]). In brief, this not only destroys the imaginary distinction between productive and unproductive labour, but also the very distinction between labour and everything else. There is quite simply no labour anymore in the specific sense of the term. And Marx really made the right decision by not writing that chapter of *Capital*, since it was doomed from the outset.

It is precisely at this moment that labourers become 'agents of production'. These shifts in terminology are not insignificant: the agent of production signifies, by an antiphrasis, the status of those who no longer produce anything. The semi-skilled worker [*O.S.*] had already ceased to be a labourer, but was now a worker confronted with the total indifferentiation of labour — a worker no longer engaged in the struggle over working conditions and fixed wages, but over the generalised form of labour and the political wage. Accompanying this 'agent of production' is the most abstract form of detachment, much more abstract than the old semi-skilled worker exploited to death: it is the *puppet of labour*, the lowest common module, the dumb-waiter for labour's unreality principle. To say that one no longer works but performs an 'act of production' is an inspired euphemism! With the appearance *a contrario* of the term 'productive', a culture of production and labour comes to an end. What characterises this 'agent of production' is no longer its exploitation, nor its role as raw material for a certain labour process, but its mobility, interchangeability, and function as a useless inflexion of fixed capital. The 'agent of production' designates the ultimate status of the worker who, as Marx said, 'steps to the side of production'.

Parallel to this phase where 'the process of capital itself has ceased to be a production process' is that of the disappearance of factories: the whole of society now takes on the appearance of a factory. The factory had to disappear as such, and labour had to lose its specificity in order for capital to ensure this metamorphosis and extension of its form throughout all of society. If we want to analyse the real domination of capital today, we therefore need to take note of the disappearance of determinate places of work, a determinate subject of labour, and a determinate time of social labour, as well as that of the factory, labour and the proletariat.[7] That phase of society where a branching network of factories acted as a virtual reserve army for capital is finished. The principle of the factory and labour explodes and spreads across the length of society, to such an extent that the distinction between the two becomes 'ideological': to maintain, in the revolutionary imaginary, that the factory has a specific and privileged presence is one of the traps of capital. Work appears everywhere, because there is no longer any labour. It is at this moment that labour attains its definitive and perfected form, its *principle*, linking up with the principles elaborated throughout history in those other social spaces which preceded manufacture and served as its model: the asylum, the ghetto, the workhouse, and the prison — all those places of confinement and concentration created by our culture in its march toward civilisation. But even those places have lost their fixed boundaries today: they diffuse across the global society, because the asylum form and carceral form of discrimination now invests all of social space and all moments of real life.[8] Enough factories, asylums, prisons and schools still remain, and doubtless will always remain, to act as signs of deterrence and to deflect, by their imaginary substance, the reality of capital's domination. There have always been churches to conceal the death of God, or to conceal that God is everywhere (which is the same thing). There have always been animal reserves and Indian reservations to conceal that these creatures are dead, and that we are all Indians. There have always been factories to conceal that labour is dead, that production is dead, or rather that production is everywhere and nowhere. For it is useless to combat capital today in its *determinate* forms. On the contrary, once one accepts that capital is no longer determined by anything at all, and that its supreme weapon is the reproduction of labour as imaginary, then clearly it is capital itself that is close to extinction.

WAGES

Labour in its perfected form, where it has no relationship with a determinate production, has no equivalence with the wage either. The latter is only an equivalent of labour power (however illusory or unjust) from the perspective of its *quantitative* reproduction. But even this meaning is lost when the wage is a sanction of the *status* of labour power, when it becomes a sign of conformity to the rules of the game of capital. Then the wage is no longer equivalent or proportional to anything at all;[9] like baptism (or extreme unction), it is a sacrament that turns you into a true citizen of the political society of capital. It is the end of paid labour as a form of exploitation and the beginning of paid labour as a form of shareholding in the society of capital; it is a shift from the strategic function of the worker to consumption as an obligatory social service, since beyond the economic investment by capital in the wage-revenue of the labourer, there is another sense of the term 'investment' implied by the current phase of the wage as status: capital invests the wage labourer as one invests a person with a duty or responsibility, or rather it invests him as one 'invests' or lays seige to a town — it completely occupies it, controlling all access to it.

Not only does the wage as revenue enable capital to entrust the circulation of money to producers, thus becoming the true reproducers of capital, but more profoundly the wage as status enables it to turn them into purchasers of goods insofar as capital itself is a purchaser of labour. Each user makes use of his objects of consumption, reduced to the functional status of the production of services, just as capital makes use of its labour power. Thus is everyone deeply invested with the mentality of capital.

Conversely, once the connection between wages and labour power is severed, nothing can oppose unlimited and maximalist wage demands (not even the unions). For if there is a 'fair price' for a certain *quantity* of labour power, then no price can be set for this consensus and global participation. Traditional wage demands simply negotiated the *working conditions* of producers, while the maximalist demands of wage earners is a form of offensive for the reversal of their *status* as reproducers, a status to which they are condemned through wages. These demands are a challenge. Wage earners want everything. It is their way of not only deepening the economic crisis of the system, but of turning against the system all the political constraints that it imposes on them.

Maximum wages for minimal work: such is their battle cry. And the political consequence of these escalating demands could well lead to the blowout of the system, according to its own logic of labour as enforced presence. Thus wage earners no longer intervene in the role of producers, but in the non-productive role assigned to them by capital — and their intervention in this process is catastrophic, not dialectical.

The less there is to do, the more demand there is for higher wages, since this minimal employment is the sign of an even more patent absurdity of enforced presence. This is how 'class' has been transformed by capital: dispossessed of its own exploitation, and of the use of its labour power, it can't pay capital enough for this *denial of production*, this loss of identity, and this corruption. When it was exploited, it could only demand the minimum; but once it becomes *déclassé*, it is free to emand everything. [10] And the important point is that capital can quite easily keep up with these demands. It is not at all difficult for the unions to make those wage earners without consciousness aware of the very equivalence abolished by capital between wages and labour. It is not at all difficult for the unions to channel this blackmail of unlimited wages in the direction of sensible negotiations. Without the unions, workers would immediately demand increases of 50%, 100%, or 200% — and they might even be able to get them! There are examples of this in the United States and Japan. [11]

MONEY

Saussure's proposed homology between labour and the signified on the one hand, and wages and the signifier on the other, provides a sort of matrix which could be extrapolated to the whole of political economy. But the contrary proves to be true today: there is a severed connection between signifiers and signifieds, as well as between wages and labour. And there is a parallel escalation in the movement of signifiers and wages. Saussure was correct: political economy is a language, since the mutation that affects linguistic signs when they lose their referential status also affects the categories of political economy. The same process proves to be true in two other areas:

(1) The severed connection of production from all social reference or finality — here production enters the phase of *growth*. We must understand growth not in the sense of an acceleration, but on the contrary as something which marks the *end of production*. Production was once characterised by a significant disparity between itself and a relatively contingent and autonomous form of consumption. But after the crisis of 1929, and above all since the end of the Second World War, when consumption becomes literally 'planned' and begins to assume the mythical force of a controlled variable, we enter into a phase where

production and consumption no longer have their own respective determinations or ends, but are both caught in a cycle, spiral, or tangle of excessive growth, leaving far behind their traditional social objectives. This growth becomes a process unto itself, pursued for itself alone. It is no longer devoted to needs or profits. It is not an acceleration of productivity, but a structural inflation of the *signs* of production propelled by their mutual reciprocation and proliferation, including of course the monetary sign. It is the era of rocket flights, Concordes, global military campaigns, burgeoning industries, centres for social or individual development, educational schemes, retraining programs, etc. Everything must be produced, under the constraint of reinvestment at all cost (and not as a function of the rate of surplus value). The centrepiece of this planned reproduction promises to be anti-pollution, in which the whole 'productive' system is to be recycled through the elimination of its own waste — an immense equation adding up to zero, but ultimately not for naught, because outlined in this pollution/anti-pollution 'dialectic' is the aspiration of endless growth.

(2) The severed connection of the monetary sign from all social production: here it enters unlimited speculation and inflation. Inflation is to money what the escalation of wages is to the selling of labour power (and what growth is to production). In all these cases, the same uncoupling triggers off the same boom and the same potential crisis. The same referential loss exists whether it is the uncoupling of wages from a 'fair' price for labour power, or whether it is the uncoupling of money from real production: in the former, it is the time of abstract social labour that loses its function as an index and criterion of equivalence, whereas in the latter it is the gold standard. Wage and monetary inflation (and growth) belong to the same order, and are therefore inseparable. [12]

Emptied of all the finalities and *affects* of production, money becomes speculative. With the passage from the gold standard (which was already no longer an equivalent representing true production, even though it still preserved a trace of this through a certain equilibrium — low inflation, the convertibility of currencies into gold, etc.) to floating currencies and the flotation of the system as a whole, money passes from the referential to the structural form of the sign. This is the very logic of the 'floating' signifier — not, as Lévi-Strauss thought, in the sense of yet having to find a signified, but in the sense of having detached itself from all signifieds (from an equivalence in the real) because this would restrict its proliferation and unlimited movement. Money can thus multiply itself by the simple move of transferences and ledgers, according to an incessant duplication and replication of its own abstract substance.

'Hot money' is the name given to Eurodollars, no doubt to convey this senseless circularity of the monetary sign. But it would be more precise to describe money as 'cool' — a word coined by McLuhan and Riesman to designate an intense but affectless relativity of terms, an activity motivated purely by the rules of the game and the commutation of terms to the point of their exhaustion. 'Hot', on the contrary, would designate the sign in its referential phase, with all its singularity and density as a real signified, as well as its powerful affect and weak commutability. We are totally in the cool phase of the sign. The present system of labour is cool, money is cool, and the whole structural mechanism in general is cool. And the supremely hot processes of 'classical' production and labour have given way to unlimited growth, linked to the cool processes of the disinvestment of the content and process of labour.

'Coolness' is the pure manipulation of linguistic values and ledger commutations. It is the ease and aloofness with which figures, signs and words are purely manipulated, with all the omnipotence of operational simulation. So long as there is still an affect or reference, we are in the hot era. So long as there is still a 'message', we are in the hot era. But when the medium becomes the message, we enter the cool era. This is really what has happened with money. Having arrived at a certain stage of severed connection, money ceases to be a medium or a means of circulating commodities, but becomes the realisation of the system in all its spiralling abstraction: it is *circulation itself*.

Money was the first 'commodity' to achieve the status of a sign and to *escape use value*. Ever since then it has duplicated the system of exchange value in the form of a visible sign, and in this way renders visible the market (and thus also scarcity) in all its transparency. But today money goes one step further: *it even escapes exchange value*. Freed from the market itself, it becomes an autonomous simulacrum cut adrift from every message and from every sign of exchange, becoming itself a message exchangeable with itself. Since it no longer has use value or exchange value, it has ceased to be a commodity. It is no longer the general equivalent, nor even the abstracted mediation of the market. It is what circulates faster than everything else, and out of all proportion to everything else. Of course it might be argued that, since the rise of the market economy, money has always circulated the fastest, sweeping along with its acceleration all the other sectors. And throughout the entire history of capital there has been a disparity between the different sectors (financial, industrial, agricultural, but also consumer goods, etc.) relative to the speed at which money circulates. This disparity still persists today, as with the example of national currencies (those tied to a local market, production, or trade) and their resistance to the speculation of international currency. But the latter now leads the offensive, since it is what circulates, floats, or drifts the fastest: the simple move of flotation can destroy any national economy. Thus all sectors are regulated, according to the differential rate of their turnover, by this upwardly spiralling flotation — which, far from being an epiphenomenal or antiquated process ('what use is the Stock Exchange?'), has become the purest expression of the system. This scenario is to be found everywhere: the inconvertibility of currencies into gold or the inconvertibility of signs into their references; the general flotation and mutual convertibility of currencies or the indeterminate fluidity and structural manipulation of signs. There is a flotation of all the categories of political economy once they lose their gold referent of labour power and social production (work and non-work, labour and capital have become convertible — it is the dissolution of all logic), just as there is a flotation of all the categories of consciousness once the subject, which is *the mental equivalent of the gold standard*, has been lost. There is no more referential agency under whose jurisdiction producers might exchange value according to fixed equivalences: it is the end of the gold standard. There is no more referential agency under whose aegis the subject might enter into a dialectical exchange with objects, or mutually exchange determinations on the basis of a stable identity and according to established rules: it is the end of the subject of consciousness. One is almost tempted to call it the reign of the unconscious. The logical conclusion is that if the subject of consciousness is the mental equivalent of the gold standard, then *the unconscious is the mental equivalent of financial speculation and floating capital*. Since all individuals are in fact now disinvested as subjects and dispossessed of their object relations, they drift relative to one another in the form of incessant transferential fluctuations. Flows, connections and disconnections, transferences and counter-transferences: the whole of sociality could well be described in terms of a Deleuzian unconscious or monetary mechanism (or even in terms of Riesman's 'otherdirectedness', which already refers to this floating of identities — but alas, in terms that are all too Anglo-Saxon and hardly schizophrenic). But why would the unconscious be privileged (even when orphaned and schizophrenic)? The Unconscious as a mental structure is contemporaneous with the current phase of exchange in its most radical and dominant form — it is contemporaneous with the structural revolution of value.

STRIKES

Strikes were justified historically in a system of production as a form of organised violence which, in opposing the violence of capital, attempted to extract a portion of surplus value, if not power. Today, this type of strike is dead:

(1) Because capital is in the position to allow all strikes to continue until they rot — and this is because we are no longer in a system of production (one involving the maximalisation of surplus value). Damn the profits so long as the reproduction *of the form of social relations* is saved!

(2) Because nothing is fundamentally altered by these strikes: today capital is redistributed by itself, and that is a matter of life or death for it. At best strikes extract from capital, according to its own logic, what it eventually would have conceded in any case.

So if the relations of production, and with them the class struggle, become ensnared in orchestrated political and social relations, then clearly the only thing that can break out of this cycle is what escapes the organisation and definition of class as:

— the historical instance of *representation*;

— the historical instance of *production*.

Only those who escape the whirligig of production and representation can throw its mechanism off balance and inadvertently bring about a reversal of the 'class struggle', which could well mean its end as the focal point for the 'political'. It is here that the intervention of immigrants in recent strikes takes its meaning. [13]

Because millions of workers find themselves, through the mechanism of their discrimination, deprived of all representative authority, their emergence on the stage of class struggle in the West has brought the crisis of representation to a critical point. These immigrant workers are barred entry to a class by all of society, including the unions (and moreover with the economic and racist complicity of their 'membership': for an organised proletarian 'class' centered on its economic and political relationship with the forces of a bourgeois capitalist class, immigrants are 'objectively' class enemies). And because of this social exclusion, immigrants function as analysers of the relation between workers and the unions, and more generally between 'class' and all authorised representatives of 'class'. Being deviants with regard to political representation, they infect with their deviance the whole proletariat, which also gradually learns to do without the system of representation and every authority pretending to speak in its name.

But this situation will not last: the unions and the bosses have sensed the danger and make every effort to promote immigrants to a 'full supporting role' on the stage of 'class struggle'.

Autopsy of the Unions

The Renault strike in March and April 1973 was a sort of dress rehearsal for this crisis. In appearance it seemed confused, uncoordinated, distorted, and ultimately a failure (except for the extraordinary terminological victory brought about by the replacement of the now taboo 'semi-skilled worker' with 'agent of production'!). But in reality it revealed the exquisite agony of the unions trapped between their membership and the bosses. In the beginning, it was a 'wild-cat' strike triggered off by immigrant workers. But the Trade Union Congress [*C.G.T.*] already had a weapon up its sleeve for dealing with this type of incident: the extension of strikes to other factories or other sectors of the workforce, thus taking advantage of the now ritual mass demonstrations that occur every Spring. But even though this method of control had been well tested ever since 1968, and was counted on by the unions as remaining useful for another generation, it failed to work this time. No sooner had the rank-and-file (at Seguin, Flins, Sandouville) gone out on strike than they immediately returned to work, and more significantly without heeding the 'advice' of their unions. The latter were constantly caught off-guard. Whatever the unions won from management to put before the workers was totally rejected. And whatever concessions the unions gained from the workers to put before management were rejected as well: management closed down the factories and appealed to the workers behind the unions' back. In fact, it deliberately extended the crisis to force the unions to the wall — couldn't they control *all* the workers? The real issue was the social existence or legitimacy of the unions. This is why the employers (and all the government departments) 'hardened' against them. It no longer involved a test of strength between the organised (unionised) proletariat and the bosses, but a *test of the power of representation* of those unions trapped between their membership and the bosses. And this test was the culmination of all wild-cat strikes over recent years, which is to say those detonated by non-unionists, rebellious youth, immigrants, and all the classless.

The implications of this are immense. The whole social edifice is in danger of collapsing with the collapse of the unions' legitimacy and power of representation. The legislature and other arbitrating bodies have become unwieldy. Even the police become useless when the unions prove incapable of maintaining law and order in factories or elsewhere. In May 1968, the unions saved the regime. But now their hour has come. The very confusion of these recent events demonstrates their profound implications (this is as true for student demonstrations as it is for the Renault strikes). To strike or not to strike. Which side should one take? Nobody can decide anymore. What are the objectives? Who is the enemy? For whom does one speak? Those geigercounters used by the unions, political parties, and action groups for measuring the combativity of the masses have gone haywire. The student movement slips through the fingers of those who want to structure it according to their own objectives — so did this movement have none? In any event, it did not want *to be objectified behind its own back*. The Renault employees went back to work with nothing gained, even though they had refused to do so eight days before when they received a reasonable offer, etc. This confusion is in fact similar to what happens in dreams: it betrays a resistance or censorship acting on the dream's very content. But what is essentially betrayed by the confusion surrounding the Renault strikes, and which even the proletarians themselves have difficulty in accepting, is that the traditional external class enemy of social struggle (the bosses and capital) has been *displaced* by the true internal class enemy, its own authorised class representatives (the parties and unions). The authority to which the workers delegate their power turns against them because of the power delegated to it by the bosses and the government. Capital, because it only monopolises *production*, can only alienate labour power and its product; whereas parties and unions, because they monopolise *representation*, alienate the social power of the exploited. Calling unions into question is a step forward in the historical process of revolution. But this step forward pays the price of an apparent regression to greater confusion and indecisiveness, with all its absence of continuity, logic, objectives, etc. Everything becomes uncertain and a cause for resistance when people have to confront the agent of their own oppression, and to dispel *from their own head* the unionist, shop steward, official or spokesperson they find there. But at least the murkiness of those events of Spring 1973 went to the heart of the problem: that the unions and parties are dead, and that all they have to do now is die.

The Corruption of the Proletariat

This crisis of representation is the crucial *political* aspect of recent social movements. On its own, however, it hasn't proved fatal for the system, since what we can already see everywhere (even among the unions themselves) is its formal supersession (and recuperation) through the general scheme of *worker-management*. There is no more delegation of authority — everyone is now fully responsible for production! A new ideological generation has arisen! But it will have its work cut out for it, because this crisis intersects with one that goes far deeper, one related to production itself and the very system of productivity. And here again immigrants are in the position, no doubt indirectly, of analysers. Just as they analysed the relationship of the 'proletariat' to its representative authorities, they now analyse *the relationship of workers to their own labour power*, as well as their relationship to themselves as the force of production (and no longer simply to those representative authorities in their ranks). This is because immigrants have been uprooted far more recently from a non-productivist tradition, and because their social structures had to be dismantled in order to hurl them into the labour process in the West. But it is also why in return they profoundly dismantle this general process and the dominant morality of productivism in Western societies.

Everything unfolds as if the enticement of their productive force into the European labour market has provoked an increasing corruption of the European proletariat with regard to labour and production. This involves not only 'clandestine' practices aimed at the obstruction of work ('go-slow', petty theft, absenteeism, etc.), which have never stopped — but this time the workers suddenly ceased work, without any warning, openly, collectively, spontaneously, and, to the great despair of the unions and bosses, without making demands or negotiating anything, and then just as spontaneously returned to work *en masse* on the following Monday. Neither a victory nor a defeat, it was not a strike but a '*stop-work*' — a euphemism far more revealing than the word 'strike'. And its outcome was the collapse of the whole discipline of labour, as though all the ethical and practical norms imposed by two centuries of industrial colonisation in Europe had been shattered and forgotten — without apparent effort, and without 'class struggle' as such. Interruptions, laxity, erratic hours, indifference to overtime, bonuses, promotions, benefits and savings: they do the barest minimum and then stop work, coming back to it as the mood strikes them. Colonists reproached the 'underdeveloped' for precisely this sort of behaviour: it proved impossible to teach them the value of work, the rational utilisation of time, the concept of saving wages, etc. It was only by exporting them overseas that they ultimately came to be integrated into the labour process. And this was the very moment that workers in the West began to increasingly 'regress' to the behaviour of the 'underdeveloped'. For it would not be an inconsiderable revenge on this most advanced form of colonisation (the importation of cheap labour) to witness the corruption now gripping the Western proletariat itself — with the result that one day it may have to be exported in turn to the underdeveloped countries in order to relearn the historical and revolutionary values of work.

There is a close relationship between the ultra-colonisation of immigrant workers (since colonies were not profitable *in situ*, they were imported) and the industrial decolonisation now influencing all sectors of society (this passage from the *hot* stage of labour as investment *to the cool and cynical exercise of tasks* can be seen everywhere, from the school to the factory). Because immigrants (and young or rural semi-skilled workers) have most recently left behind their 'savage' indifference to the 'rationality' of work, they are in the position to analyse Western society and the whole recent, fragile, superficial, and arbitrary character of its forced collectivisation through labour, its collective paranoia, out of which such a morality, culture or myth has been created. We have forgotten that this industrial discipline was only imposed on the West two centuries ago, and at the cost of unprecedented violence — even though it has never really taken hold and is now beginning to come apart at the seams (it won't even last as long as that other colonisation beyond the seas).

Strike for Strike's Sake

The motto of all struggle today is strike for strike's sake. With no political motivation, goal or reference, it responds by opposing this production itself with no motivation, reference, social use value, or finality other than itself — it responds to *production for production's sake*, namely to a system now entirely become that of *reproduction*, turning round on itself in an immense tautology of the labour process. Strike for strike's sake is an inversion of this tautology, but a subversive inversion since it exposes a new form of capital, corresponding to the last phase of the law of value.

Strikes have finally ceased to be a means, and the sole means, for putting pressure on *political* relations of force and the game of power. They have become an end in themselves. They negate through a radical parody on its own ground that sort of finality without end which production has become.

Waste no longer exists in production for production's sake. Although this notion had validity in a limited economy of use, it has now become inapplicable. It relies on a pious critique of the system. There is no waste with Concorde, the space race, etc. Quite the contrary: this is because, when a system has reached the height of 'objective' uselessness, what it produces and reproduces *is work itself*. Besides, it is above all what everyone (including the workers and the unions) demands of it. Everything revolves around employment, since the social is now based on the creation of jobs—the British unions were quite prepared to transform Concorde into a supersonic bomber if it meant saving jobs. When it comes down to a choice between inflation and unemployment, long live inflation! Work, as much as social welfare and consumer goods, has become an article of social redistribution. It is an immense paradox: the less labour is a productive *force*, the more it becomes a *product*. This is not an insignificant aspect of the current transformation taking place in the capitalist system, and of its revolutionary passage from a specific phase of production to that of reproduction. The less the system needs labour power in order to function and expand, the more demand there is for it to supply and 'produce' work.

The demands of strike for strike's sake (and today even most 'protest' strikes are heading in this direction) correspond to this absurd circularity of a system where one works in order to produce work. 'Pay us for the days we are on strike' simply means: pay us so that we can *reproduce* strike for strike's sake. It is a reversal of the general absurdity of the system.

Since products, *all* products, and even work itself, are now beyond the useful and the useless, there is no more productive labour, but simply *reproductive* labour. The same holds true for consumption: there is no more 'productive' or 'unproductive' consumption, but simply *reproductive* consumption. Leisure is as 'productive' as work, and factory labour is as 'unproductive' as leisure or the tertiary sector—it doesn't matter which formula is used, because *it is precisely this indifference which marks the terminal phase of political economy.* Everyone is now reproductive, having lost the concrete finality which once distinguished them. No one produces anymore. Production is dead. Long live reproduction!

A Genealogy of Production

What the present system reproduces is capital in its most rigorous definition: as *a form of social relations*, and not in the ordinary sense of money, profit, or as an economic system. Reproduction has always been understood as an 'extension' of the mode of production, and as being determined by the latter; whereas the mode of production should really be conceptualised as one modality (and not the only one) of the *mode of reproduction*. Productive forces and the relations of production—otherwise known as the sphere of material production—are perhaps only one possible, and thus historically relative, conjuncture of the reproduction process. Reproduction in this form goes far beyond economic exploitation. The movement of productive forces is thus not its necessary condition.

And historically, wasn't the original status of the 'proletariat' (or industrial wage earners) one of social confinement, concentration, and exclusion?

The confinement in factories is a fantastic extension of the 17th-century mechanism described by Foucault. Wasn't 'industrial' labour (one that is non-artisanal, collective, controlled, and deprived of the means of production) born in the first great workhouses? In the beginning, and as part of its rationalisation, this society confined its indigents, its vagrants and its deviants, keeping them occupied and held in place by the imposition of its rational principle of labour. But the contamination worked both ways, since this rupture by which society founded its principle of rationality struck back at the entire society of labour: confinement became a microcosm of what was later to be extended to the whole of society in the form of the industrial system — since this society was to become, under the sign of labour and its productivist finality, a concentration camp, detention house and quarantine centre.

Instead of using the concept of proletarian exploitation to explain racial, sexual, and other kinds of oppression, we should ask ourselves whether the reverse is not the case — whether the status of workers, like that of the mad, the dead, nature, animals, children, blacks and women, is first one of *excommunication* rather than *exploitation*, and of discrimination and isolation rather than of theft and abuse.

My conjecture would be that no true class struggle has ever existed except on the basis of this discrimination: the struggle of sub-humans against their status as beasts, and against this caste division whose abjection condemns them to the sub-humanity of labour. This is what lies behind every strike, every uprising, and even those 'wage' actions of today: it is the source of their virulence. Even so, the proletarian has now become a 'normal' being: the worker has been promoted to the rank of full 'human being', and in this capacity takes up the mantle of all dominant discriminations — he is racist, sexist, and oppressive. Compared with actual deviants and all classes of discriminated people, the worker is on the same side as the bourgeoisie, on the side of the human and the normal. The fact remains that the fundamental law of this society is not the law of exploitation, but the *code of normality*.

May '68: The Illusion of Production

The first shock-wave of this passage from production to reproduction pure and simple was May '68. The academic profession was the first to be affected, and above all the Human Science Faculties, because it was more evident there than anywhere else (even without an explicit 'political' consciousness) that *no one was productive anymore*, but simply reproductive (that those who taught science and culture were themselves bearers of the general reproduction of the system). It was this sense of total uselessness, irresponsibility ('What good are sociologists?') and irrelevance that led to the student movement of 1968 (and not the lack of opportunities, since there are always plenty of them *in a system of reproduction* — what no longer existed were places for the genuine *production* of anything).

This shock-wave continues to spread. Nothing will prevent it from progressively flowing to the very edges of the system, one sector of society after another falling from the rank of *productive forces* to the status of *reproductive forces* pure and simple. If the cultural, educational, judicial, familial, or so-called 'superstructural' sectors were the first to be affected by this process, then it is clear that all of the so-called 'infrastructural' sector is progressively being affected as well: this new post-'68 generation of fragmented, wild-cat, serial, or other such strikes no longer testify to the 'class struggle' of a proletariat assigned to production, but testify to the rebellion of those who, even in the factories, are assigned to reproduction.

However, even in this sector, the first to be affected are those marginal and unorganised groups like young semi-skilled workers brought in from the countryside to fill the factories, immigrants, non-unionised labour, etc. In fact, and for all the reasons mentioned, there is every likelihood that the last to react will be the 'traditional', organised and unionised proletariat, since it has the capacity to entertain for the longest time *the illusion of 'productive' labour*. Reinforced and sanctioned by the labour movement, this 'proletarian' consciousness of being the true 'producers' unlike everybody else, and of being at the centre of social wealth despite everything, even at the cost of exploitation, must surely constitute the greatest *ideological* defense against the disintegration of the present system — which, far from 'proletarianising' whole segments of the population or extending the exploitation of 'productive' labour as good Marxist theory would have it, assigns everyone to the status of reproductive workers.

More than anything else, manual or 'productive' workers labour under *the illusion of production* — just as in their leisure they labour under the illusion of freedom.

Things are tolerable so long as they are perceived as a source of wealth or satisfaction, *as a use value*, even under the most alienated and exploited forms of labour. The worst individual or historical situations are tolerable so long as there still exists (even in the imaginary) a correspondence between 'production' and personal or social needs (this is why the concept of 'need' is so fundamental and so mystifying), because *the illusion of production is always the illusion of its ideal correspondence with use value.* And those proletarians who today believe in the use value of their labour power are potentially the most mystified by, and the least susceptible to, this resistance that seizes upon people in the depths of their total uselessness, this circular manipulation that turns them into mute signposts of senseless reproduction.

On the day when this process will have spread throughout the whole of society, May '68 will take on the appearance of a general blowout of the system, and the problem of those links between students and workers will no longer be posed: it simply exposed the rift between those in the present system who still believe in their own labour power, and those who don't.

NOTES

1. [See Daniel Verres et al., *Le Discours du capitalisme*, Paris, L'Herne, 1971, p. 36. The passage quoted directly below, and somewhat modified by Baudrillard, is on p. 74.]

2. [Karl Marx, *Grundrisse*, tr. Martin Nicolaus, London, Allen Lane, 1973. All page numbers in parenthesis refer to this edition.]

3. [Karl Marx, *Capital*, vol. I, tr. Ben Fowkes, Harmondsworth, Penguin, 1976, pp. 1044-45. Note that this passage appears in the appendix entitled 'Results of the Immediate Process of Production', in Section II of the Penguin edition, and is not included in the 1965 Moscow edition published by Progress Publishers. It should also be noted that discrepancies exist between the French version of this passage and Fowkes' translation, particularly with regard to the last sentence, which has been modified here to make sense of the statement by Baudrillard immediately following it.]

4. Marx, that dissembling imp, came close to recognising this with his concept of the collective labourer: 'The product is transformed from the direct product of the individual producer into a social product, the joint product of a collective labourer, i.e. a combination of workers, each of whom stands at a different distance from the actual manipulation of the object of labour. With the progressive accentuation of the co-operative character of the labour process, there necessarily occurs a progressive extension of the concept of *productive labour*, and of the concept of the bearer of that labour, the *productive worker*. In order to work productively, it is no longer necessary for the individual himself to put his hand to the object; it is sufficient for him to be an organ of the collective labourer, and to perform any one of its subordinate functions. The definition of productive labour given above, the original definition, is derived from the nature of material production itself, and it remains correct for the collective labourer, considered as a whole. But it no longer holds good for each member taken individually' (ibid., pp. 643-644).

5. Free time is, in a manner of speaking, a form of 'complex labour', in the sense that the latter, in opposition to simple labour, links up with the definition of a service: the close bond between prestation and the prestator, the non-equivalence of a service with the time of abstract social labour, or with a wage reproductive of labour power. Marx would have been able to see this if he hadn't been blinded by productive labour and all the many distinctions by which he attempted to save the subject of history — the productive labourer. As Marcuse argues in *One Dimensional Man* [London, Abacus, 1972, p. 43]: 'The reification of labour power, driven to perfection, would shatter the reified form by cutting the chain that ties the individual to the machinery . . . [Automation] would open the dimension of free time as the one in which man's private and societal existence would constitute itself.' Instead of indulging in a fantasy about free time, Marcuse has understood that the system, thanks to technical progress and automation, produces free time as the extreme reification of labour power, as the perfected form of the time of abstract social labour, and precisely through an inverse simulation of non-labour.

    Others types of 'complex' labour are job training, qualification, education, etc. There is also a temptation to analyse them in terms of surplus value, as the reinvestment by capital in science, training and research, and as constant capital superadded to the ordinary worker. Adam Smith: 'A man produced at the cost of much labour and time can be compared to an expensive machine . . .' But this is mistaken. Instruction, education and training are not indirect investments, but a direct form of social domestication and control. Capital does not seek a type of complex labour in these mechanisms; it writes them off completely, and sacrifices to them an enormous portion of its 'surplus value' for the reproduction of its hegemony.

6. Paid unemployment already amounts to the same thing (currently one year's severance pay in France). But this is surpassed by the proposed 'negative tax', already in use in some countries, heralding a basic minimum wage for all — housewives, handicapped people, unemployed youth — to be deducted against the income derived from their *eventual* employment. Quite simply, unemployment loses its role as a critical force (and all that this implies politically). Work becomes an *option*, and the wage becomes a certificate of existence, an automatic matriculation into the social apparatus. Capital still remains the wage system, but this time in its pure form — detached from labour, like the signifier (according to Saussure's analogy) is detached from the signified, a labour which was only the transitory material of capital.

7. The social evolution of housing clearly reveals how the strategy of capital has shifted from an economic process to a process of expansion.

    The worker was first housed in the hovel attached to factories, a locus whose function was the reproduction of labour power, but whose strategic focus remained the factory and industry. Housing was not a form of capital investment.

    Little by little, housing becomes invested as a means of partitioning space and time, as a direct and universalised process for the control of social space:

housing is no longer a locus for the reproduction of labour, but for the reproduction of *the habitat itself as a specific function*, as a direct form of social relations. It is no longer the locus for the reproduction of the labourer, but for the reproduction of the inhabitants themselves, the *users*. The ideal type of industrial slave, once the proletarian, has now become the 'user': the user of goods, the user of words, the user of sex, the user of labour itself (the 'agent of production', once the worker, has now become the user of his factory and of his labour as an individual and collective tool, as a *social service*), the user of public transport, but also the user of his own life and death.

As a decentered, expansionary and global strategy, use or the appropriation of use value is the perfected form of social control through self-management.

8. So it is with the Californian utopia of the cybernetic disintegration of the 'tertiary metropolis'; in other words, the utopia of work delivered to the home via computers. Work infiltrates every corner of society and daily life. Not only does labour power cease to exist, but so does the space and time of labour: society is nothing but one continuous process of the production of value. Work has become a *way of life*. It is useless rebuilding factory walls or returning to the golden age of the factory and the class struggle in order to counteract the ubiquity of capital, surplus value and labour, because this ubiquity is linked to their very disappearance. Nowadays the worker sustains the imaginary of struggle, like the cop sustains the imaginary of repression.

9. The concept of surplus value is quite simply meaningless in relation to a system which, once reproductive of labour power as the source of profit and surplus value, has now become reproductive of the whole of existence through the advanced redistribution or reinjection of the total equivalent of social surplus labour. Surplus value is consequently everywhere and nowhere. In fact, there are no more 'hidden costs of capital', or conversely there are no more 'profits' in the sense of a unilateral extortion. The law of the system is one of relinquishing and redistributing these profits, so that they can be circulated, so that each and every person caught in the fine mesh of this endless redistribution can become a manager, and so that the whole population can self-manage surplus value, thus becoming deeply ensnared by the whole political and quotidian order of capital. And just as surplus value is meaningless when viewed from the perspective of capital, it is no less so when viewed from the perspective of the exploited. The distinction between that fraction of labour recovered in a wage and the remainder called surplus value is meaningless in relation to the labourer who, once reproductive of his labour power through his wage, has now become reproductive of his whole existence through a general process of 'labour'.

10. Other related forms of maximalist demands are equal wages for all and the struggle against job qualification. The aim of these demands is the end of the division of labour (the end of labour as a social relation) and the end of the law of equivalence as applies to wages and labour power, which is fundamental for the system. Thus their aim is indirectly the very form of political economy.

11. The same phenomenon occurs with underdeveloped countries. The price of

raw materials begins to soar once they lose their economic content and become signs or tokens of the submission to a global political order, to a planetary society of peaceful coexistence—which, under the thumb of the super powers, inevitably leads to the socialisation of underdeveloped countries. This escalation of prices then becomes a challenge, not only to the wealth of Western countries, but to the political system of peaceful coexistence, since it is confronted with the domination of a global political class, no matter whether it is capitalist or socialist.

The Arabs, before the petrol crisis, made traditional wage demands: pay for petrol *at a fair price*. But now their demands change direction, becoming maximalist and unlimited.

12. And the energy crisis provides both types of inflation with an alibi as well as a perfect deterrent. From now on it will be possible to blame inflation, or the internal structural crisis of the system, for the 'spiralling prices' demanded by those countries producing energy and raw materials. And it will be possible to counteract the disaffection caused by the productivist system, expressed among other things by the challenge of maximalist wages, by the blackmail of poverty or the destruction of *the use value of the whole economic system*.

13. But this intervention does not exclude all those other groups *deprived of social representation*. Young women, students, homosexuals, and 'proles' themselves—when they go 'wild-cat', or when we accept that the unions don't really represent them at all, but only themselves—are all 'immigrants' in this sense. Conversely, when everyone becomes an immigrant, then there are no 'immigrants as such', since they would not constitute a new historical subject or proletariat taking over from the old one.

The Ecliptic of Sex

Nothing today is less certain than sex, behind the liberation of its discourse. Nothing is less certain than desire today, behind the proliferation of its figures.

In sexual matters too, proliferation is close to total destruction. This is the secret of the escalating production of sex, of the signs of sex, and the hyperrealism of pleasure [*jouissance*], particularly feminine pleasure: the uncertainty principle has extended itself to sexual reason as it has to political and economic reason.

The period of sexual liberation is also that of sexual indeterminacy. No more lack, no more interdict, no more limits: it is the loss of the whole referential principle. Economic reason can only sustain itself through penury: it vanishes with the realisation of its objective, which is the abolition of the spectre of penury. Desire, too, can only sustain itself through lack. When all desire is channeled into the demand for enjoyment, when it becomes limitlessly operational, it is without reality because without imaginary—it is everywhere, but everywhere a simulation. It is the spectre of desire that haunts the defunct reality of sex. Sex is everywhere, except in sexuality (Barthes).

The transition to the feminine in sexual mythology is contemporaneous with the passage from determinacy to general indeterminacy. The feminine is not substituted for the masculine according to a structural inversion of the sexes. This substitution marks the end of the determinate representation of sex, the floating of the law governing sexual difference. The rise of the feminine corresponds to the apogee of pleasure and to the catastrophe of the reality principle of sex.

Thus, in this mortal conjuncture of a certain hyperreality of sex, it is femininity which is all-absorbing—as it always was, but for different reasons, through irony and seduction.

Freud was right. There is only one sexuality, only one libido: the masculine. Sexuality is that strong, discriminating structure centred on the phallus, castration, the name-of-the-father, repression. There is no other kind. It is useless dreaming of a non-phallic, barless, or unmarked sexuality. It is useless, within this structure, trying to move the feminine to the other side of the bar, and mixing up the terms: either the structure remains the same (the feminine is entirely absorbed by the masculine), or else it collapses and the masculine and the feminine disappear (the degree zero of the structure). This is really what happens simultaneously today: behind the ferment of the sexual paradigm, with its erotic polyvalence, infinite potentiality of desire, and libidinal connections, diffractions and intensities, all the various forms of this liberatory alternative — which originates in a psychoanalysis liberated of Freud, or in a desire liberated of psychoanalysis — combine to bring about the indifferentiation of the structure and its potential neutralisation.

The trap of the sexual revolution is that it confines the feminine to this sole structure, condemning it to a negative discrimination when the structure is strong, or to a derisory triumph in a weakened structure.

However the feminine is elsewhere, it has always been elsewhere: this is the secret of its strength. Just as something is said to endure because its existence is inadequate to its essence, we need to say that the feminine seduces because it is never where it is thought to be. So it is not in its alleged history of suffering and oppression either: the historical calvary of women (its ruse is to disguise itself as such). It only takes the path of servitude in this structure where it is delimited and repressed, and where the sexual revolution delimits and represses it more dramatically still — but through what aberrant complicity are we being asked to believe that this is the history of the feminine, if not precisely a complicity with the masculine? Repression is already absolute in the *recitation* of the sexual and political suffering of women, to the exclusion of any other form of strength or sovereignty.

There is an alternative to sex and power unacceptable to the sexual axiomatic of psychoanalysis, and this alternative unquestionably belongs to the order of the feminine — quite outside the male/female opposition, which is masculine in essence, sexual in destination, and impossible to invert without it literally ceasing to exist.

This strength of the feminine is seduction.

Thus the decline of psychoanalysis and sexuality as strong structures, their debasement in a 'psy'[1] and molecular universe (which is none

other than that of their ultimate liberation) allows us to glimpse a
parallel universe (in the sense that they never meet) which can no
longer be interpreted in terms of psychical and psychological relations,
or in terms of repression and the unconscious, but in terms of play,
challenge, dual [*duelles*] relations, and the strategy of appearances: in
terms of seduction, not at all in structural terms or distinctive oppositions, but seduction as reversibility — a universe where the feminine is
not what opposes the masculine, but what *seduces* the masculine.

In seduction, the feminine is a term neither marked nor unmarked.
Nor does it recover an 'autonomy' of desire or pleasure, an autonomy of
body, speech, and writing which it would have lost(?). It does not insist
on its truth; it seduces.

Of course this sovereignty of seduction can be called feminine by
convention, the same convention that claims sexuality is fundamentally
masculine. But the important point is that seduction has always
existed — tracing, in the background, the feminine as that which is
nothing, which never 'produces' itself, and which is never where it is
produced (certainly not in any 'feminist' demands): not seduction as
seen from the perspective of a psychic or biological *bisexuality*, but of a
certain *transsexuality*, one which the whole sexual organisation, including psychoanalysis, has a tendency to diminish, according to the axiom
that there is no other structure than that of sexuality, rendering seduction constitutionally incapable of referring to anything else.

What do women contest in their opposition to the phallocratic structure? An autonomy, a difference, a specificity of desire and pleasure,
another use of their body, a speech, a writing — *but never seduction*. They
are ashamed of seduction as an artificial staging of their bodies, as a
destiny of bondage and prostitution. They don't understand that *seduction represents the mastery of the symbolic world, whereas power only represents the
mastery of the real world*. The sovereignty of seduction is not directly
comparable to the possession of political or sexual power.

There is a strange and tenacious complicity of the feminist movement with the order of truth. For seduction is combatted and rejected
as an unnatural deviation from the truth of woman, one which is to be
found ultimately inscribed in her body and in her desire. Thus is
abolished in a single blow the immense privilege of the feminine, which
has never consented to truth or meaning, and which has always
retained absolute mastery of the reign of appearances. It abolishes the
immanent capacity of seduction to divert everything from its truth and
to return it to play, to the pure play of appearances, and thus to over-
turn in an instant all the systems of meaning and power: to turn

appearances on themselves, to turn the body into appearance, and not to treat it as depth of desire — since the reversibility of all appearances is the only level at which systems are fragile and vulnerable, and since meaning is only vulnerable to sorcery. It is an act of extraordinary blindness to renounce this strength which alone is equal or superior to all others, since it reverses all of them by a simple move in the *strategy of appearances*.

Anatomy is destiny, said Freud. And in the feminist movement it is quite astonishing how the refusal of this destiny — phallic by definition, and confirmed by anatomy — still leads to a fundamentally anatomical and biological alternative. Luce Irigaray:

> . . . woman's pleasure does not have to choose between clitoral activity and vaginal passivity . . . The pleasure of the vaginal caress does not have to be substituted for that of the clitoral caress. They each contribute, irreplaceably, to woman's pleasure. Among other caresses . . . Fondling the breasts, touching the vulva, spreading the lips, stroking the posterior wall of the vagina, brushing against the mouth of the uterus, and so on. To evoke only a few of the most specifically female pleasures.[2]

The word of woman? But always it speaks the language of anatomy, that of the body. Feminine specificity lies in the diffraction of erogenous zones, in a decentered erogeneity, with its polyvalent diffusion of pleasure and its transfiguration of the whole body by desire: such is the leitmotiv traversing the whole sexual and feminine revolution, but also our whole culture of the body, from Bellmer's 'anagrams' to the machinic connections of Deleuze. It always concerns the body, if not the anatomical body, then at least the organic and erogenous body — the functional body for which, even in this fragmented or metaphorical form, pleasure would be its destination, and desire its natural manifestation. This means one of two things: either the body in all this is only a metaphor (but then what is the sexual revolution and our whole culture of the body talking about?), or else we have permanently entered, with this discourse of the body and of woman, into anatomical destiny, into anatomy as destiny. Nothing in all of this is radically opposed to Freud's formula.

Nowhere do we find seduction, the body operating by artifice and not by desire, the seduced body or the body to be seduced, the body passionately diverted from its truth, from this ethical truth of the desire that haunts us — this solemn, profoundly religious truth which is incarnated by the body today, and for which seduction is just as malevolent and cunning as it once was for religion. Nowhere do we find the body given over to appearances.

For *only seduction is radically opposed to anatomy as destiny*. Only seduction destroys the distinctive sexualisation of bodies, and the phallic economy that inevitably results from it.

It is naive for any movement to think that it can subvert systems via their infrastructure. Seduction is smarter than that, and spontaneously so, with a striking certainty. It doesn't have to prove or justify itself: it comes about instantaneously in the reversal of all so-called depth of the real, in the reversal of all psychology, all anatomy, all truth, all power. It secretly knows that *there is no anatomy*, that there is no psychology, and that all signs are reversible. Nothing is intrinsic to it, save appearances — all the powers elude it, but it makes all their signs reversible. Who can resist seduction? The only genuine stakes are to be found in the strategy and mastery of appearances, as opposed to the power of being and of the real. It is useless playing one being against another, one truth against another: this is the trap of trying to subvert foundations, when a *slight* manipulation of appearances will suffice.

For woman is but appearance. And it is the feminine as appearance that defeats the masculine as depth. Instead of protesting against this 'offensive' formula, women would do well to let themselves be seduced by the fact that here lies the secret of their strength, which they are beginning to lose by setting up feminine depth against masculine depth.

It is not even really the feminine as surface which should be contrasted with the masculine as depth, but the feminine as the indistinction of surface and depth, or as the indifference between the authentic and the artificial. This is Joan Rivière's basic proposition in 'La Féminité comme mascarade' (*La Psychanalyse*, no. 7), which encapsulates all of seduction: 'Whether femininity is authentic or superficial, it is fundamentally the same thing.'

This can only be said of the feminine. The masculine itself discriminates on the basis of an infallible and absolute criterion of veracity. The masculine is certain, while the feminine is insoluble.

Curiously, this proposition concerning the feminine — that the very distinction between the authentic and the artificial is groundless — defines the space of simulation as well: not only is there no possible distinction here between the real and its models, there is no other real than that generated by the models of simulation, just as there is no other femininity than that of appearances. Simulation is also insoluble.

This strange coincidence brings us back to the ambiguity of the feminine: it is both an incontestable proof of simulation and the only possibility of going beyond simulation — through seduction in fact.

THE ETERNAL IRONY OF THE COMMUNITY

> Femininity — the eternal irony [in the life] of the community.
>
> Hegel[3]

Femininity as the uncertainty principle.

It makes the sexual poles waver. It is not the polar opposite of the masculine: it is what abolishes distinctive oppositions and thus sexuality itself, as it has been historically embodied in masculine phallocracy, as it may soon be embodied in feminine phallocracy.

If femininity is the uncertainty principle, then it is in the game of femininity — where it is itself uncertain — that this uncertainty will be the greatest.

Transvestism: neither homosexual nor transsexual, what transvestites love is the game of gender confusion. The spell they cast, on themselves as well, comes from sexual wavering and not, as is customary, from the attraction of one sex for the other. They truly love neither men/men nor women/women, nor those who tautologically define themselves as distinct sexed beings. For a sex to exist, signs must redouble the biological being. But here signs are detached from the body — there is no sex strictly speaking, for what transvestites are enamoured with is this game of signs, what excites them is *the seduction of signs themselves*. Everything for them is makeup, theatre, seduction. They seem obsessed with sexual games, but all the more so with acting; and if their life seems to have a greater sexual investment than ours, it is because they make sex into a whole gestural, sensual, ritual game, into an exalted, but ironic invocation.

Nico only seemed so beautiful because her femininity was purely an act. Something more than beauty, almost sublime emanated from her, a different seduction. The deception to be uncovered was that she was a false drag, a real woman playing at drag. This is because a non-woman/woman, set in motion by signs, can take seduction further than a real woman already fixed by her sex. She alone can exert a pure fascination, pure because more seductive than sexual. This fascination is lost when the true sex reveals itself, where of course another desire can profit — but no longer in fact from perfection, which can only belong to artifice.

Seduction is always more remarkable and more sublime than sex, for it is seduction that we prize above all.

We should not seek for transvestism a foundation in bisexuality. Whether confused or ambivalent or indefinite or inverted, the sexes and sexual roles are still real, they still testify to the psychic reality of sex. On the contrary, it is this very definition of the sexual [instance] that is eclipsed. And this is not a perverse game. The perverse is that which perverts the order of terms. But here there are no longer any terms to pervert: there are only signs to be seduced.

Nor should we look toward the unconscious or 'latent homosexuality' — that old casuistry of latency which is itself produced by the *sexual* imaginary of surface and depth, and which always underscores a symptomatic reading and a corrected meaning. *But there is nothing latent here*: everything calls into question the very hypothesis of a secret and determinant sexual instance, the hypothesis of an underlying play of phantasms directing the superficial play of signs — on the contrary, everything is at play in the vertigo of this reversal, *this transsubstantiation of a sex into signs which is the secret of all seduction.*

Then again, perhaps the seductiveness of the transvestite comes directly from parody — a parody of sex in the oversignification of a sex. The prostitution of transvestites thus differs from the ordinary prostitution of women. The former is closer to the sacred prostitution of Antiquity (or to the sacred status of the hermaphrodite). It reestablishes the link between makeup and theatre as the ritual and parodic display of a sex whose own pleasure is absent.

Seduction is, in this case, coupled with a parody revealing a quite relentless hostility towards the feminine, and so could be interpreted as the annexation by men of the seductive armory of women. The transvestite would thus represent the position of the primitive warrior, who alone is seductive — the woman is nothing (a wink in the direction of fascism, and its affinity for the transvestite). But isn't this a nullification rather than an incorporation of the sexes? Isn't the masculine, its status and privileges, negated in this derision of femininity, becoming a contrapuntal element in a ritual game?

In any case, this parody of the feminine isn't as hostile as might be thought, since it is the parody of femininity *as men imagine it*, in their representations as well as their phantasms. An exacerbated, degraded, and parodic femininity (the drag queens of Barcelona grow their moustaches and expose their hairy chests), it announces that in this society femininity is nothing but the signs men dress it up in. To oversimulate femininity is to say that woman is only a model of male simulation. There is a challenge to the *model* of woman by the *game* of woman, a challenge to the woman/woman by the woman/sign; and it is possible that this lifelike but simulated denunciation, which plays on the edge of the artificial, which simultaneously enacts and counteracts the mechanisms of femininity to perfection, may be more lucid and more radical than all the ideological and political protestations of a femininity 'alienated in its being'. Transvestism says that femininity has no being (no nature, writing, or pleasure of its own — or as Freud said, no specific libido). Contrary to the whole quest for an authentic femininity, feminine discourse and so forth, here it is said that woman is nothing, and that this is her strength.

It is a more subtle response than the frontal attack by feminists on the theory of castration. For here they run up against not an anatomical but a symbolic fatality, which potentially burdens all sexuality. The reversal of this law can only reside in its *parodic resolution*, in the eccentricity or doubling of the signs of femininity, which puts an end to the whole insoluble biology or metaphysics of the sexes. Makeup is nothing else: a triumphant parody, a resolution by excess, by hypersimulation on the surface of that simulation-in-depth which is the symbolic law of castration. Such is the transsexual game of seduction.

Such is the ironic practice of artifice — the capacity, specific to the made-up or prostituted woman, to exacerbate a trait in order to render it more than a sign, not of the false versus the true, but of the falser than the false; and in so doing, to embody the height of sexuality while simultaneously dissolving it in simulation. Such is the irony specific to the constitution of woman as idol or sexual object, since it is precisely through her enclosed perfection that she puts an end to the game of sex and returns the man, lord and master of sexual *reality*, to his *imaginary* transparency as a subject. Such is the ironic strength of the object, which woman loses in her promotion to a subject.

All masculine strength is that of production. Everything that is produced, even the woman producing herself as woman, falls within the category of masculine strength. The sole strength of femininity is the opposite and irresistible one of seduction. Being and having nothing in its own right, this strength is only that of nullifying the strength of production. But nullify it it always does.

Besides, has there ever been a phallic power? The whole history of patriarchal domination, phallocracy, and the ageless privilege of the masculine is perhaps only a story to be enjoyed undefeated. It begins with the exchange of women in primitive societies, foolishly interpreted as the first phase of the woman as object. Everything told to us about it, the universal discourse on the inequality of the sexes, with its leitmotiv of egalitarian and revolutionary modernity, which is reinforced in our time with all the energy of a *failed* revolution — all this is only a gigantic misconception. But the reverse hypothesis is perfectly plausible, and in a way more interesting: that the feminine has never been dominated, that it has always been dominant — the feminine not really as a sex, but as the transversal form of all sex and all power, as a secret and virulent form of non-sexuality, and as a challenge whose ravages can be felt today across all of sexuality. And hasn't this challenge of the feminine, as well as that of seduction, always been triumphant?

In this sense, the masculine has never been more than a residue, a secondary and fragile formation, which must be defended by means of exclusions, institutions, and stratagems. Indeed, the phallic fortress gives every sign of being a fortress: namely, of weakness. It totally relies on the protection of a manifest sexuality, of a sex whose finality is exhausted in reproduction or in pleasure.

One might argue that the feminine is the sole sex, and that the masculine only exists by a superhuman effort to depart from it. A momentary distraction, and one slips back into the feminine. It may well be that the feminine has the definite privilege, and that the masculine has the definite handicap — it is clearly absurd to want to 'liberate' one in order to elevate it to the fragile 'power' of the other, to that altogether bizarre, paradoxical, paranoid, and tiresome state of the masculine.

This sexual fable is the inverse of the phallic one, where woman arises from man by subtraction — here man arises from woman as the exception. It is a fable that would be easily reinforced by Bettelheim's arguments in *Symbolic Wounds*: men have established their power and their institutions simply to counteract the quite superior primordial powers of women. Penis envy isn't the driving force; on the contrary, it is man's jealousy of woman's procreative powers. This privilege of woman is irreconcilable: the only recourse was to invent a different social, political, and economic order, a masculine order where this natural privilege could be redressed. In the ritual order, those practices which appropriate signs of the opposite sex are largely masculine: scarifications, mutilations, artificial vaginisations, 'the man-childbed', etc.

All this is about as convincing as a paradoxical hypothesis can be (which is always more interesting than the accepted hypothesis), but ultimately it is only an inversion of terms, equivalent to turning the feminine into a primordial substance, into a sort of anthropological infrastructure. Its conclusion is the opposite of anatomy, but it is still anatomy as destiny — and again, the whole 'irony of femininity' is lost.

The feminine loses its irony as soon as it is instituted as a sex, even and most especially when denouncing its oppression. This is the eternal lure of Enlightenment humanism, whose aim is to liberate the servile sex, the servile races, the servile classes in the very terms of their servitude. Let the feminine become a full sex! But this would be an absurdity other than in terms of sex and power.

The feminine has really nothing to do with either equivalence or value, and thus is insoluble through power. It is not even subversive: it is reversible. Power, by contrast, is soluble through the reversibility of the feminine. And so if it is impossible to tell from the 'facts' whether it is the masculine or the feminine which has dominated the other throughout the centuries (once again, the thesis of feminine oppression rests on a caricature of the phallocratic myth), it is nonetheless clear that, in sexual matters as well, the reversible form secretly triumphs over the linear form, the excluded form triumphs over the dominant form, and the seductive form triumphs over the productive form.

Femininity is, in this sense, related to madness. This is because madness secretly harbours the wish to be normalised (thanks to the hypothesis, among others, of the unconscious). This is because femininity secretly harbours the wish to be readapted and normalised (particularly in sexual liberation).

And in sexual pleasure.

One of the proofs often advanced for the oppression of women is the theft of pleasure, their lost enjoyment — a flagrant injustice which everyone must immediately try to redress, by a sort of sex marathon or rally. Sexual pleasure has assumed the form of a necessity or fundamental right. The last born of the Rights of Man, it has been elevated to the rank of a categorical imperative. It is immoral to transgress it. But it doesn't even have the Kantian charm of finalities without end. It is enforced as the management and self-management of desire — and, as with the law, ignorance is no excuse.

But this ignores the fact that sexual pleasure is also reversible, for there can be a greater intensity in its absence or denial. Even at those moments when the sexual goal becomes a matter of chance, something emerges which can be described as seductive or pleasurable. Or rather, sexual pleasure may only be the pretext for another, more exciting, more passionate game. This is what happens in the film *In the Realm of the Senses*, where the pursuit of sexual pleasure is really more a circuitous path beyond pleasure — a challenge which triumphs over the pure workings of desire, because its logic is far more intoxicating and because it is a passion, whereas the former is merely a drive.

But this intoxication can exist just as much in the *refusal* of sexual pleasure. Who knows if women, far from being 'robbed', haven't always triumphantly exercised the right of sexual reserve, hurling a challenge from the depths of their non-pleasure, or rather challenging the pleasure of men to be simply what it is? No one knows how far this destructive provocation may go, nor what is the extent of its capability. Man has never reached the end of it, being reduced to a solitary enjoyment and restricted to adding up the total of sexual conquests.

Who has won in this game of conflicting strategies? Apparently, the man on every count. But it is just as likely that he has lost his way or has been engulfed in this game, as he has in the seizure of power, by a sort of flight in advance where no accumulation or calculation can assure his salvation, nor remove the secret despair of what eludes him. That had to cease, and women had to enjoy. Steps had to be taken to liberate them and to make them enjoy, putting an end to that unbearable challenge by which pleasure is ultimately nullified by a possible strategy of non-pleasure. For sexual gratification has no strategy: it is simply an energy in search of its end. Thus it is quite inferior to any strategy which can use it as a subterfuge, and desire itself as a tactical device. This is the central theme of libertine sexuality in the 18th-century, from Laclos to Casanova and Sade (including Kierkegaard in *Diary of a Seducer*), for whom sexuality still remains a ceremony, ritual or strategy, before being submerged, with the Rights of Man and psychology, in the revealed truth of sex.

Thus arose the era of the pill and the assignation to pleasure. The right of sexual reserve is finished. Women must have grasped that they were being deprived of something essential by strongly resisting, through the whole spectre of 'barren' acts, the 'rational' adoption of the pill. It is the same resistance as that of entire generations to education, medicine, welfare, and work. It is the same profound intuition of the ravages of liberty, free speech, and unlimited pleasure: here there is no longer any possibility of challenge, of the other challenge, since all symbolic logic is exterminated through the blackmail of permanent erection (not to mention the tendency of the rate of pleasure to fall?).

The 'traditional' woman wasn't repressed or forbidden pleasure: she was entirely within her own keeping, not at all dominated or passive, and certainly not dreaming of her future 'liberation'. There are kind souls who retrospectively see woman as alienated throughout history, but today as liberated in her desire. But this vision reveals a profound contempt, the same contempt for the so-called 'alienated' masses when they are perceived as never being anything other than mystified cattle.

It is facile to paint a picture of woman as alienated down through the ages, and of the portals of desire opening up for her today in the name of the revolution and psychoanalysis. All this is so simple, so obscene in its simplicity. Worse: it is the very expression of sexism and racism — it's pity.

Happily, the feminine has never conformed to this image. It has always had its own strategy, the unrelenting and victorious strategy of challenge (the chief form of which is seduction). It is useless shedding tears over the injustices it has suffered, and wanting to redress them. It is useless acting as judge and jury of the weaker sex. It is useless mortgaging everything on a liberation and desire whose secret would finally be revealed in the 20th-century. All the cards and all the trumps have always been played, at every moment of history. And men haven't won, not at all. It is rather women who would now appear to be losing, and precisely under the sign of sexual pleasure — but that's another story.

It is the present history of the feminine in a culture that produces everything, divulges everything, enjoys everything, discourses everything. It is a culture that promotes the feminine as a full sex (equal rights, equal pleasure), the feminine as a value, at the expense of the feminine as uncertainty principle. The whole strategy of sexual liberation is dedicated to laying down the rights, or the law, of feminine pleasure — to the overexposure and staging of the feminine as a sex, and of multiple pleasures as the proof of sex.

Porno clearly indicates this. A trilogy of gaping, enjoyment, and meaning [*de la béance, de la jouissance et de la signifiance*], porno only promotes the feminine pleasure-seeker so excessively all the better to hide this uncertainty hovering over the 'dark continent'. The 'eternal irony of the community' that Hegel spoke about is finished. Henceforth woman will be gratified, and will know the reason why. All femininity will be rendered visible — woman the emblem of pleasure, pleasure the emblem of sexuality. There is no more uncertainty, no more secrecy: it is the beginning of absolute obscenity.

Pasolini's *Salo, or The 120 Days of Sodom* is the veritable twilight of seduction: all reversibility has been abolished in it according to a relentless logic. Everything here is irreversibly masculine and dead. Even the complicity, the promiscuity of tormentor and victim in torture has disappeared: it is an inanimate torture, an affectless perpetration, a cold machination (where one can see that sexual possession, contrary to all seduction, is really the industrial exploitation of bodies: enjoyment is a product of extraction, the technological product of a machinery of bodies, of a logistics of pleasures that goes straight to the core of the matter, only to discover a lifeless object).

What the film clearly illustrates is that in a dominant masculine system, in every dominant system (which becomes masculine by this very fact), it is femininity which embodies reversibility, the possibility of play and symbolic engagement. The world of *Salo* is completely purged of that minimum of seduction which is the wager not only of sex, but of every relation, including death and the exchange of death (this is expressed, in *Salo* as much as Sade, by the predominance of sodomy). Here it appears that the feminine is not one sex as opposed to the other, but is what returns to haunt the masculine — the sex with free rein and with full rights, the sex with the monopoly on sex — with something other than sex, *and of which sex is only the disenchanted form*: seduction. The latter is a game, while sex is a function. Seduction belongs to the ritual order, while sex and desire belong to the natural order. The masculine and the feminine confront each other as these two fundamental orders, and not as some biological difference or as rivals in a naive power struggle.

The feminine is not only seduction, it is also a challenge to the masculine to be the only sex, to take upon itself the monopoly of sex and pleasure, challenging it to go to the limit of its hegemony and to wield it unto death. The constant pressure of this challenge throughout the whole sexual history of our culture leads to the collapse of phallocracy today, as it is powerless to take it up. It is also possible that our whole conception of sexuality collapses at the same time, since it is built around the phallic function and a positive definition of sex. Every *positive* form can readily accommodate its *negative* form, but recognises the mortal challenge of a *reversible* form. Every structure can accommodate inversion or subversion, but not the reversal of its terms. Seduction is this reversible form.

Not the form to which women have been historically relegated — a culture of the gynaeceum, of powder and lace, a seduction viewed through the mirror (and imaginary) stage of woman, an arena of sexual games and ruses (although preserved here is the sole surviving ritual of the body in Western culture, while all the others, including courtesy, have disappeared) — but alternatively seduction as an ironic form, which shatters the sexual reference: not seduction as the space of desire, but of move and countermove.

This is what transpires in the most banal game of seduction: I steal away, you don't turn me on, for it is I who plays with you, and who robs you of your pleasure. A fickle game, but it is wrong to assume that this is merely a sexual strategy. It is really more a strategy of displacement (*se-ducere*: to lead astray, to stray from one's course), a diversion of the truth of sex: to 'play with' is not to 'turn on' [*jouer n'est pas jouir*]. There is a kind of sovereignty in this seduction, a passion or game belonging to the order of signs — an order which prevails in the long run, because it is reversible and indeterminate.

The charms of seduction are far superior to the Christian consolations of sexual fulfilment. We are led to believe that this is a natural end — and many go mad when they don't achieve it. But love has nothing to do with drives, except in the libidinal design of our culture. To love is a challenge or wager, for it challenges the other to love in return — to be seduced is to challenge the other to be seduced (no argument is more subtle than to accuse a women of being incapable of being seduced). Perversion, from this point of view, takes on a different meaning: it is to *pretend to be seduced* without being seduced, and to be incapable of being seduced.

The first rule of seduction is that of interminable ritual exchange, of endlessly escalating bids between the seducer and the seduced, for the simple reason that the dividing line between winning and losing is blurred, and that there is no limit to this challenge to the other to be even more seduced — to love me more than I love you, till death do us part. On the contrary, the sexual [instance] has an immediate and banal end: pleasure is a form of unmediated fulfilment of desire.

As Roustang writes in *Un Destin si funeste*:

> In analysis, one can see the extreme danger that may be incurred by a man who begins to listen to a woman's demand for sexual pleasure. If, through her desire, a woman alters the unalterability within which a man cannot help but enclose her, if she herself becomes an immediate and limitless demand, if she no longer remains within this enclosure and is no longer held by it, the man finds himself cast into a sub-suicidal state. A demand that tolerates no delay, no excuse, that is limitless with regard to intensity and duration, shatters the absolute represented by woman, by feminine sexuality, and even by feminine pleasure . . . Feminine sexual pleasure can always be rendered divine again . . ., whereas the demand for enjoyment made by a woman to the man who is bound to her without being able to flee causes him to lose his bearings and the feeling of pure contingency . . . When all desire is channeled into the demand for enjoyment, the world turns upside down and bursts asunder. This is doubtless why our culture has taught women to demand nothing in order to induce them to desire nothing . . .[4]

What is all this desire 'channeled into the demand for enjoyment'? Is it even a question of woman's 'desire'? Isn't it a characteristic form of madness that has little to do with 'liberation'? What is this new, and feminine, configuration of unlimited sexual demand, of the endless demand for pleasure? Indeed, it is the point at which our whole culture disappears. And Roustang is right, it betrays a form of collective sub-suicidal violence — not just for men, but for women as well, and for sexuality in general.

> We say no to those men and women who love only women, those who love only men, those who love only children (the old, sadists, masochists, dogs, cats) . . . The new militant, refined and egocentric, demands the right to his sexual racism, to his sexual singularity. But we say no to all sectarianism. If we must become misogynists in order to be pederasts, androphobes in order to be lesbians, . . . if we must refuse the pleasures of the night, chance encounters, or the occasional come-on in order to defend ourselves against rape, it is simply to carry on in the name of struggle against the prohibitions of certain other taboos, other moralisms, other norms, other slavish blinkers . . .
>
> We feel our bodies to have not one sex, nor two, but a multitude of sexes. We don't see men or women, but anthropomorphic human beings [!] . . . Our bodies are weary from all these stereotypes and cultural barriers, from all these physiological segregations . . . We are all males and females, adults and children, whores, dykes and queers, the fucker and the fucked, the sodomised and the sodomiser. We don't accept the reduction of our whole sexual diversity to one sex. Our Sapphism is only one facet of our sexualities. We refuse to limit ourselves to what society demands of us, namely to be hetero, lesbo or homo, and the whole range of advertising products. We are unreasonable in all our desires.
>
> (Judith Belladonna Barbara Penton, *Libé*, July 1978)

Isn't this frenzy of unlimited sexual activity, this exacerbated dissipation of desire in the demand for pleasure the reverse of what Roustang says? For if women have been taught up until now to demand nothing in order to induce them to desire nothing, aren't they taught today to demand everything in order to desire nothing? Isn't the whole dark continent decoded by pleasure?

The masculine is thought to be closer to the Law, and femininity to be closer to pleasure. But is not pleasure itself the axiomatic of a universe decoded sexually — pleasure as that feminine and liberatory reference produced by the gradual relaxation [*exténuation*] of the Law, and thus as an extension of the Law which has now become the injunction to pleasure, after having been its prohibition. It is an effect of inverse simulation when pleasure is said or wants to be autonomous, whereas it is truly a product of the Law. Or else the Law collapses, and in its place pleasure is ushered in as the new contract. No matter: nothing has changed, for this inversion of signs is simply a strategic effect. This is the meaning of the present reversal, and of the dual prerogative of the feminine and pleasure over the masculine and prohibition which previously dominated sexual reason. The exaltation of the feminine is a perfect instrument for this unprecedented general-isation and organised extension of Sexual Reason.

An unforeseen destiny interrupts all the illusions of desire and all the rationalisations of liberation. Marcuse:

> What has been considered the *feminine* antithesis to masculine qualities in patriarchy, in reality a repressed social, historical alternative, would be the socialist alternative . . . Ultimately, a social revolution that does away with male domination would end the allocation of specifically feminine charac-teristics to the woman as woman, would bring these qualities into all sectors of society, and develop them in the sphere of work as well as that of leisure. In that case, the liberation of women would also be the liberation of men . . .[5]

In other words, the feminine liberated in the service of the new collective Eros (the same mechanism as with the death drive — the same dialectical folding back upon the new social Eros). But what happens if, upon 'liberation', the feminine does not prove to be a set of specific qualities (which may have been possible only in repression), but simply the expression of an *erotic indeterminacy*, and the loss of specific qualities, in the social as much as the sexual sphere?

In seduction there was a potent irony of the feminine, whose indeter-minacy and ambiguity is just as ironic today — ensuring that its pro-motion to subject is accompanied by the resurgence of its status as object, which is to say by universal pornography. It is upon this strange coincidence that women's liberation founders, which would really like to keep the two quite separate. But it is a hopeless task, for the libera-tion of the feminine is only significant in terms of its radical ambiguity. Even Roustang's text, which tends to valorise the irruption of the feminine demand for enjoyment, cannot but foreshadow the equal catastrophe for women caused by this channeling of all desire into demand. Leaving aside the powerful argument concerning the sub-suicidal state provoked in men by such a demand, there is still no way of distinguishing the *monstrosity* of this feminine demand for sexual pleas-ure from the total interdiction formerly imposed on it.

This ambiguity can just as easily be found on the side of the mascu-line and its powerlessness. The panic provoked in men by the 'liberated' feminine subject only equals their fragility before the gaping of the 'alienated' feminine sex or object in pornography. Whether woman demand pleasure 'in becoming conscious of the rationality of her own desire', or offer herself for pleasure in a state of total prostitution; whether the feminine be subject or object, liberated or prostituted, it [she] is everywhere promoted as the sum total of sex, as a gaping voracity, a devourment. It is no accident that all porno revolves around the feminine sex. This is because the erection is never certain (there are no scenes of impotency in porno: it is exorcised throughout by the hallucination of an inexhaustible supply of women). For a sexuality now become questionable because summoned to prove itself and to manifest itself unflaggingly, the position marked masculine is fragile. The feminine sex, however, is constant — in its availability, in its gaping, in its degree zero. This constancy of the feminine, as opposed to the intermittency of the masculine, is sufficient to assure it an ultimate superiority at the level of the organic representation of pleasure, at the level of the infinitude of sex which has become our phantasmatic dimension.

Sexual liberation, like the liberation of productive forces, is potentially limitless. It demands an overabundance, a 'sex affluent society'. It can no more tolerate a scarcity of sexual goods than a scarcity of material goods. Only the feminine sex can embody this *utopia* of constant availability. This is indeed why everything in this society will be feminised, will be sexualised in feminine terms: objects, goods, services, and relations of every kind. The aim of advertising is not so much to link sex with a washing machine (which is absurd), but to confer on this object the imaginary quality of the feminine — that of being totally available, never retractile, never uncertain.

Such is the gaping monotony cherished by porno sexuality, where men, whether flaccid or erect, have only a ludicrous role to play. Hard core changes nothing: the masculine is unappealing because too determinate, too marked (as the canonical phallic signifier), and thus too fragile. Fascination is more readily directed toward the neuter, toward an indeterminate gaping, toward a mobile and diffuse sexuality. The historical revenge of the feminine after so many centuries of repression and frigidity? Perhaps: but it is more likely to be the attenuation of the sexual mark, either the historical mark of the masculine which once nourished all the systems of erectility, verticality, lineage, growth, production, etc., and which disappears today in an obsessive simulation of all these themes — or that of the feminine mark as it has always been embodied in seduction. Behind the mechanical objectification of sex, what prevails today is the masculine as fragility and the feminine as degree zero.

We have in fact entered a new phase of sexual abuse and violence — a violence against the 'sub-suicidal' masculine by unrestrained feminine pleasure. But this violence is not an inversion of the historical violence against women by the sexual prowess of men. The violence in question is the neutralisation, deflation, or collapse of the marked term before the irruption of the unmarked term. It is not full, generic violence, but the violence of deterrence, *the violence of the neuter*, the violence of the degree zero.

The same applies to porno: it is the violence of neutralised sex.

STEREO-PORNO

'Take me into your motel room . . . and screw me.'
'There is, somehow, in your language, something, which I can't put my finger on, that somehow leaves something to be desired.'
Philip K. Dick, *We Can Build You*

Turning everything into reality
Jimmy Cliff

Trompe l'oeil subtracts a dimension from real space, and this is what makes it seductive. Porno, by contrast, adds a dimension to the space of sex — it makes it more real than the real, and this is why it lacks seduction.

It is useless trying to discover which phantasms haunt porno (fetishism, perversion, the primal scene, etc.), since they are barred from it by the excess of 'reality'. Moreover, perhaps porno is only an allegory; in other words, a forced cultivation of signs, a baroque enterprise of oversignification literally bordering on the 'grotesque' (the 'grotesque' art of gardening added a touch of raw nature, like porno adds picturesque anatomical details).

The very obscenity inflames and consumes its object. It is seen too close up, you see what you have never seen before — your sex, you have never seen it function so close up, and indeed, happily for you, not at all. It is all too real, too close up to be real. And this is what is fascinating — the excess of reality, the hyperreality of the whole thing. Thus the only phantasm at work in porno, if there is one, is not the phantasm of sex, but that of the real and its disappearance into something other than the real, into the hyperreal. The voyeurism of porno is not sexual voyeurism, but a voyeurism of representation and its loss, an intoxication [*vertige*] with the loss of the scene and the irruption of the obscene.

By means of the anatomical zoom, reality loses its dimension of depth. The distance of the gaze gives way to an instantaneous and exacerbated representation: that of a sex in its pure state, stripped not only of all seduction, but of the very virtuality of its image — a sex of such immediacy that it becomes indistinguishable from its own representation. It is the end of perspectival space, as well as the space of the imaginary and of the phantasm. It is the end of the scene, the end of illusion.

However obscenity is not porno. Traditional obscenity still has a content that is sexually transgressive, provocative, and perverse. It operates through repression, and with a specifically phantasmatic violence. But this obscenity disappears with sexual liberation: Marcuse's 'repressive desublimation' has come to pass (even if the lifting of repression hasn't passed into general morality, its mythical triumph, like repression before it, is total). The new obscenity, like the new philosophy, arises from the ashes of the old, and its meaning is different. It doesn't deal with violent sex, with the real risks of sex, but with a sex neutralised by tolerance. Sex is graphically 'rendered' by it, but it is the rendering of something that has been concealed. Porno is the artificial synthesis of sex; it is the festival of sex, not its feast. It is something neo, or retro, as you will, like the chlorophyll effect of those green belts substituted for a defunct nature, which thus participate in the same obscenity as porno.

Modern unreality has nothing to do with the order of the imaginary. It belongs to the order of too much reference, too much truth, too much exactitude — it consists of making everything manifest in its absolute reality. This extraordinary microscopy is just like those hyperrealist paintings where you can see the pores on a face, and which doesn't even have the charm of a disquieting strangeness. For hyperrealism is not surrealism: it is a vision which immobilises seduction by sheer visibility. It 'gives you more'. This is already true of colour in film or television: the colour, the sharp resolution, the sex in high fidelity, with bass and treble (true to life!) — it gives you so much that you have nothing more to add, which is to say give in exchange. It is totally oppressive: by giving you *a little too much*, everything is taken away from you. Beware of that which is so well 'rendered' to you without you having ever given it!

How bewildering, stifling, and obscene is the total recall of Japanese quadriphonics: a room ideally climatised, fantastically engineered, with music in four dimensions, not just the three of ambient space, but a fourth, visceral one of internal space — it is the technical delirium of a perfect restoration of music (Bach, Monteverdi, Mozart!) *which has never existed*, which no one has ever heard like this, and which wasn't meant to be heard like this. Besides, one doesn't 'hear' it: quite the contrary. The distance that allows music to be *understood*, at a concert or elsewhere, is abolished. You are hemmed in on all sides; there is no longer any musical space, but a totally simulated environment where you are dispossessed of even that minimum of analytical perception which constitutes the *charm* of music. The Japanese have, in all good faith, quite simply mistaken the real for the most dimensions possible. If they could invent hexaphonics, they would. But this fourth dimension they add to music is precisely the one that castrates you of all *musical* pleasure. Hence you are fascinated by something else (but it is no longer seduction): the technical perfection, the 'high fidelity' which is every bit as obsessional and puritanical as that other, conjugal kind of fidelity. But this time there is no way of knowing to what object it is faithful, since nobody can tell where the real, or the vertiginous perfection with which it is persistently reproduced, begins or ends.

In this sense, the technology digs its own grave. For while it perfects the means of synthesis, it makes the criteria for analysis and definition more stringent, with the result that absolute fidelity and exhaustivity in matters of the real becomes evermore impossible. The real is turned into a vertiginous phantasm of exactitude, vanishing into the infinitesimal.

'Normal' three-dimensional space, when compared for example to trompe l'oeil, which saves on one dimension, already constitutes a degradation, an impoverishment *by its surfeit of means* (everything that is real or wants to be real already constitutes a degradation of this kind). Quadriphonics, superstereo and hi-fi constitute the final degradation.

Porno is the quadriphonics of sex. It adds a third and fourth channel to the sexual act. The hallucination of detail predominates — science has already accustomed us to this microscopy, this surfeit of reality in microscopic detail, this voyeuristic exactitude of the close-up on the cell's invisible structures, this notion of a relentless truth which will never again find its measure in the play of appearances, and which only the sophistication of a technical apparatus can reveal. It is the end of the secret.

What else does porno itself reveal to us, with its trick vision, but this same relentless and microscopic truth of sex? It is the direct heir of a metaphysics entirely dependent upon the phantasm of concealed truth and its revelation, upon the phantasm of 'repressed' energy and its *production* — on the obscene stage of the real. Whence the impasse of enlightened thought on the matter: should we censor porno and adopt a well-tempered repression? It is insoluble, for porno is right: it belongs to the ravages of the real, to the insane illusion of the real and of its objective 'liberation'. You can't liberate productive forces without also wanting to 'liberate' the animal function of sex: one is as obscene as the other. The realist corruption of sex and the productivist corruption of work — it is the same symptom, the same struggle.

The worker in chains finds an equivalent in something more extraordinary than any strip-tease: that vaginal sideshow in Japan. The girls are arranged along a platform, their legs spread apart, with Japanese proles in shirt sleeves (it is a popular spectacle) free to bury their noses and their eyes right into the girl's vagina, in order to look, to get a better look — but at what? — and climbing over each other to reach the girls who speak gently to them all the while, or snub them as a matter of form. The remaining spectacle of flagellations, mutual masturbations, and traditional strip is nothing compared to this moment of absolute obscenity, with its voracious inspection that far exceeds sexual possession. Sublime porno: if they could, the guys would completely bury themselves in the girls. Is it an exaltation of death? Perhaps: but at the same time they comment upon and compare respective vaginas, without ever bursting into laughter, with deadly seriousness, and without ever trying to touch them, except by accident. There is nothing lubricious here: it is an extremely solemn and childlike act, an undivided fascination with the mirror of the feminine organ, like that of Narcissus with his own image. At this sublime point, which goes far beyond the conventional idealism of strip-tease (where perhaps seduction may still exist), porno reverts to a purified obscenity, extending deep into the visceral domain. Why stop at nudity, at the genitals? If the obscene belongs to the order of representation and not to the sexual order, shouldn't the very interior of the body and its viscera be explored? Who knows what profound pleasure in visual dismemberment, in mucosa, and in smooth muscles awaits to be uncovered there? Our definition of porno is still quite restricted. But obscenity has an unlimited future.

But wait! What is at issue here is not the deepening of a drive, but simply an *orgy of realism* and an orgy of *production* — the mania (which is perhaps a drive too, but one that replaces all the others) for making everything appear, for placing everything under the jurisdiction of signs. Let everything be rendered in the light of the sign, in the light of a visible energy. Let every word be liberated, and spiced with desire. We wallow in this liberalisation which is only the expanding process of obscenity. Everything that is hidden, that still delights in the forbidden will be unearthed, rendered unto the word and to the manifest. The real is growing, the real is expanding: one day the whole universe will be real, and when the real becomes universal, it will be death.

Simulation porno: nudity is only ever a sign of more. Nudity, when veiled by clothing, functions as a secret and ambivalent referent; when unveiled, it surfaces as a sign and returns into the circulation of signs. Nudity as design. The same process exists in 'hard core' or blue movies:

the sexual organ, gaping or erectile, is only a sign of more in the hyper-sexual panoply. Phallus as design. The more desperately you pursue the truth of sex in its naked function, the deeper you are immersed in the accumulation of signs, the more you are ensnared in the infinite oversignification of an already nonexistent reality, and of a body which has never existed. Our whole culture of the body, consisting in the 'expression' of its 'desire', in the stereophonics of its desire, is a culture of monstrosity and incurable obscenity.

Hegel: 'Now as the pulsating heart shows itself all over the surface of the human, in contrast to the animal, body, so in the same sense it is to be asserted of art that it has to convert every shape in all points of its visible surface into an eye, which is the seat of the soul and brings the spirit into appearance.'[6] Thus there is never nudity, never the naked body, or the body which would only be naked — quite simply, there is never the body. As the Indian said to the Whiteman who asked him why he went around naked: 'For me, it's all face.' The body in a non-fetishist culture (which does not fetishise nudity as objective truth) is not opposed, as it is for us, to the face as the sole source of expression, and alone endowed with the gaze: it is itself a face, and it gazes at you. Thus the body is not obscene, which is to say meant to be seen naked. It *can't* be seen naked, no more than the face can for us, because the body *is* a symbolic veil, and is nothing but that; it is seduction that is to be found in this play of veils, where strictly speaking the body is abolished 'as such'. This is where seduction plays, and never where the veil is torn away in order to reveal a desire or truth.

The indistinction of body and face in a whole culture of appearances is followed by their distinction in a culture of meaning (where the body becomes monstrously *visible*, or the sign of a monster called desire); and then, with porno, there is the total triumph of this obscene body, to the point of obliterating the face. According to the erotic models of porno, the actors are faceless; they couldn't be beautiful, ugly, or expressive, for this is inconsistent with a functional nudity that effaces everything in the sheer spectacularity of sex. Some films are nothing but visceral sound-effects of coitus in close-up: even the body has disappeared in them, fragmented into grotesque partial objects. Any facial expression at all is unseemly, since it shatters the obscenity and again introduces meaning in the place where everything conspires to abolish it in sexual excess and the vertigo of non-entity.

The end result of this degradation to a terroristic visibility of the body (and its 'desire') is that appearances lose all their secrecy. In a culture where appearances are desublimated, everything is material-ised in its most objective form. Porno culture par excellence is simply one that everywhere and always endorses the function of the real. Porno culture is simply an ideology of the concrete and facticity, of use and the pre-eminence of use value, of the material infrastructure of things and the body as the material infrastructure of desire. It is a one-dimensional culture where everything exults in the 'concrete material-ity of production' or in the concrete materiality of pleasure — in endless work or mechanical copulation. The obscenity of this world is that nothing in it is left to appearances or left to chance, since everything is necessarily a visible sign. It is like the obscenity of those gendered dolls dressed up in a sex, and which piss, speak, and one day will make love. As a little girl remarked: 'My dolly knows how to do that, too. Can't you make me a real one?'

From the discourse of work to the discourse of sex, from the discourse of productive forces to the discourse of drives, there runs the same ulti-matum of *pro-duction* in the literal sense of the word. Its original sense is not in fact manufacture; rather, it means to render visible, to cause to appear or be made to appear. Sex is produced as one produces a docu-ment, or as an actor is said to 'make an appearance' on stage.

To produce is to force what belongs to another order (that of secrecy and seduction) to materialise. Seduction is that which is everywhere and always opposed to production. Seduction withdraws something from the order of the visible, whereas production brings everything into view, be it an object, number, or concept.

Let everything be produced, be read, let everything become real, visible, and marked with the sign of efficacy; let everything be tran-scribed into relations of force, into conceptual systems or into quanti-fiable energy; let everything be said, accumulated, catalogued, and recorded: such is sex in porno, but more generally such is the whole enterprise of our culture, whose natural condition is obscenity. Ours is a culture of 'monstration' and demonstration, of productive mon-strosity.

There is never any seduction in it; nor in porno with its immediate production of sexual acts, with its frenzied immediacy of pleasure — there is no seduction in these bodies penetrated by a gaze literally sucked into the void of transparency. There is not a shadow of seduc-tion in this universe of production, ruled as it is by the principle of transparency governing all forces in the order of visible and quanti-fiable phenomena — objects, machines, sexuals acts, or gross national products.

What an insoluble ambiguity: porno puts an end to all seduction *by sex*, but at the same time it puts an end *to sex* by the accumulation of signs of sex. It is both the triumphant parody and simulated agony of sex: such is its ambiguity. In this sense, porno is true: it shows things as they are in a system of sexual deterrence by hallucination, of the deterrence of the real by hyperreality, and of the deterrence of the body by its forced materialisation.

Porno is usually treated as a double process: sexual manipulation for the well-known goals of defusing class struggle (always the old 'mystified consciousness'), as well as the venal corruption of sex — the true, good, or liberating type of sex that belongs to natural law. Thus either porno masks the truth of capital and its infrastructure, or else it masks the truth of sex and desire. But porno masks nothing at all (now is the time to say it): it is not an ideology, that is to say it does not conceal the truth. It is a simulacrum, that is to say a truth effect that conceals there is no truth.

Porno says: somewhere there is true sex, since I am its caricature. In its grotesque obscenity, porno is an attempt to save the truth of sex, to lend a bit of credibility to the faltering sexual model. Here is the real question: does true sex, or quite simply any sex, exist somewhere as the body's ideal use value, as a potential for pleasure which can and must be 'liberated'? The very same question should be put to political economy: beyond exchange value as the inhumane abstraction of capital, does a 'true' material of value exist, an ideal use value of commodities and social relations which can and must be 'liberated'?

SEDUCTION/PRODUCTION

In reality, porno is only the paradoxical limit of the sexual [instance]. An exacerbation of the realistic, a maniacal obsession with the real: this is the obscene, etymologically and in every sense. But isn't the sexual [instance] already a forced materialisation, isn't the advent of sexuality already part of the Western notion of what is realistic, of the obsession peculiar to our culture with the instantiation and instrumentalisation of all things?

Just as it is absurd to divide other cultures into religious, economic, political, juridical, even social [instances] and other such phantasmagorical categories, for the simple reason that they do not occur there, and that these concepts are like so many venerial diseases with which we infect them in order to 'understand' them better, so too is it absurd to autonomise the sexual as an instance, as an irreducible given, indeed one to which all other givens can be reduced. We need to do a critique of Sexual Reason, or rather a genealogy of Sexual Reason as Nietzsche did a genealogy of morals, since that is our new morality. One could say of sexuality as of death: 'It is a habit to which consciousness has not long been accustomed.'

We fail to understand — or we vaguely sympathise with — those cultures for which the sexual act has no finality in itself, and for which sexuality is not a deadly serious preoccupation with a release of energy, a compulsory ejaculation, a production at all cost, or a hygienic inspection of the body. These are cultures which maintain lengthy processes of seduction and sensuousness, a lengthy procedure of gifts and countergifts; lovemaking is only the eventual outcome of this reciprocity set to the rhythm of an ineluctable ritual. This no longer has any meaning for us: the sexual has now become strictly *the actualisation of a desire in a moment of pleasure* — all the rest is literature. What an extraordinary fixation on the function of orgasm, and more generally on the material function of energy!

Ours is a culture of premature ejaculation. Increasingly, all seduction, all manner of seduction (which is itself a highly *ritualised* process) disappears behind the *naturalised* sexual imperative, behind the imperative and immediate realisation of desire. Our centre of gravity has in fact shifted towards a libidinal economy, which only allows for the naturalisation of a desire attached either to drives or to a mechanical functioning, but above all to the imaginary of repression and liberation.

Nowadays, one no longer says 'You have a soul and you must save it,' but:

'You have a sexual nature, and you must try to put it to good use.'

'You have an unconscious, and it [id] must speak.'

'You have a body, and you must enjoy it.'

'You have a libido, and you must expend it.' Etc.

This compulsion for liquidity, flows, and an accelerated circulation of the psychical [instance], the sexual [instance], and bodies is the exact replica of the imperative that rules market value: capital must be made to circulate, no longer around a fixed point, but as an endless chain of investments and reinvestments, just as value must be made to radiate in all directions. This is the form that value now takes; and sexuality, the sexual *model*, is the form that value takes at the level of bodies.

The sexual model takes the form of an *individual* activity based on a *natural* energy: to each his desire, and may the better man win (in pleasure). This is the very form that capital now takes, and this is why sexuality, desire and pleasure are in fact *subordinate* values. When they emerged not so long ago as a system of reference on the horizon of Western culture, it was as outcast and residual values, as an ideal of the

lower classes (first bourgeois and then petit-bourgeois), in contradis-
tinction to the aristocratic values of blood and birth, of challenge and
seduction, or to communal, religious and sacrificial, values.

Besides, this body which is our constant reference has no reality
except as a sexual and productive model. It is capital that gives birth in
the same movement to the energised body of labour power and to the
body we dream of today as a sanctuary for desire and the unconscious,
for psychical energy and drives — the body which, dominated by drives
and haunted by primary processes, has itself become primary process,
and thus an anti-body: the ultimate revolutionary reference. Both are
simultaneously conceived in repression, and their apparent antagonism is yet another effect of its intensification. To discover the secret of
bodies in 'unbound' libidinal energy, as opposed to the bound energy of
productive bodies, and to discover the phantasmatic and instinctual
truth of the body in desire, is again simply to unearth the psychic
metaphor of capital.

Such is desire, such is the unconscious: the slag-heap of political
economy, the psychical metaphor of capital. And sexual jurisdiction is
the ideal means, by a fantastic extension of the jurisdiction governing
private property, to assign each individual to the management of a
specific capital: psychical capital, libidinal capital, sexual capital, unconscious capital — a capital for which each individual will be answerable to himself, and under the sign of his own liberation.

What a fantastic depreciation of seduction! Sexuality, as it has been
changed by the revolution of desire, as a mode of production and circulation of bodies, is precisely what it is, can only enter speech in the very
terms of 'sexual intercourse' by ignoring every form of seduction — just
as the social [instance] can only enter speech in the very terms of 'social
intercourse' or 'social relations' when it has lost all of its symbolic
content.

Sex can only be elevated to a function, to an autonomous instance, in
the place where it has liquidated seduction. It mostly occurs even today
in lieu of a missing seduction, or as the residue and staging of a failed
seduction. *Thus it is seduction in the form of an absence that is sexually
hallucinated* — in the form of desire. The modern theory of desire derives
all its force from this liquidation of the process of seduction.

What is to be found in the place of a seductive form is now the
proceedings of a productive form, a sex 'economy': the retrospective
phantasy of a drive, the hallucination of a stock of sexual energy, and an
unconscious where repression and the facilitations of desire are inscribed. All of this, and the psychical [instance] in general, springs
from a form of autonomised sex — just as nature and the economical

[instance] were once the deposits of a form of autonomised production. Nature and desire, equally idealised, succeed one another in the progressive stages of liberation: once it was the liberation of productive forces, today it is the liberation of the body and sex.

The sexual [instance] and the discourse of sex were born, as with the birth of the clinic and the clinical gaze, *in the place where there was nothing before*, except for undirected, insensate, unstable, or highly ritualised forms, and thus where there was no repression either — that leitmotiv with which we burden all earlier societies even more than our own, those which we condemn as primitive from a technological point of view, but even more emphatically from a sexual and psychical point of view, since those societies have understood neither the sexual [instance] nor the unconscious. Happily, psychoanalysis came along to prepare the ground for this repression by revealing what was hidden. What an incredible racism of truth, an evangelical racism of psychoanalysis and the coming of the Word!

We behave as if the sexual [instance] was repressed wherever it does not appear as an end in itself: this is our way of saving it. But to speak in this way of repressed or sublimated sexuality in primitive, feudal, or other societies, to speak of 'sexuality' and the unconscious is quite simply a mark of profound stupidity. We can't even be sure that sexuality is the best key to our own society either. And in regard to questioning the very hypothesis of sexuality, and to questioning sex and desire as specific instances, it is possible to agree with Foucault (but for different reasons) when he says that *there is not, and never has been repression in our society either*.

Sexuality as it is related to us, and as it enters speech, is undoubtedly, like political economy or any other system, only a montage or simulacrum which has always been by-passed, confounded, and exceeded by practical experience. Coherence and transparency have never existed any more for *homo sexualis* than they have for *homo oeconomicus*.

A lengthy process simultaneously institutes the psychical and the sexual [instances], and the 'other scene' of the phantasm and the unconscious, as well as the energy produced there. This psychical energy is simply the result of a 'scenic' hallucination of repression, an energy hallucinated as the material of sex; and an energy that becomes, depending on the type of instance involved (topical, economical, etc.), a metaphor or metonymy for all the modalities of secondary or tertiary repression — that marvellous edifice of psychoanalysis, or as Nietzsche would say, that most beautiful hallucination of the hinterworld. Such is the extraordinary efficacy of this model of simulated energy and its scene; such is the extraordinary theoretical psychodrama of this staging of the psyche, of this scenario of sex as an instance, as an incontestable reality (just as production has been hypostatised by others). Besides, no matter whether the economic, the biological, or the psychical [instance] defrays the cost of this *mise-en-scène*, or whether it is the 'scene' or 'the other scene', what should be called into question is the whole scenario of sexuality (and psychoanalysis) as a model of simulation.

It is true that in our culture the sexual [instance] has triumphed over seduction, annexing it and making it subordinate to itself. Our instrumentalist perspective has inverted everything; since, in the symbolic order, seduction is present from the beginning, while sex only occurs as an extra. It is the same for sex as for recovery in the analytical cure, or for childbirth in Lévi-Strauss' account: it comes about in addition, with no relation of cause and effect. This is the whole secret of 'symbolic efficacy': the world operates by a process of mental *seduction* — as it does for Chuan Tzu's butcher,[7] whose intuition of the ox's interstitial structure enables him to dissect it without ever blunting his knife: it is a sort of symbolic resolution which, *as an extra*, leads to a practical end.

Seduction also operates according to this form of symbolic articulation or dual affinity with the structure of the other — sex may come about as an extra, but not necessarily. Seduction would instead be a challenge to the very existence of the sexual order. And if the 'liberation' of our era has appeared to invert these two terms, and to offer a victorious challenge to the order of seduction, then this victory is almost certainly a superficial one. The question of the inherent superiority of the ritual logic of challenge and seduction over the economic logic of sex and production remains completely unanswered.

For all liberations and revolutions are fragile, and seduction is inevitable. It is always there, lying in wait for them — since they are seduced, despite themselves, by an endless series of reversals that diverts them from their truth. Even at the very moment of their triumph, it is there waiting for them. This is why sexual discourse itself constantly runs the risk of meaning something quite different from what it says.

Take an American film: a guy tries to pick up a girl, cautiously, tactfully. The girl objects, aggressively: 'What do you want? Do you want to jump me? Then, change your appproach! Say: I want to jump you!' And the guy replies, sheepishly: 'Yes, I want to jump you.' 'Then, go fuck yourself!' But later, when he drives her home, she says: 'I'll make coffee, and then you can jump me.' And so it goes. In fact, this cynical

dialogue which professes to be objective, functional, physical, and
without subtlety is simply a game. A wager, challenge, or provocation
implicitly transpires. Its brutality actually abounds with amorous
inflexion and complicity. It is a new method of seduction.

Or again, take this excerpt from Philip K. Dick's *We Can Build You*:
'Take me into your motel room . . . and screw me.'

'There is, somehow, in your language, something, which I can't put
my finger on, that somehow leaves something to be desired.'[8]

This can be understood to mean: What you propose is unacceptable,
it lacks the poetry of desire, it is too direct. But in a sense these words
say the opposite: there is something indefinable about this proposition
that consequently *opens* the way for desire. The direct sexual approach
is too direct to be really genuine, because it instantly refers to something else.

The first version laments the obscenity of this dialogue. The second
is more subtle: it understands that obscenity is just a detour, that it is
seduction in disguise, and thus an 'indefinable' allusion to desire — an
obscenity too blunt to be true, too unpolished to be impolite. Obscenity
is revealed to be a challenge, and thus again seduction.

This is because the pure demand for sex, a direct sexual statement is
fundamentally impossible. One can never be free of seduction, and this
anti-seductive discourse is simply the latest metamorphosis of seductive
language.

Directly stating a sexual demand is not only absurd in relation to the
complexity of human emotions — you just can't make such a statement.
To believe in the reality of sex and in the possibility of stating it without
further ado is the trap of every discourse dedicated to transparency, as
well as every discourse dedicated to functionalism, science, and truth.
Fortunately, this illusion is constantly eroded, consumed, and destroyed — or rather, it is circumvented, diverted, *seduced*, surreptitiously
turning against itself to be dissolved in a different game or wager.

Of course, there is not a trace of seduction in porno and sexual
commerce. Like nudity, and like truth, these are abject practices. All
this is the body in its disenchanted form, just as sex is seduction in its
banished and disenchanted form, just as use value is the object in its
disenchanted form, just as the real in general is the world in its
banished and disenchanted form.

Nor will nudity ever abolish seduction, because again it immediately
becomes something else — the hysterical disguise for a different game,
which surpasses nudity. There can never be any degree zero, any objective reference, any neutral state, but always and ever higher stakes. As
with the body in nudity, and meaning in truth, all signs in our culture

seem to gravitate toward an ultimate objectivity, toward an entropic and metastable form of neutrality—what else is that naked and ideal type of body on vacation, exposed to the screened and neutralised rays of the sun, in a satanic parody of bronzed objects? And yet do signs ever come to rest at a neutral zero point of the real? Isn't there always a reversal of the neuter itself in a new spiral of stakes, in seduction and death?

What seduction was concealed in sex? What other kind of seduction or challenge is concealed in the abolition of the wager of sex? (The same question exists on another level: what fascination or challenge is concealed in the masses, in the abolition of the wager of the social?)

The whole description of disenchanted systems is perhaps false, as is the entire hypothesis itself about the disenchantment of systems, the irruption of simulation and deterrence, the abolition of symbolic processes and the death of referential systems. The neuter is never neutral. It is reseized by fascination. But does it again become an object of seduction?

Seductive and agonistic logics, ritual logics are stronger than sex. *Sex never has the final word in history, no more than has power.* This is borne out by *In the Realm of the Senses*, a film entirely composed of the sexual act, but where pleasure, in its dogged pursuit, is again seized by the logic of a different order. The film is sexually unintelligible, since pleasure in the accepted sense leads to anything but death. For the madness that overwhelms the couple (but it is only madness to us, since in reality it has a rigorous logic) drives them to the point where sense no longer has any meaning, and where the exercise of the senses no longer has anything to do with sensuality. Nor is it mystical or metaphysical. It is the logic of challenge, whose impulse originates in an outbidding between the partners. More precisely, the crucial turning point occurs when the logic of pleasure, which dominated at the beginning of the game when the man was in control, shifts to the logic of challenge and death at the prompting of the woman—she who now becomes, after being a mere sexual object, mistress of the game. This reversal of the value of sex into a seductive and agonistic logic is brought about by the feminine.

There is no perversion or morbid instinct here, no 'mutual attraction' of Eros and Thanatos, no ambivalence of desire, no interpretation of a psycho-sexual origin. It is not a question of sex or the unconscious. The sexual act is seen as a ritual, ceremonial, or martial act, for which death is the inevitable outcome (as in those ancient tragedies on the theme of incest), the emblematic form of fulfilment of the challenge.

Thus the obscene can be seductive, sex and pleasure can be seductive. Even the most anti-seductive figures can become seductive figures (feminist discourse could be said to have discovered, despite its total lack of seduction, a sort of homosexual seduction). All they have to do is overstep the bounds of truth, in a reversible configuration tantamount to their death. The same goes for power, which is the most anti-seductive figure of all.

Power seduces — but not in the vulgar sense of a desire of the masses, a complicit desire (a tautology that amounts to basing seduction on the *desire of others*). No, power seduces by this reversibility which haunts it, and upon which a minimal [symbolic] cycle is established. Dominators and dominated no more exist than do victims and torturers. (To be sure, 'exploiters' and the 'exploited' really do exist, as completely separate and opposed entities, because there is no reversibility in production; but that is precisely the point, for nothing fundamental happens at this level). There are no *separate* positions: power is exercised according to a *dual [duelle]* relation, hurling a challenge at society which in return challenges it to exist. If power cannot be 'exchanged' according to this minimal cycle of seduction, challenge or artifice, it quite simply disappears.

Basically, power does not exist. In a relation of forces there never exists a unilateral position upon which a 'structure' or 'reality' of power, and its perpetual motion, could be established. That is simply the dream of power imposed on us by reason. But nothing wants it that way. Everything seeks its own death, including power — or rather, everything wants to become exchangeable, reversible, or eradicable in a cycle (this is why there is in fact no repression or unconscious, since reversibility is always already present). *That alone is profoundly seductive.* Power is not seductive unless it becomes a sort of challenge to itself, otherwise it is merely an exercise satisfying the hegemonic logic of reason alone.

Seduction is stronger than power, because it is a reversible and mortal process; whereas power, like value, pretends to be irreversible, to be cumulative and immortal like value. Power shares all the illusions of the real and production; it wants to belong to the order of the real, and thus teeters into an imaginary and irrational belief about itself (assisted by the theories that analyse it, even when they contest it). Seduction, however, doesn't belong to the order of the real. It never belongs to the order of force or to relations of force. This is precisely why seduction envelops the whole *real* process of power, as well as the whole real order of production, with endless reversibility and dis-accumulation — *without which neither power nor production would exist.*

This is the void behind power, or at the very heart of power and production, and it is this void which today gives them a final glimmer of reality. Without that which enables their reversibility, which nullifies or *seduces* them, they would have never attained the force of reality.

Besides, no one has ever been interested in the real. It is the place of disenchantment, the place of a simulacrum of accumulation against death. Nothing could be worse. It is the imaginary catastrophe behind the real and truth which sometimes makes them fascinating. Do you think that power, economy and sex — all the great parlour tricks of *the real* — would have survived for a single moment without the support of a fascination precisely originating in the inverted mirror that reflects and continually reverses them, and where their imaginary catastrophe generates a tangible and imminent gratification?

Particularly today, the real is no more than a stockpile of dead matter, dead bodies, dead language — a sedimentary residue. And even more so today, our whole security rests on a *stocktaking of the real* (the ecological argument hides the fact that what disappears on the horizon of the species is not energy reserves, but the *energy of the real*, the reality of the real, and every possibility, capitalist or revolutionary, of managing the real). If the horizon of production is vanishing, then the horizon of speech, sex and desire can still arise to save the day. To liberate, to enjoy, to give speech to others, to speak out — now that's real, that's substantial, that's stock in reserve. That's power.

Unhappily, no — that is, not for long. All this consumes itself in the process. We have wanted to make sex, like power, into an irreversible instance, and to make desire into an irreversible energy (needless to say, into a *stock* of energy, since desire is never far from capital). In our imaginary, only irreversible things like accumulation, progress, growth and production have meaning. Value, energy, and desire are all irreversible processes for us — this is the very meaning of their liberation (inject the smallest dose of reversibility into our economic, political, institutional or sexual apparatuses, and everything immediately collapses). This is today what guarantees sexuality its mythical authority over body and soul. But it is also what makes it fragile, just like the whole edifice of production.

Seduction is stronger than production. It is stronger than sexuality and must never be confused with it. It is not an internal process of sexuality (although it is generally relegated to that), but a circular and reversible process of challenge, of outbidding and death. On the contrary, the sexual [instance] is seduction in a reduced form, restricting it to the material energy of desire.

What we need to analyse is the intrication of the procedure of seduction in the procedure of production and power, as well as the irruption of that minimum of reversibility which exists in every irreversible process, secretly ruining and dismantling it while simultaneously ensuring that a minimal continuity of pleasure traverses it, without which it would be nothing. We should bear in mind that production everywhere and always seeks to eradicate seduction in order to establish itself as the sole economy of relations of force. And we should also bear in mind that sex, and the production of sex, seeks everywhere to eradicate seduction in order to establish itself as the sole economy of relations of desire.

This is why Foucault's argument in *The History of Sexuality* needs to be turned on its head, while accepting its basic premise. For Foucault can only see the *production* of sex as discourse: he is fascinated by the irreversible unfolding and interstitial saturation of a field of speech, which simultaneously institutes a field of power, and which culminates in a field of knowledge that reflects (or invents) it. But from where does power draw this somnambulistic functionality, this irresistible urge to saturate space? If no sociality or sexuality exists which has not been cultivated and staged by power, then perhaps no power exists which has not been cultivated and staged by knowledge (or theory) — in which case it is advisable to bring the whole thing into simulation, and to reverse this all too perfect mirror, even if the 'truth effects' it produces are miraculously decipherable.

And besides: isn't this equivalence of power and knowledge, this coincidence of their apparatuses that seems to rule us in a field totally permeated by it, this conjunction presented to us by Foucault as complete and fully operational — isn't it perhaps more like the relationship between two dead stars, whose final flickerings shed light on each other because they have lost their own radiance? In their original phase, power and knowledge were specifically opposed to one another, and sometimes violently (just as sex and power were opposed to one another). And if they are confused today, isn't it due to the gradual extinction of their reality principle, of their distinct characteristics and individual energy? Their conjunction would thus herald not an intensified positivity, but a mutual indifferentiation, whose end result would be that only their ghosts combine to haunt us.

Behind this apparent *stasis* of power and knowledge that seems to hover or spring up from everywhere, there would finally be only the *metastases* of power, or the cancerous proliferations of a structure henceforth thrown into total disorder. And if power spreads everywhere and can now be detected at every level ('molecular' power), if it becomes a cancer in the sense that its cells proliferate in every direction and no longer obey the good old 'genetic code' of the political, then it is because the political itself is stricken with cancer and is in a state of advanced decomposition; or else if it attains this universal propagation and saturation, this somnambulistic functionality, then it is because it is afflicted with hyperreality and is in an advanced crisis of simulation (or a cancerous proliferation of the mere *signs* of power).

Thus everywhere and always we need to take up the wager of simulation, and to grasp the reverse side of signs — those signs which of course, taken at face value and in good faith, always lead us to the tangible reality of power, just as they lead us to the tangible reality of sex and production. We need to grasp this positivism in reverse, and we need to dedicate ourselves to this reversal of power through simulation. Power itself will never arrive at this conclusion, and we should reproach Foucault's text for not doing it either, since in failing to do so it again falls under the spell of power.

To all those obsessed with the plenitude of power and the plenitude of sex, we need to pose the question of the void; and to those obsessed with power as continuous expansion and investment, we need to pose the question of the reversal of the space of power, as well as the reversal of the space and discourse of sex — to their fascination with production, we need to pose the question of seduction.

NOTES

1. [Fr. '*psy*' refers broadly to psychology, psychiatry, psychoanalysis, and is slightly pejorative. It is commonly used to designate anything having to do with this milieu.]

2. [Luce Irigaray, *This Sex Which Is Not One* (1977), tr. Catherine Porter and Carolyn Burke, New York, Cornell University Press, 1985, p. 28.]

3. [G.W.F. Hegel, *Phenomenology of Spirit* (1807), tr. A.V. Miller, Oxford University Press, 1977, p. 288 (translation slightly modified).]

4. [François Roustang, *Dire Mastery: Discipleship From Freud to Lacan*, tr. Ned Lukacher, Baltimore, Johns Hopkins University Press, 1982, pp. 104-105.]

5. [Herbert Marcuse, 'The Failure of the New Left?', *New German Critique*, *18* (Fall 1979), p. 11 (tr. Biddy Martin — slightly modified). This is an expanded version of a talk delivered at the University of California, Irvine, in April 1975.]

6. [Hegel, *Aesthetics*, vol. I, tr. T.M. Knox, Oxford University Press, 1975, p. 153.]

7. [See Tchouang-Tseu III, *Principe d'hygiène*, as described by Baudrillard in *L'Echange symbolique et la mort*, Paris, Gallimard, 1976, pp. 187-189.]

8. [Philip K. Dick, *We Can Build You* (1972), London, Collins, 1986, pp. 127-128.]

Figures of
The Transpolitical

The transpolitical is the transparency and obscenity of all structures in a destructured universe, the transparency and obscenity of change in a dehistoricised universe, the transparency and obscenity of information in a defactualised universe, the transparency and obscenity of space in the promiscuity of networks, the transparency and obscenity of the social in the masses, of the political in terror, of the body in obesity and genetic cloning . . . The end of the scene of history, the end of the scene of the political, the end of the scene of the phantasm, the end of the scene of the body—it is the irruption of the obscene. The end of secrecy—it is the irruption of transparency.

The transpolitical is the mode of disappearance of all this (what fascinates is no longer the mode of production, but the mode of disappearance); it is that malefic curvature which puts an end to the horizon of meaning. The saturation of systems brings them to the point of inertia: the balance of terror and of deterrence, the orbital circulation of floating currencies, H-bombs, communication satellites . . . and theories, themselves orbiting like the satellites of a referential void. It is the obesity of memory systems and information banks which are now and forevermore unmanageable—it is the obesity and saturation of a system of nuclear destruction which now and forevermore exceeds its own ends, becoming excrescent, hypertelic. The transpolitical is also this: the passage from growth to excrescence, from finality to hypertely, from organic equilibria to cancerous metastases. It is the locus of catastrophe, and no longer of crisis. Here things rush headlong to the rhythm of technology, including 'soft' and psychedelic technologies, which take us ever further from all reality, all history, all destiny.

But don't despair! If secrecy is increasingly hounded by transparency, if the scene (not only that of meaning, but also the power of illusion and the seduction of appearances) is increasingly hounded by the obscene, then the enigma still remains intact — including that of the transpolitical.

The era of the political was one of anomie: crisis, violence, madness and revolution. The era of the transpolitical is one of anomaly; aberrations without consequence, contemporaneous with events without consequence.

Anomie is that which escapes the jurisdiction of the law, while anomaly is that which escapes the jurisdiction of the norm. (The law is a rule [*instance*], whereas the norm is a curve; the law is a transcendental, whereas the norm is a mean.) Anomaly operates in an aleatory and statistical field, a field of variations and modulations now oblivious to that margin or transgression characteristic of the field of law, since all of this is neutralised in a statistical and operational equation — a field so normalised that abnormality no longer has any place in it, even in the form of madness or subversion. Yet anomaly still exists.

There is something mysterious about anomaly, because we do not know its precise origin. As regards anomie, we know how matters stand: the law is still presumed knowable — anomie is not an aberration, but the infraction of a determinate system. Whereas with anomaly, it is uncertain which very law it escapes and which rule it infringes. Either this law no longer exists, or it is unknowable. There is infraction, or rather errancy in relation to a state of things such that we can no longer tell whether its system is one of cause and effect.

Anomaly no longer has the tragic face of abnormality, nor even the dangerous and deviant face of anomie. It is anodyne in a sense, anodyne and inexplicable. It quite simply belongs to the order of appearance, to the emergence of something on the surface of the system, of our system, from somewhere else. From another system?

Anomaly has no critical incidence with the system. Rather, it forms the figure of a mutant.

THE OBESE

As regards anomaly, I wish to discuss that fascinating obesity one encounters everywhere in the United States, that sort of monstrous conformity to empty space, that deformity of excessive conformity which expresses the hyperdimension of a sociality at once saturated and empty, and into which the scene of the social and that of the body are vanishing.

This strange obesity has nothing to do with protective padding, nor with the neurotic fat of depression. It is not obesity as compensation for the undernourished, nor the dietary obesity of the overfed. Paradoxically, it is the body's mode of disappearance. The rule which secretly demarcates the sphere of the body has vanished. The mirror form through which the body secretly watches over itself and its own image has been abolished, giving way to the unrestrained superfluity of a living organism. No more limits, no more transcendence: it is as if the body no longer stood in opposition to the outside world, but sought to assimilate space into its own appearance.

The obese are fascinating for their total neglect of seduction. In any event, it doesn't bother them: they live their lives without complexes, unselfconsciously, as if they no longer even possessed an ego ideal. They are not ridiculous, and they know it. They aspire to a sort of truth; indeed, they manifest something of the system and its empty inflation. They are its nihilist expression, that of the universal incoherence of the signs, morphologies and forms of alimentation and of the city — that hypertrophic cellular tissue proliferating in all directions.

A foetal, primal and placental obesity, it is as if they were pregnant with their own bodies, of which they will never finally be delivered. The body swells, swelling without ever giving birth to itself. But there is also a second obesity, that of simulation, in the image of those contemporary systems pregnant with so much information to which they never give birth: it is the obesity characteristic of operational modernity, with its frenzy to stockpile and commit everything to memory, to produce an exhaustive and totally useless inventory of information about the world, and at the same time one of such monstrous potentiality that its representation or even implemention is no longer possible — a hollow superfluity recalling Père Ubu's celebrated 'Strumpot' of the last century, but this time in a cool universe, without irony, without the acid of pataphysics.

Whether pataphysical or metaphysical, this hysterical pregnancy is in any case one of the strangest signs of American culture, of that spectral environment where each cell (each function, each structure) is free in a sense, like cancer, to ramify and divide itself to infinity, to fill up potentially all space solely with itself, to monopolise all information for itself ('feedback' is already an obese structure, the matrix for all structural obesities), and to revel in the bliss of genetic superfluity, each molecule content in the paradise of its own formula . . .

So it is not a question of the obesity of a few individuals, but the obesity of an entire system, of an entire culture. It is when the body loses its rule and its scene that it attains this obscene form of obesity. It is when the social body loses its rule, its scene and its stakes that it itself also attains this pure and obscene form as we know it, its visible and all too visible operation, its ostentation — this investment and overinvestment of all space by the social, without in any way altering its totally spectral and transparent character.

This obesity is itself also spectral, weightlessly floating in the good conscience of sociality. It embodies the formless form, the amorphous morphology of the social today: the ideal individual paradigm of reconciliation, of a closed and self-contained niche. These are no longer bodies strictly speaking, but exemplars of a certain cancerous inorganicity which everywhere now lies in wait for us.

To stay in the oral domain (even though this obesity has nothing to do with compulsion or oral regression), we could say that what applies to the social also applies to taste in American cuisine. It is a monumental attempt to deter taste in food: it is as if their savour is isolated, expurgated and resynthesised in the form of fanciful and artificial sauces. *Flavour* is everything, just as *glamour* used to be in cinema — all individual characteristics are obliterated in favour of the studio's aura and the fascination with models. So it is with the social: just as the function of taste is isolated in a sauce, the social is isolated as a function in all the therapeutic sauces with which we are drenched. A sociosphere of contact, of surveillance [*contrôle*], of persuasion and dissuasion, of the exhibition of inhibitions in massive or homeopathic doses ('Have a problem? We'll solve it!'): that's obscenity — all structures turned inside out and exhibited, all operations rendered visible. In America, this extends from the incredible web of telephone lines and overhead electric cables (the whole network is on the surface) to the concrete delegation of all bodily functions in the habitat, the litany of ingredients on the most basic can of food, the display of income or IQ, including the barrage of signposts, the obsession with distributing the organs of power, equal to the mania for pinpointing the critical function in the lobes of the brain . . .

Life's determinacy is lost in a desperate programming; everything is conceived as overdetermination and seeks its hysterical hypostasis. So it is that the social, formerly the mirror of conflict, class and the proletariat, finds its definitive hypostasis with the handicapped. Historical contradictions have taken on the pataphysical form of mental or physical defects. There is something strange about this hysterical redirection of the social — the most probable diagnostic is that, with the handicapped as with the retarded or the obese, *the social is haunted by its disappearance*. Having lost its credibility and the rule of its political game, the social seeks in its living detritus a kind of transpolitical legitimacy—after crisis management, there is the open self-management of deficiency and monstrosity.[1]

Formerly, it was: 'To each according to their merits', then: 'To each according to their needs', later on: 'To each according to their desires', and today: 'To each according to their deficiencies.'

The obese in a sense escape all sexualisation, all sexual division by the indivisiblity of their full body. They resolve the gap of sex by absorbing the surrounding space. They are symbolically pregnant with all the objects from which they are no longer capable of separating themselves, or with those for whom they can no longer find the distance to love them. Body and non-body are inseparable in the obese. Their body is a convex or concave mirror, having failed to generate that plane mirror which would reflect them.

The mirror stage that enables the child, through the distinction of limits, to open itself up to the scene of the imaginary and representation—this schism has not happened in the obese who, for want of attaining their internal division, enter into the proliferation of an indivisible and imageless body.

Just as there are no obscene animals, neither are there obese animals. Would it be because animals are never confronted by this scene or their image? As they are not subject to this obligation of a scene, they couldn't be obscene. With man, on the contrary, this obligation is total; but with the obese, there is something like a release from this obligation, from the whole vanity of representation, from every hint of seduction—the loss of body as face. The pathology of the obese is thus not hormonal, but a pathology of the scene and of the obscene.

It is quite difficult to tell what constitutes the scene of the body. But at the very least: it is the place where it *plays*, and most particularly with itself, where it escapes itself in elliptical forms and movement, in dance, where it escapes its inertia in gesture, where it comes unbound in the aura of the gaze, where it becomes allusion or absence—in brief, where it offers itself as seduction. And it is the absence of all these things that transforms the obese into an obscene mass.

In their superfluity, the obese make sex suddenly appear superfluous. They have this in common with clones—those other mutants whose emergence we have yet to see, but which the obese prefigure fairly well. For don't the latter entertain the dream of becoming hypertrophic so that one day they will divide into two alike beings?

Transsexual in a fashion, isn't their aim to surpass sexual reproduction and to rediscover the reproduction of fissiparous beings? The proliferation of the body is not far from genetic proliferation . . .

The paradox of cloning in fact concerns the fabrication of beings genetically (non-oedipally) identical to their parent, and thus beings with a sex, even though sexuality has become perfectly useless in this affair. The sex of clones is superfluous, but not like Bataille's superfluity as excess — it is quite simply a useless vestige, just like certain animal organs or appendages for which there is no identifiable purpose, and which appear anomalous or monstrous. It has become an excrescence, an eccentric difference which no longer makes sense as such (many of these moribund differences litter our history and that of the species).

Does there perhaps exist in every organic unity the instinct to evolve through pure contiguity, this tendency toward linear and cellular monotony? It is what Freud called the death drive, which is nothing other than the undifferentiated excresence of the living being. This process knows neither crisis nor catastrophe: it is hypertelic, in the sense that it has no other end than growth, with no consideration for limits.

At a given moment, something manages to stop this process. In obesity, this process is unstoppable. The body, losing its specific traits, pursues the monotonous expansion of its tissue. No longer even individuated or sexed, it is nothing but an indefinite, metastatic extension.

In his essay 'Uber den Begriff der Ekstasis als Metastasis' (On the Concept of Ecstasy as Metastasis), Franz von Baader defines metastasis, which is comparable to ecstasy, as the anticipation of death, of the beyond of one's own end, within the heart of life itself. And certainly something like this exists in the obese, who can be thought to have swallowed their own dead body into their living being — something which produces *a surplus of body*, and which makes the body suddenly appear superfluous. It is the engorgement of a useless organ. They have also in a sense swallowed their own sex, and it is this swallowing of their sex which constitutes the obscenity of their hypertrophied body.

Baader's ecstatic or metastatic form — this form of death which comes to haunt the living being and make it appear a useless incarnation — could easily be extended to contemporary information systems, which are also metastatic in the sense of anticipating dead meaning in living signification, and thus of producing a surplus of meaning, or of producing superfluous meaning, like a useless prosthesis. So it is with porno too: its phantasmal ambience derives from the anticipation of dead sex in living sexuality, of the weight of all dead sex (as one spoke of the weight of all dead labour on living labour). Porno makes sexuality suddenly appear superfluous — it is this that is obscene: not its surplus of sex, but ultimately the superfluousness of its sex. It is this that makes the obese obscene: not their surplus of body, but the superfluousness of their body.

What secret goal is the aim of all this (for there would almost certainly have to be one)? What carnal demon is able to hold up this distorting mirror to the body (for there is something lubricious about it)?

Maybe it concerns rebellion, as with cancer? Once rebellions were political, those of groups or individuals oppressed in their desire, energy, or mind. Today, rebellions hardly ever break out. In our quaternary world, rebellion has become *genetic*. It is the rebellion of cells in cancer and in metastases: an irrepressible vitality and undisciplined proliferation. This is also rebellion, but a non-dialectical, subliminal rebellion, one which escapes us. But who understands the destiny of cancerous formations? Their hypertely perhaps corresponds to the hyperreality of our social formations. Everything happens as if the body cells rebel against a genetic *decree*, against the commands (as one aptly says) of DNA. The body rebels against its own 'objective' definition. Is this a pathological act (like the mutiny of antibodies elsewhere)? In traditional somatic or psychosomatic pathology, the body reacts to external physical, social, and psychological attacks: it is an exoteric reaction. Whereas with cancer, it concerns an *esoteric* reaction: the body rebels against its own internal organisation, it destroys its own structural equilibrium. It is as if the species was fed up with its own definition and had plunged headlong into organic delirium.[2]

The obese are also in this advanced state of delirium. For they are not simply fat, with a fatness opposed to normal morphology: they are *fatter than the fat*. Their meaning no longer exists in distinctive opposition, but in their excess, in their superfluity, in their hyperreality.

They exceed their own pathology: this is why they elude dietary regimes as much as psychotherapy, and link up with this other logic, this exponential strategy by which things deprived of their finality or their reference replicate themselves in a sort of game *en abyme*.

Obesity would thus be a fine example of this vicissitude which stalks us, of this revolution in things no longer through their dialectical sublation (*Aufhebung*), but through their potentialisation (*Steigerung*), through their elevation to the power of two, to the nth power — of this raising to extremes in the absence of the rule of play.

In the image of speed, which alone is the expression of perfect mobility, because unlike movement, which has direction, speed has none, it goes nowhere, and has nothing to do with movement (it is the ecstasy of movement), so is there something about the body for which obesity, in its aberration, would be a perfect verification or ecstatic truth, because in it the body, instead of being reflected, takes itself as its own swelling mirror. As Canetti said: 'Only tautological statements are perfectly true'.

HOSTAGES

Violence is anomic, while terror is anomalous.

Terror, in the image of obesity, is also a sort of convex and distorting mirror of order and the political scene — the mirror of its disappearance. It too seems to be related to another, aleatory and vertiginous succession, to a panic of contiguity, and no longer to be answerable to the determinations of violence alone. More violent than the violent: such is terrorism, whose transpolitical spiral corresponds to the same raising to extremes in the absence of the rule of play.

Neither dead nor alive, hostages are suspended in an incalculable term of expiry. It is not their destiny that stalks them, nor their death proper, but an anonymous chance which can only seem absolutely tyrannical to them. There is no longer even any rule for the game of their life and death. This is why they are beyond alienation, beyond the terms of alienation and exchange. They are in a state of radical exception, of virtual extermination.

They can't even run the risk of their own lives: these are stolen from them to serve as a cover. In a certain way, the worst thing is that hostages themselves risk nothing — they are perfectly covered, deprived of their own destiny.

They are no longer victims at all, since it is not they who die, and since they are simply made to answer for the death of others. Their sovereignty is not even alienated — it is frozen.

So it is in wartime, according to a law of equivalence which strictly doesn't apply to war: ten hostages are shot for the murder of an officer. But the entire population can serve as hostages for their leader: the German people were to be condemned to death by Hitler if he failed to be victorious. And in the nuclear strategy, civil populations and the major urban centres serve as hostages for the super powers: their death and their destruction serve as the rationale for deterrence.

We are all hostages. All of us now serve as the rationale for deterrence. As objective hostages, we are collectively answerable for something—but for what? It is a sort of rigged predestination, whose manipulators we are no longer able to identify; but we know that the scales of death are no longer in our own hands, and that we are henceforth in a permanent state of suspense and exception, for which the nuclear is a symbol. As objective hostages of a terrifying divinity, we don't even know what event or accident will trigger the ultimate manipulation.

But we are also subjective hostages. We are answerable for ourselves, we act as our own cover, and the responsibility for our risks rests on our own heads. This is the law of an insurance society, where all risks must be covered. This situation corresponds to that of hostages. We are *hospitalised* by society, held *hostage*. Neither life nor death: such is security—so paradoxically is also the status of hostages.

An extreme and caricatural form of responsibility, anonymous, statistical, formal and aleatory—this is what the terrorist act or taking hostages brings into play. But if we really think about it, terrorism is no more than the hangman for a system whose contradictory aim is also both the total anonymity and total responsibility of us all. Through the death of *no matter whom*, it executes the sentence of anonymity which is already ours, that of the anonyomous system, the anonymous power, the anonymous terror of our real lives. The principle of extermination is not death, but statistical indifference. Terrorism is no more than the operative of a concept which negates itself in its realisation: the concept of unlimited and indefinite responsibility (anybody can be responsible for anything at any time). In its extreme consequences, terrorism does no more than execute the very proposition of liberal and Christian humanism: all men are bound together—you, yes even you are bound up with and responsible for the suffering pariahs of Calcutta. In the process of questioning the monstrosity of terrorism, we should perhaps ask ourselves whether it does not itself stem from this essentially monstrous and terrorist proposition of universal responsibility.

Such is our paradoxical situation: since there is no sense to anything anymore, everything has to function to perfection. Since there is no more responsible subject, each event, even the most minor, must at all cost be imputed to someone or to something—everybody is responsible, a maximal floating responsibility is always present, ready to be invested in any incident whatsoever. Any anomaly whatsoever must be accounted for, any irregularity whatsoever has to have its guilty party, its criminal association. Such is terror, and such is also terrorism: this search for responsibility out of all proportion to the event—this hysteria of responsiblity which itself results from the disappearance of causes and from the omnipotence of effects.

The problem of security, as we know, haunts our societies and has long since replaced the problem of liberty. This is due less to a change of philosophy or morality than to an evolution in the objective state of systems:

— a relatively loose, diffuse, extensive state of the system produces *liberty*;

— a different (tighter) state of the system produces *security* (self-regulation, surveillance, feedback, etc.);

— a subsequent state of the system, that of proliferation and saturation, produces panic and *terror*.

There is nothing metaphysical in all this: they are objective states of the system. You can apply them to the movement of cars or to the system for circulating responsibility—it amounts to the same. Liberty, security, terror: in every domain, we have passed through these successive stages. First there is personal responsibility, then surveillance (the taking over of responsibility by an objective authority), and then terror (universal responsibility and blackmail of responsiblity).

It is to redress or bring to a halt the scandal of random death (unacceptable for our system of liberty, rights, and the pursuit of profit) that the great systems of terror, which is to say those for the prevention of random death by systematic and organised death, have been installed. This is the monstrous logic of our situation: the systems of death put an end to accidental death. And this logic of systematic death (terror) is what terrorism desperately tries to destroy by replacing it with an elective logic: that of hostages.

(In offering himself as a substitute for the hostages of Mogadiscio, the Pope also sought to substitute anonymous terror with *elective* death, with sacrifice, similar to the Christian model of universal atonement — but this offer was parodic without meaning to be so, since it designates a solution and a model which are totally unthinkable in our contemporary systems, whose incentive is precisely not sacrifice, but extermination, not elected victims, but spectacular anonymity.) Even the 'sacrifice' of terrorists, in attempting to resolve the situation through their own death, has nothing to do with expiation, since it does no more than momentarily unmask anonymous terror.

There is nothing to atone for, because terrorists no less than hostages have become nameless and unnameable.

Nor do they have a territory any longer. One used to refer to 'the space of terrorism': those fractal or non-territorial zones like airports and embassies. The embassy is a miniscule space by means of which an entire foreign nation can be held hostage. The plane with its passengers is a patch or wandering molecule of enemy territory, thus almost already no longer a territory, and thus almost already a hostage, since to take something hostage or remove it from its territory is to transfer it to the balance of terror. Everywhere today terror is our normal and silent condition, but it manifests itself most clearly in that orbital space, that astral space which everywhere today overshadows our own.

It is from this 'no man's land' of terror that the order of the world is now governed: it is from this sort of extraterritorial and extraplanetary place that the world is literally held hostage. This is what the balance of terror means: *the world is made collectively responsible for the order which governs it* — if something were to seriously threaten this order, *the world would have to be destroyed* . . . And what location would be more effective to do this from than one outside the world, with its satellites and orbiting bombs? It is from this place, which is no longer strictly a territory, that all territories are ideally neutralised and held hostage. We have become the satellites of our own satellites.

The space of terrorism is no different from the space of orbital surveillance. Through satellites and space flights, as much civilian as military, planetary space is brought to the edge of an abyss — suspended, like hostages in their place of detention, in uncertain imminence: literally 'ex-stasied', to be exterminated at some later time.[3]

Just as there is a space of terrorism, so is there a circulation of hostages. Each taking of hostages, each terrorist act is linked to another; and just as one has the impression at the global level of a chain or succession of transpolitical acts of terrorism (even though the political scene doesn't at all give the impression of being a chain reaction), one also has the impression of an endless orbital circulation around the planet of a sort of sacrificial information, somewhat like the 'kula' circulated throughout the Melanesian archipelago.

Nothing resembles this circulation of hostages — both an absolute form of human convertibility *as a pure and impossible form of exchange* — more than the circulation of Euro-petro-dollars and other floating currencies, which are deterritorialised to such a point, beyond gold and local currencies, that in reality they are virtually no longer interchangeable, but pursue among themselves their own orbital cycle, embodying the abstract and unrealisable delirium of total exchange, just as artificial terrestrial satellites embody the abstract delirium of superiority and surveillance. And it is also *a pure and impossible form of war* that is embodied in orbital bombs.

We are all hostages, we are all terrorists. This circularity has replaced the other kind, that of masters and slaves, dominators and dominated, exploiters and exploited. The constellation of slaves and proletarians is finished: it is henceforth the constellation of hostages and terrorists. The constellation of alienation is finished: it is henceforth one of terror. Terror is worse than alienation, but at least it frees us from nostalgic liberalism and the ruses of history. The era of the transpolitical has commenced.

We have entered this constellation of blackmail not only in the 'political' sphere, but everywhere. Everywhere this senseless delegation of responsibility acts as deterrence.

Even to the point where we become hostages of our own identity — summoned as we are to assume an identity, to assume personal responsiblity for our identity (such is the name of security, eventually social security), to be ourselves, to speak, enjoy, be fulfilled under pain of . . . but of what? It is under pain of provocation. As opposed to seduction, which permits things to operate in the guise of secrecy, the duel and ambiguity, provocation allows you no freedom to be, but summons you to reveal yourself just as you are. It is always a blackmail of identity (and thus a symbolic murder, since you are never *that one*, except to be precisely condemned under it).

The whole sphere of manipulation belongs to the same order. Manipulation is the soft technology of violence through blackmail. For the practice of blackmail is always to take hostage a portion of the other, a secret, an emotion, a desire, a pleasure, his suffering, his death — the exploitation of these things through manipulation (which covers the whole psychological field) is our way of forcibly soliciting a demand equivalent to our own.

In the interpersonal regime of demand (contrary to love, passion or seduction), we are subjected to emotional blackmail, we become the other's emotional hostage: 'If you don't give me that, you will be responsible for my breakdown — if you don't love me, you will be responsible for my death.' And of course: 'If you don't allow yourself to love, you will be responsible for your own death.' In short, a hysterical entrapment — the summons and solicitation to *respond*.

To avoid capture, take others hostage. Don't hesitate. In any case, it's the accepted rule or general condition. The only transpolitical condition is that of the masses. The only transpolitical act is terrorism, one which reveals our transpolitical affliction and draws out its extreme consequences — and this, unhappily for our critical minds, for any side whatsoever. Taking hostages has no message; it has no meaning, nor any political efficacy. It is an event without consequences (it always leads to a 'dead end'). But don't political events themselves simply offer a false continuity? It is the resolution of continuity that is interesting. In the past this resolution took the form of revolution, whereas today it only results in special effects — terrorism itself is only one immense special effect.

Yet it is not for lack of wanting meaning. Contrary to general transparency, terrorism attempts to summon things to recover their meaning, without doing anything other than hastening this sentence of death and of indifference. But this effect of transparency is of such a specific type that it needs to be distinguished from and opposed to others as a catastrophic, crystalline, or intensive form of transparency — in contrast to all those extensive forms surrounding us. It reflects the dilemma, in which all of us are unhappily caught, that there is undoubtedly no solution to the *latent* extension of terror other than through its *visible* intensification.

The only revolution in things is no longer to be found today in their dialectical sublation (*Aufhebung*), but in their potentialisation, in their elevation to the power of two, to the nth power, be it that of terrorism, irony, or simulation. What is in progress is no longer the dialectical but the ecstatic. So it is that terrorism is an *ecstatic* form of violence, so it is that the State is an ecstatic form of society, so it is that porno is an ecstatic form of sex, the obscene an ecstatic form of the scene, etc. It seems that things, having lost their critical and dialectical determination, cannot avoid replicating themselves in their exacerbated and transparent form. So it is with Virilio's pure war: the ecstasy of unreal, eventual, omnipresent war. It isn't just space exploration that brings this world to the edge of an abyss. Everywhere it is the virus of potentialisation and of *mise en abyme* which triumphs, transporting us to ecstasy and ecstatic indifference.

Terrorism or taking hostages would be a political act if it were simply that of the hopelessly oppressed (this may still be true in some cases). But in reality, this act is part of the ordinary general behaviour of all nations and all groups. So the Soviet Union neither liquidates Sakharov nor annexes Afghanistan: it holds both of them hostage: 'If you disturb the balance of power, then I'll take a hard line in the Cold War . . .' The Olympic Games are used by the United States as hostage against the Soviet Union: 'If you don't back off, the Games are finished . . .' Petroleum is used by the oil-producing countries as hostage against the West. It is useless lamenting this situation in the name of the rights of man or whoever. We've already moved far beyond that, since those who take hostages do no more than bring out into the open the truth of the system of deterrence (which is why they are opposed by the system of morality).

More generally, we are all thus hostages of the social: 'If you don't participate, if you don't manage your own financial assets, health, or desire . . . If you aren't part of society, then you'll destroy yourself.' The bizarre idea of holding oneself hostage in order to have one's demands met is thus not so strange — this is indeed the act to which 'psychopaths' are driven when they hole themselves up and fight to the bitter end.

Blackmail is worse than interdiction. Deterrence is worse than sanction. In deterrence, it is no longer said: 'You can't do that', but: 'If you don't do that . . .' And indeed this is where it stops — its menacing eventuality is left suspended. The whole art of blackmail and manipulation lies in this suspension — a 'suspense' which is strictly that of terror (like hostages kept in suspense about their fate: they are suspended in an eternal stay of execution). It goes without saying that this is how we live collectively under nuclear blackmail — not under direct nuclear threat, but under the *blackmail* of the nuclear, which strictly speaking is not a system of planetary destruction, but of its manipulation.

This institutes quite a different type of power relation than that based on the violence of interdiction. For the latter still had a determinate reference or object, and thus its trangression was possible; whereas blackmail is allusive — it is no longer based on an imperative nor on the utterance of a law (it became necessary to invent a mode of *deterrence*, which rests on the non-utterance of the law, and on floating retaliation), but makes use of an enigmatic form of terror.

Terror is obscene, in that it puts an end to the *scene* of interdiction and violence, which at least was familiar to us.

Backmail is obscene, in that it puts an end to the scene of exchange.

Hostages themselves are obscene. They are obscene because they no longer represent anything (this is the very definition of obscenity). They are in a state of exhibition pure and simple. Pure objects, objects without image. Made to disappear before their death. Frozen in a state of disappearance. In their own way, cryogenised.

The Red Brigades' victory in kidnapping Aldo Moro was to have demonstrated, by taking him out of the picture (aided and abetted by the Christian Democrats who couldn't wait to wash their hands of him), that he represented nothing, instantly rendering him equivalent to the void of the State. Power, in so being stripped down to its anonymous remains, no longer even has importance as a cadaver, and can end up in the boot of a car — in a shameful way for all concerned, and thus also in an obscene way, since it no longer meant anything (in the traditional political order, a king or prince would never have been held hostage: possibly he is killed, but even then his corpse is powerful).

The obscenity of hostages is confirmed by the impossibility of getting rid of them (the Red Brigades also experienced this with Moro). It is the obscenity of those *who are already dead* — this is why they are politically useless. Obscene in their disappearance, they become a mirror of the manifest obscenity of power (in this regard, the Red Brigades were perfectly successful — but Moro's death, on the other hand, proved quite problematic, because if it is true that *when dying serves no purpose one must know how to disappear*, it is also true that when killing serves no purpose one must know how to make disappear).

Let us also consider Judge D'Urso, discovered bound and gagged in a car — not dead, but with symphonic music playing at full blast through headphones: transistorised. Sacred shit that the Red Brigades had each time thrown at the feet of the Communist Party.

This bias of terrorism toward the obscene and exhibitionism, as opposed to the option of secrecy in the ritual of sacrifice, explains its connection with the media — themselves the obscene phase of information. One says: without the media, there would be no terrorism. And it is true that terrorism does not exist by itself, as an isolated political act: it is the hostage of the media, just as the media are the hostage of terrorism. There is no end to this chain of blackmail — everyone is the hostage of the other, which is the *ne plus ultra* of our so-called 'social' relations. Besides, there is another end [*terme*] behind all this, something like the matrix for this circular blackmail: it is the masses, without which there would be neither the media nor terrorism.

The masses are the perfect prototype of hostages, of something held hostage, which is to say nullified in its sovereignty, abolished and nonexistent as subject — but wait! also *absolutely inexchangeable as object*. Like hostages, you can't do anything with them, and it's impossible to get rid of them. Such is the incredible revenge of hostages, such is the incredible revenge of the masses. Such is the fatality of manipulation that it can never be nor take the place of strategy.

It is still in fact due to nostalgia that we continue to distinguish active manipulators from those passively manipulated — thus echoing the old relations of domination and violence in the new era of soft technologies. Take one of the figures of manipulation: the restricted options for answering questions in surveys, polls, and other forms of market research. To be sure, the answer is prompted by the question, but those posing the questions have even less autonomy, since they can only pose questions with the chance of receiving a circular answer — they are thus caught in exactly the same vicious circle. There can be no strategy on their part, and there is manipulation on both sides. The game is equal, or rather the stakes are equally nil.

The Moro case already offered a good example of this strategy with zero outcome, for which the media are its black box, and the inert and fascinated masses its amplifier. An immense four-part cycle of protagonists, between whom circulates a shifting responsibility. The revolving stage of the transpolitical.

Translucent in the person of Moro, it is the empty, absent State (the power which penetrates us without striking us, and which we also penetrate without striking it) that is held hostage by these terrorists who are themselves clandestine and elusive — one desperately mimicking power, and the other counter-power. Impossible to negotiate, the death of Moro signifies that there is no longer anything to negotiate between two protagonists who are in fact each other's hostage, as in every system with unlimited liability. (Traditional society is a society of limited *liability*, which is what enables it to function — in a society of unlimited liability, which is to say one where the terms of exchange no longer exchange anything, but endlessly exchange among themselves, then everything begins to spin, producing nothing but effects of vertigo and fascination. It should be noted that Italy, which has already furnished history with its most beautiful spectacles, like the Renaissance, Venice, the Church, tromp l'oeil and opera, again presents us today, with the spectacle of terrorism, one of its most fertile and bizarre episodes, and with the total complicity of the whole of Italian society: *terrorismo dell'arte!*)

With the kidnapping of Judge D'Urso, everything is taken one step further. It is no longer so much the official State versus the free terrorists still in hiding, but those captured terrorists promoted to judges deep within their prison cells (while Judge D'Urso fell symbolically into captivity) versus the solitary confinement of information (the media pretends to be ignorant of their existence). The roles are reversed: the captured terrorists, in a way liberated from having to hide, no longer negotiate with the political class, but with the 'media' class.

In reality, it also appears that:

— there is nothing to negotiate: the texts whose circulation the Red Brigades demand are political nonsense, and moreover a public sideshow [*un secret de Polichinelle*];

— the State has no more idea of what to do with their captives, who are even more trouble in prison than in hiding, than the Red Brigades know what to do with their hostages.

There nonetheless remains this effect of swirling responsibility that the Red Brigades succeeded in creating, such that the State, the political class, and the media themselves become answerable, to the same degree as the terrorists, for the potential death of D'Urso. To circulate maximal but empty responsibility is equivalent to unleashing general irresponsibility, and thus to shattering the social contract. The rule of the political game is abolished not by the specific use of violence, but by the demented circulation of facts and innuendos, of causes and effects, and by the enforced circulation of State values, like violence, responsibility, justice, etc.

This pressure is fatal for the political scene. It is accompanied by an implicit ultimatum which goes something like: 'What price are you willing to pay to get rid of terrorism?' — the implication being that terrorism is still a lesser evil than the Police State capable of ending it. And it is entirely possible that we secretly accept this fantastic proposition; though you don't need 'political consciousness' to do this, since a secret balance of terror makes us suspect that the spasmodic eruption of violence is far better than its rational deployment in service of the State, than its total prevention at the cost of fully draconian measures.

It is preferable in every respect for something to counterbalance the omnipotence of the State. If the mediations which assured this relative equilibrium and the rule of the political game have disappeared; if the social contract has disappeared along with the possibility for everyone of involving themselves socially, which is to say of spontaneously sacrificing a portion of their liberty in the name of the collective well-being, for the simple reason that the State has already assumed responsibility for virtually everything (here again, it is the end of exchange: the individual can no longer even *negotiate* his share of liberty, for want of which he feels himself hostage, a living surety) — then it is inevitable that the State gives rise, in direct proportion to the disappearance of this political scene, to a radical but phantasmal form of opposition: to the spectre of terrorism, which plays the same game as the State, and with whom it forges a sort of new and perverse social contract.

In any event, this ultimatum leaves the State without an answer, because it summons it to become more terrorist than the terrorists. And it hurls the media into an insoluble dilemma: if you no longer want terrorism, then it is going to be necessary to renounce even information.

The question of hostages is fascinating because it raises the question of the inexchangeable. Exchange is our law, and echange has its rules. For we exist in a society where exchange is becoming increasingly more improbable, where increasingly fewer things can actually be negotiated because rules have abandoned them, or because exchange, in becoming universal, has brought about the appearance of objects finally irreducible to exchange, and because these latter have become the genuine stakes.

We are living at the end of exchange. For only exchange protects us from destiny. Wherever exchange is no longer possible, one finds oneself in a fatal situation, a situation of destiny.

The inexchangeable is the pure object, one with the power to prohibit either its possession or its exchange — something very precious that we are unable to get rid of. It scorches, it is non-negotiable. It is killed, but takes revenge. The cadaver always plays this role. As does beauty. And the fetish. It has no value, but is priceless. It is an object without interest, and at the same time absolutely unique, without equivalent — in a word, sacred.

The hostage simultaneously embraces these two things: it is a nullified, absent and anonymous object, as well as an absolutely different, exceptional, highly charged, dangerous and sublime object (as dangerous as the terrorists: ask those responsible for freeing hostages if they do not instill, by their very existence, by their very presence, the same terror as the terrorists — besides, in order to resolve the situation, the destruction of hostages is objectively equivalent to that of terrorists: depending on the circumstances, governments will sometimes choose the former, sometimes the latter).

For all these reasons, hostages are secretly no longer negotiable — precisely owing to their total convertibility. No other situation so closely realises this paradox: removed from the circuit of exchange, hostages become exchangeable for anything at all. Having become sacred by their removal, by the state of total exception in which they are placed, hostages become the fantastic equivalent of everything else.

Hostages are closely related to the fetish, or to the talisman — objects themselves also isolated from the worldly context so as to become the focus for a specific operation, that of the omnipotence of thought. Games, particularly games of chance, seek nothing else: money removed from circulation and given up for lost becomes the wager of a prodigious convertibility, of a mental multiplication by thought which is only possible when money has assumed the form of a pure, perfectly artificial object: an imitation [*factice*], a fetish.

But we know that the fetish can no more be returned to the ordinary world (which excludes the omnipotence of thought) than gambled money can be put back into the economic circuit — it is the secret law of the other circuit. Similarly, it proves extremely difficult to convert hostages into financial or political gains. This is the illusion of terrorists, and the terrorist illusion in general: *exchange never takes place, since exchange is impossible* — just like torture for that matter, where the sufferings of the tortured are not convertible into political advantage, or even into pleasure for the torturer. So it is that terrorists can never really reconvert hostages, since in a sense they have torn them too violently from reality to be able to return them to it.

Taking hostages is both the desperate attempt to radicalise relations of force and to re-establish exchange at the highest level, to restore inestimable value to an object or individual through kidnapping and disappearance (thus through absolute rarity), and the paradoxical failure of this attempt — since, kidnapping being equivalent to the nullification of the subject, this exchange value falls to pieces in the very hands of the terrorists. On the other hand, once this situation has been created, the system rapidly comes to the conclusion that it can function without these particular individuals (Moro for example) and that in a sense it is far better not to rescue them, because released hostages are more dangerous than dead ones: they are contaminated, since their only power is one of malefic contamination (a good strategy for the Red Brigades would have been, after neutralising Moro as a statesman, to put back into circulation this living dead whom no one wanted anymore, this tainted card which had upset the whole political pack — it would then have been left to others to get rid of him).

If convertibility is impossible, then it inevitably follows that terrorists only ever exchange their own lives for those of hostages. And this explains the strange complicity which ends up uniting them. By violently removing hostages from the circuit of value, terrorists themselves are also removed from the circuit of negotiation. Both are put out of circulation, complicit in their state of exception, and what is established between them, beyond the impossibility of their conversion, is a *dual* [*duelle*] figure, perhaps the figure of seduction; it is the only modern figure of shared death, while being the opposite figure of indifferent death — so inexchangeable as to be indifferent.

Or else we should understand that taking hostages never has negotiation as its goal: it *produces the inexchangeable*. 'How do we get rid of them?' is a false problem. The situation is original in that it is inextricable. We should understand terrorism as a utopian act violently proclaiming direct inexchangeability, experimentally staging an impossible exchange, and thus verifying in the extreme a banal situation, our own, that of the historical loss of the scene of exchange, of the rule of exchange, of the social contract. For where is the other now, with whom to negotiate what still remains of freedom and sovereignty, with whom to play the game of subjectivity and alienation, with whom to negotiate my image in the mirror?

It is indeed this which has disappeared, that good old alterity of relations, that good old investment by the subject in the contract and rational exchange, that locus of both profitability and hope. All this gives way to a state of exception, to senseless speculation, either in the nature of a duel or of provocation. Taking hostages is a speculation belonging to this order — ephemeral, senseless, instantaneous. It is thus not political in essence, but all at once adheres to the dream of a bizarre transaction, the dream of an impossible exchange, and the denunciation of the impossibility of this exchange.

THE OBSCENE

All these figures, which would appear to be those of an exacerbated indifference, an exacerbation of the void, of obesity and terror, are also those of the loss of illusion, of play and the scene, thus figures of the OBSCENE.

The loss of the scene of the body with the obese, the loss of the scene of exchange with hostages, the loss of the sexual scene in obscenity, etc. But also the dwindling of the scene of the social, of the political, of the theatrical stage. Everywhere there is the loss of secrecy, of distance and of the mastery of illusion.

We have completely overlooked that form of sovereignty comprising the use of simulacra as such. For culture has never been any more than this: the collective distribution of simulacra, opposed for us today to the enforced distribution of the real and of meaning. The only sovereignty comprises the mastery of appearances, the only complicity comprises the collective distribution of illusion and secrecy.

Everything that overlooks this scene and this mastery of illusion in order to lapse into the simple hypothesis and mastery of the real falls into the obscene. The mode of appearance of illusion is that of the scene, the mode of appearance of the real is that of the obscene.

There exists a terror of, as well as a fascination for, the perpetual engendering of the same from the same. This confusion is precisely that of nature, it is the natural confusion of things, since only artifice can put an end to it. Only artifice can conjure this indifferentiation, this pairing of the same with the same.

Nothing is worse than the truer than the true: like the clone, or the automaton in that story of the illusionist. In the latter case, what is terrifying is not the disappearance of the natural in the perfection of the artificial (this automaton fabricated by the illusionist perfectly imitated all human movements, to the point where the illusionist himself could not distinguish them), but on the contrary the *disappearance of artifice* in manifest naturalism. Here there is a sort of scandal which is unbearable. This indifferentiation refers us to a terrifying nature. This is why the illusionist in return tries to disguise the genuine automaton, by giving its gestures just a hint of mechanical rigidity, thus restoring against the terror of resemblance the play and power of illusion.

That which no longer causes illusion is dead, and inspires terror. So does the cadaver, but so does the clone as well, and so more generally does everything that is so indistinguishable from itself that it is no longer capable of playing with its own appearance. This ultimate disillusion is that of death.

Against the truth of the true, against the truer than the true (which immediately becomes pornographic), against the obscenity of manifestness, against that despicable promiscuity with oneself called resemblance, we must reforge illusion, retrieve illusion — that ability, at once immoral and malefic, to *tear the same from the same* which is called seduction. Seduction versus terror: such is the wager, since no other exists.

The obliteration of every scene, of every power of illusion, the obliteration of distance, of that distance maintained by ceremony or the rule of play — it is the triumph of promiscuity in all domains. Eroticisation and sexualisation are no more than the expression of this mixing or confusion of all roles. Psychology in particular, forever ambiguous and discontent, is linked to the loss of distinct spaces of the scene and the whole rule of play. The 'other scene', that of the unconscious and the phantasm, would be incapable of consoling us for the loss of this once fundamental scene of illusion.

Illusion is not false, since it does not make use of false signs, but insensate ones. This is why it frustrates our demand for sense, but in a captivating way.

So does the image in general, which is more subtle than the real, since it has only two dimensions, and thus is always more seductive (it is truly the devil who has populated the world with images). So does trompe l'oeil: by adding the illusion of reality to painting, it is in a sense falser than the false — it is a simulacrum in the second degree.

Seduction itself is also falser than the false, since it makes use of signs, which are already semblances, in order to make them lose their meaning — it abuses signs and men. Those who have never, with a word or gaze, lost meaning know nothing of being in this state of perdition, that of abandoning oneself to the total illusion of signs, to the immediate grip of appearances, which is to say of moving beyond the false into the absolute abyss of artifice.

The false does no more than perplex our sense of the true, whereas the falser than the false sweeps us beyond, ravishing us with no possibility of recall. In the real world, the true and the false balance each other, since what is gained by one is lost for the other. In the movement of seduction (let us also think of the work of art), it is as if the false shines with all the power of the true. It is as if illusion shines with all the power of truth. What can we do against this? It is no longer the real nor signification that holds sway. When a form shines with its inverse energy, when the energy of the false shines with the power of the true, or when Good shines with the energy of Evil; when, instead of opposing them, a sort of anamorphosis leads one form to appear through another, an energy to appear through its opposite, what can be opposed to this strange movement?

In this raising to extremes operates a logic of the simultaneity of inverse effects. Perhaps the effects of obscenity and seduction should be radically opposed, but perhaps they should also be merged, and grasped together in their inextricable anamorphosis.

So are the total obscenity and the secret illusion of value strikingly resolved in games for money.

Gambling is extraordinary because it is the locus of both the ecstasy and the disappearance of value. Not the locus of its transgression, as with the potlatch and expenditure — that is still Bataille's utopia of transcendence, the final dream of political economy. Not at all: in gambling, money is neither produced nor destroyed, but disappears as value and re-emerges as appearance, restored to its pure appearance through the instantaneous reversibility of winning and losing.

The obscenity of gambling is total, since there is no appeal to any depth or value whatsoever: here money is unadorned, metamorphosed into pure circulation, into pure fascination, into an absolute passion, into a transparent, cool and superficial pleasure. Lubricity disembodied, it is the ecstatic form of value.

But the secret of gambling is also total: it is that money doesn't exist. It is just like the secret of power, which is that it doesn't exist — or of seduction, which is that desire doesn't exist. Money exists neither as essence, nor as substance, nor as value. And gambling restores it to this nonexistence.

It is the complete opposite of political economy and exchange, where money is burdened with the whole symbolic operation of value. Here, it is the distribution of money as pure simulacrum, unburdened of all obscenity so that it can no longer circulate except according to the arbitrary rule of play.

The secret of gambling is that money has no meaning. It only exists as appearance. And the substance of value is volatilised in it by the play of appearances, by the arbitrariness of the rule.

If money can be self-generated at a dizzying pace like figures can be multiplied by a simple operation of the mind, then this is only possible because it doesn't exist. It is just like that game which involves memorising the greatest number of terms possible: one can carry it infinitely further when one succeeds in forgetting the meaning of words.

It doesn't involve consumption or expenditure: for one must passionately believe in money and value in order to consume them, just as one must passionately believe in the law in order to transgress it. These are *hot* passions. Here, one need not believe in anything, one must have a secret — that money has no existence except as the power of appearance and metamorphosis (or, which amounts to the same, when raised to the power of the absolute simulation of gambling). It is a cool passion, a cold form of ecstasy. Computation forms part of it, like the rule and everything that partakes of the savage ritual of appearances. Computation functions here as a mask, and with the same intensity as masquerade. It rules, beyond appearances, the game of fluid divinities, the occult objectivity behind the subjectivity of appearances.

But if through the false can appear all the power of the true — such is the sublime form of illusion and seduction — then through the true itself can also appear all the power of the false; and this is the form of obscenity.

The obscene is this: it is the truer than the true, it is the plenitude of sex, the ecstasy of sex, it is the pure and empty, truly tautological form of sexuality (only the tautology is perfectly true). It is the pairing of the same with the same. It is sex captivated with its own display, transfixed in its organic, orgasmic excrescence, just like the body in obesity, just like cells in cancerous metastases. Not a debased, caricatural and reduced form of sexuality, but the logical exacerbation of the sexual function, the more sex than sex, sex raised to the power of sex — it is not the copulation of bodies which is obscene, but the mental superfluity of sex, the escalation of truth which leads to the cold vertigo of pornography.

But it is the same process that leads to the enchanted vertigo of seduction. The plenitude through which appears the void (the failing of the pornographic universe, with its spectacular absence of sensuality and pleasure): that's the obscene. The attenuation of meaning, the ephemerality of the sign through which appears the height of pleasure:

that's seduction. But in both cases, it is the outbidding of itself by a quality to its pure form, its ecstatic radiance.

And it is not only a quality which can thus become ecstatic, but so too can the absence of quality: there is an ecstatic radiance of the neuter, since the neuter itself can become potentialised. This presents something indefinably monstrous, in which obscenity plays a major part. Pornography is precisely an art of the exhibition of the neuter, of the inevitable radiance of the neuter.

An essentially sexual obscenity is pious and hypocritical, since it draws our attention away from the general form of obscenity. The latter characterises every form which is transfixed in its apparition, which loses the ambiguity of absence in order to vanish into exacerbated visibility.

More visible than the visible, such is the obscene.

More invisible than the invisible, that is secrecy.

The scene belongs to the order of the visible. But there is no more scene of the obscene, there is nothing but the expansion of the visibility of all things to the point of ecstasy. *The obscene is the end of the whole scene.* In addition, it is an ill omen, as its name suggests. For this hypervisibility of things is also the imminence of their end, the sign of apocalypse. All signs bear apocalypse upon themselves, and not just the infra-sensual and disembodied signs of sex. Apocalypse is, with the end of secrecy, our fatal condition. If all enigmas are resolved, then the stars flicker out. If all secrecy is rendered visible, more than visible, obscenely manifest, and if all illusion is rendered transparent, then the sky becomes indiscernible from the earth. In our culture everything is sexualised before disappearing. It is no longer a sacred prostitution, but a sort of spectral lubricity which seizes hold of idols, signs, institutions, discourse—an obscene allusion or inflection which seizes hold of every discourse, this should be considered the surest sign of their disappearance.

There is no obscenity when sex is in sex, when the social is in the social, and nowhere else. But today the social flows into everything, just like sexuality—one speaks of social 'intercourse' like one does of sexual 'intercourse'. It is no longer a mythic transcendent sociality, but a pathetic sociality of rapprochement, of contact (like lenses), of pros-thesis, of reinsurance. It is a *society of mourning*, an endless mass hallucination of lost determination. The group is haunted by sociality like the individual is haunted by sex—both are sexually haunted by their disappearance.

We are all social workers today. What is this social that is nothing but work? Who even believes any longer in their own factual or legal existence, who believes in anything other than their own enforced reproduction, in the context of a market where they see themselves subject, like any other commodity, to the law of rarity, production, and exchange? Including subject to advertising, since everywhere in the media, in its ideology and discourse, it is the social which becomes an advertisement for itself.

In a world where the energy of the public scene, the energy of the social as myth and as illusion (whose intensity is greatest in utopias) is in the process of disappearing, the social becomes monstrous and obese, it swells to the contours of a niche, to a mammary, cellular or glandular body, which formerly was glorified in its heroes, but which today is linked to its handicapped, its depraved, its degenerates, its defectives and its maladjusted in an immense enterprise of therapeutic mothering.

The social has no existence except within certain limits, those within which it imposes itself as wager, as myth, I would almost say as destiny, as challenge, and not ever as reality, in which case it annihilates itself in the game of supply and demand. The body also annihilates itself in the game of sexual supply and demand, as well as losing that mythic power which turns it into an object of seduction . . .

As for the social, one could say that its obscenity has fully ripened today, like that of the cadaver of which one cannot rid oneself, or more precisely which enters that accursed stage of putrescence. It is at this point, before withering and assuming the beauty of death, that the body passes through a truly obscene stage and must at all cost be conjured and exorcised, since it no longer represents anything, no longer has any name, and its unspeakable contamination invades everything.

Everything that imposes itself through its objective, which is to say abject, presence; everything that no longer has secrecy nor the lightness of absence; everything that, like the rotting body, is surrendered solely to the material operation of its decomposition; everything that, without the possibility of illusion, is surrendered solely to the operation of the real; everything that, without mask, makeup, and face, is surrendered to the pure operation of sex or death — all this could be said to be obscene and pornographic.

Many things are obscene because they have too much meaning, because they occupy too much space. They thus attain an exorbitant representation of truth, that is to say the apogee of the simulacrum.

When everything is political, it is the end of politics as destiny, and the beginning of politics as culture, and the immediate destitution of this political culture.

When everything becomes cultural, it is the end of culture as destiny, and the beginning of culture as politics, and the immediate destitution of this cultural politics.

And so it goes for the social, history, the economy, and sex. The saturation point of these formerly distinct and specific categories marks the point of their banalisation and the inauguration of a transpolitical sphere which is first that of their disappearance. The end of fatal strategies — it is the beginning of banal strategies.

It was thought a subversive discovery had been made in affirming that the body, sport and fashion were political. It thus did no more than precipitate their indifferentiation in an analytical and ideological fog — a bit like discovering that all illnesses are psychosomatic. A beautiful discovery, but which advances nothing: it assigns them to a category of greater indefinition.

Everywhere the received manifestness of the generality of this order — political, cultural, social, sexual, psychological — marks its death sentence. Multidisciplinarity in all its forms is one of its symptoms: each discipline aligns itself with concepts degenerated from others.

But of course we should consider, in the mixing of concepts and categories as in the mixing and promiscuity of races, those bizarre effects of transfiguration in the United States — effects evident in the violence of indifference, the violence of juxtaposition, the violence of promiscuity: new scene of the obscene. But then it is as if obscenity is transfigured by acceleration, by the corpuscular speed of bodies, signs, and images.

Obscenity embraces all aspects of modernity. We are accustomed to seeing it above all in the perpetration of sex, but it extends to everything that can be perpetrated in the visible — it becomes the perpetration of the visible itself. A murderous prostitution, in the image of that hyperreal footage from South America, where the sadistic violence on the screen is actually perpetrated during filming. A murderous aberration? It's not at all clear, since this footage is in a direct line with the phantasm of the complete restoration of the real, with the resurrection of details characteristic of pornography, but just as much with the retro in the register of the past, or with the 'rendered' and the 'live' in the register of life pure and simple.

Porno aims at rendering sex, while the retro aims at rendering events, cultural traits, historical personages — they aim at hallucinating details, purged of all nostalgia by means of too-exact signs. It is indeed a question of *exaction*: things are dragged forcibly into the real, forced to signify as real. But perhaps things are only ever 'true' at this cost: that of being brought forth under too harsh a light, with too high a register of fidelity.

So it is that the whole of the real has already passed into pornographic hyperreality, that the whole of the present has passed into the retro, that the whole sweet melody of meaning has passed into our soothing stereophony of signals.

It is the obscenity of everything tirelessly filmed, filtered, revised and corrected under the wide angle of the social, morality, and information. Those people extorted of their lives on TV, the furthest reaches of France exposed to public acts of confession, and even animals are subjected to educative blackmail: once we could watch a live broadcast of a giraffe giving birth — what a miracle! — but nowadays the broadcast is relayed via a schoolroom, so we can watch the animals being watched by children, etc. The most minor film can only be projected at the cost of pointless and trivial discussion: it is the soft technology of culture, socialisation to the extreme, the rampant obscenity of uninterrupted social commentary.

Solicitation, sensitising, linking, targeting, contact, connection — this whole terminology is that of a *white obscenity*, of dejection and uninterrupted abjection. It is the obscenity of change, of that corrosive fluidity of signs and values, of that total operational extraversion of all behaviour . . . The white and impersonal obscenity of polls and statistics — the masses are faced with divulging their secret, even if they have none. The whole world has to divulge its secret, cross the threshold of silence and enter the immanent space of communication, a space where even that minimal dimension of the gaze is effaced. The gaze is never obscene, whatever one may say. Obscene, on the contrary, is that which can no longer be gazed at, and thus seduced; it is everything, animate or inanimate, which can no longer be shrouded in that minimal seduction of the gaze and which, naked and without secrecy, is doomed to an all-devouring immediacy.

Obscenity is the absolute proximity of the thing seen, an interment of the gaze in the screen of vision — hypervision in close-up, dimension in recoil, the total promiscuity of the gaze with what it sees. A prostitution.

We, particularly us Westerners, devour faces like sexes, in their psychological nudity, in their affectation of truth and desire. Denuded of their mask, signs and ceremony, they shine in effect with the obscenity of their demand. And we subject ourselves to the call of this elusive truth, we lose all our energies in this empty deciphering. Only appearances, which is to say *signs that prevent meaning from filtering through*, protect us from this irradiation, from this erosion of substance in the empty space of truth.

The face divested of its appearances is nothing but a sex, the body divested of its appearances is naked and obscene (even though nudity can clothe the body and protect it from obscenity).

It is doubtless impossible to totally divest a body or face of its appearances in order to surrender it to the pure concupiscence of the gaze, to divest it of its aura in order to surrender it to the pure concupiscence of desire, to divest it of its secret in order to surrender it to the pure operation of deciphering. But we should not underestimate the power of the obscene, its power to exterminate all ambiguity and all seduction in order to surrender us to the definitive fascination of faceless bodies, of eyeless faces and of gazeless eyes. In any case, this is perhaps what attracts us in advance: a perfectly ecstatic and obscene universe of pure objects, each transparent to the other and colliding with one another like nuclei of pure truth.

This obscenity carries with it what has remained of the illusion of depth, as well as the final question that can still be put to a disenchanted world: is there hidden meaning? When everything is oversignified, meaning itself becomes unattainable. When all values are overexposed, in a sort of indifferent ecstasy (including the social under socialism in France today), then the credibility of value is annihilated.

There could thus have been a sort of ruse on the part of traditional pornography. Porno basically says: there is good sex somewhere, since I am its caricature. There are limits, since I am at a point beyond them. Now, this is the whole question: is there good sex somewhere, sex as the ideal value of the body, as 'desire', and which must be liberated? The virtual state of things, that of the total explication of sex, replies: no. Sex can be perfectly liberated, perfectly transparent, and yet without desire, without pleasure (but it works).

It was the same question put to political economy: beyond this exchange value embodying the abstraction and inhumanity of capital, is there a good substance of value, an ideal use value of commodities, which can and must be liberated? We well know that there is not, that use value has disappeared on the horizon of exchange value, and was no more than the paradoxical dream of political economy.

It is the same question for the social: beyond, or short of this terrorist and hyperreal sociality, of this omnipresent blackmail of communication, is there a good substance of the social, an ideality of social intercourse which can and must be liberated? The answer is clearly no: the balance or harmony of a certain social contract has disappeared on the horizon of history, and we are doomed to this diaphanous obscenity of change. And there is no need to believe that we have experienced the realisation of a bad utopia—we are experiencing the realisation of utopia plain and simple, that is to say its submergence in the real.

So is it for theatre and scenic illusion.

Baroque theatre is still a sort of representational extravagance. Indissociable from festival, water displays, fireworks, and mechanical contrivances (the great machinery of technology is inaugurated here, in the production of theatrical illusion), scenic illusion is total. As with the contemporary simulacrum of trompe l'oeil, which is more real than the real, but without seeking to confuse itself with it, here on the contrary *the real is challenged according to its own rules*, by means of machines, artifact, technique, and counterfeit. So it is for perspective in painting and architecture from the 16th to 17th-centuries: its usage is very often illusionistic and operatic. It remains a *mise-en-scène*, a strategy of appearances, and not of the real—illusion preserves all its power without surrendering its secret (there is none).

Even so it will be forced to confess it. Theatre will be caught in the trap of representation. From the 18th-century onwards, it takes the 'real' upon itself; the scene moves away from machinic simulation and the metaphysics of illusion, with naturalist illusion gaining the upper hand. The scene exchanges the allure of metamorphosis for the discreet charm of transcendence. So begins the *critical era* of theatre, contemporaneous with social upheaval, psychological conflict, and the critical era of the real in general.

There nonetheless remains a wager at the level of this representation. Theatre, if it no longer has the energy of metamorphosis or the sacred effects of illusion, preserves a critical energy, and a sort of sacrilegious charm—incorporated in that division between the stage and the audience, which is itself also a critical form, the space of transcendence and judgment.

Artaud is doubtless the last to want to save theatre by snatching it from the rotting scenario of the real, by anticipating the end of representation and by reinjecting into it, through the virtue of cruelty, something even earlier than illusion and the simulacrum, something of that savage operation on reality by the sign, or that indistinction between the two which still characterises nonrealist theatre (Peking

Opera, Balinese theatre, and sacrifice itself as the scene of murderous illusion).

Today this critical energy of the scene, without mentioning of course its power of illusion, is on the point of being swept away. All theatrical energy is channeled into the denial of scenic illusion and into antitheatre in all its forms. If for a time the theatre form and the form of the real acted on each other dialectically, today it is the pure and empty form of theatre which plays with the pure and empty form of the real. Having proscribed illusion, having abolished the division between stage and audience, theatre descends to the street and the everyday, pretending to infiltrate the real, dissolving itself in it at the same time as transfiguring it. It is the height of paradox. Then all those 'fragmented' forms of animation, creativity, expression, 'happenings', and 'acting out' flourish — theatre takes on the appearance of a global therapeutic psychodrama. It is no longer that famous Aristotelian catharsis of passions, but a detoxification cure or resuscitation. Illusion is no longer in the foreground: it is truth which glitters in this free expression. We are all actors, all spectators, there is no more scene, the scene is everywhere, there is no more rule, everyone acts out their own drama, improvises their own phantasms.

This obscene form of antitheatre is present everywhere.

But so indeed is this obscene form of antipedagogy and antipsychiatry, where knowledge and madness vanish in psychodramatic complicity; and that of antipsychoanalysis, where analyst and analysand end up exchanging roles — everywhere a certain scene disappears, everywhere the poles underlying a certain intensity or difference are stricken with inertia.

Or with artificial resurrection, which is one of the forms of obscenity. One of the most significant vicissitudes can be seen in the scene of work, itself also in the process of disappearing — resuscitated, so to speak, in the vacuum of those German factory-simulacra in which is preserved for the use of the unemployed, and in the absence of any 'real' production, the psychosocial experience of the labour process. A miraculous hallucination of the modern world: the unemployed are paid to re-enact gratuitously, if one may say that, the very gestures of production, in a sphere now become perfectly useless. It is strictly the ecstasy of labour, since they experience labour in its ecstatic form. Nothing is more obscene and at the same time more melancholic than this parody of labour. Here the proletarian becomes a whore wrapped in cellophane.

This white obscenity, this crescendo of transparency reaches its summit with the collapse of the political scene.

As early as the 18th-century, this scene becomes moralised and a matter of seriousness. It becomes the locus of a fundamental signified: the people, the will of the people, social contradictions, etc. It is summoned to answer to the ideal of good representation.

Whereas earlier political life, like that of the court, was performed theatrically, with a basis in play and machination, henceforth there exists a public space and a system of representation (this break occurs simultaneously in theatre with the separation of the stage from the audience). It is the end of a certain aesthetic, and the beginning of a certain ethic of the political, henceforth assigned, like figurative space, not to scenic illusion, but to historical objectivity.

This ethical crystallisation of the political scene engenders a lengthy process of repression (just as linguistic structuration engenders a repressed of the sign). The obscene comes into being here, off-stage, in the shadowy wings of the system of representation. It is thus obscure from the outset: it is that which defeats the transparency of the scene like the unconscious and the repressed defeat the transparency of consciousness — neither visible nor representable, it thus possesses an energy of rupture and transgression, a concealed violence. Such is traditional obscenity, that of the sexual or social repressed, of that which is neither represented nor representable.

Things are different for us: conversely, obscenity today is *one of over-representation*. Ours, our radical obscenity, is no longer that of the concealed or the repressed, but that of the transparency of the social itself, of the showing through [*transparition*] of the social (and sex) as meaning, as reference, as manifestness. A total reversal has occured. And if obscenity was formerly only the secondary character of the repressed (it was the hades of representation just as one speaks of the '*enfer*' of the Bibliothèque Nationale), having about it the charm of interdiction, with its phantasms and perversions, today it glitters as its primary character — it shatters the scene of the visible in a sort of ecstasy of representation.

In the beginning there was secrecy, whose rule is the play of appearances. Then there was the repressed, whose rule is the play of depth. Finally there was the obscene, and this was the rule of play for a universe without appearances or depth — for a universe of transparency. White obscenity.

Everything surfaces in it, but there is no more secrecy in these superficial things. That which was kept secret, or even that which did not exist has become forcibly dragged into the real, represented beyond all necessity and all probability. It is the forcing of representation. Look at pornography: orgasm in full colour and in close-up is neither necessary nor credible — it is simply implacably true, even if it is the truth of nothing at all. It is simply abjectly visible, even if it is the representation of nothing at all.

For something to have meaning, there must be a scene; and for a scene to exist, there must be illusion, a minimum of illusion, of imaginary movement, of challenge to the real, one which transports you, seduces you, revolts you. Without this strictly aesthetic, mythic and ludic dimension, there is not even any scene of the political, where something might cause a stir. And this minimal illusion has disappeared for us: there is no necessity nor probability for us in the events of Biafra, Chile and Poland, of terrorism or inflation, or of nuclear war. We are given an over-representation of them by the media, but not the true picture. All this is simply obscene for us, since throughout the media it is made to be seen without being gazed at, subliminally hallucinated, or absorbed like sex absorbs the voyeur: at a distance. Neither spectators nor actors, we are voyeurs without illusion.

If we are anaesthetised, it is because there is no more aesthetic (in the true sense) of the political scene, no more wager, no more rule of play. For information and the media are not a scene, a perspectival space where something is played out, but a screen without depth, a perforated tape of messages and signals to which corresponds the receiver's own perforated reading.

Nothing can compensate for this dwindling of the whole scene and of all illusion — in the automatic simulation of the social, in the automatic simulation of the political. Especially not the discourse of political men, all of them compelled to simulate in a pathetic pantomime — pornographers of indifference whose official obscenity replicates and underscores the obscenity of a universe without illusion. And nobody, for that matter, gives a damn. We exist in the ecstasy of the political and of history — perfectly informed and impotent, perfectly bound together and paralysed, perfectly transfixed in a sterephonic world — transpoliticised beings.

Today there is no more transcendence, but the immanent unfolding of surface operations, the smooth and operational surface of communication. The faustian, promethean period of production and consumption gives way to the protean era of networks, the narcissistic and proteiform era of connection, contact, contiguity, 'feed-back', a universal interface. In the image of television, the whole of the surrounding universe, and our own body, becomes a monitoring screen.

The decisive mutations of objects and of the modern environment are derived from this tendency toward the formal, operational abstraction of elements and functions, toward their homogenisation in a single virtual process, toward the displacement of gesturalities, bodies and efforts in electrical and electronic commands, toward the miniaturisation of temporal and spatial processes whose true scene — but it is no longer a scene — is that of infinitessimal memory and microprocessing.

All times are derived from a miniaturisation of time, the body, and pleasures. There is no more ideal principle for these things on a human scale. There remains nothing but their nuclearised effects. This shift from the human scale to the nuclear shell is discernible everywhere: this body, our body, appears profoundly superfluous, useless in its extension, in the multiplicity and complexity of its organs, its tissue, its functions, given that everything is concentrated today in the brain and the genetic code, which in themselves alone summarise the operational definition of being. The open country, the immense geographical countryside seems a desert body whose very extension loses its imperative (and whose traversal is eventually boring), seeing that all events crystallise in cities, themselves in the process of reduction to a few miniaturised shrines. And as for time: what can be said about this endless free time with which we are left, this far too much time which surrounds us like a bleak terrain, a dimension rendered useless in its unfolding, seeing that instantaneous communication has miniaturised our exchanges into a succession of instants?

We are no longer in the drama of alienation, we are in the ecstasy of communication.

The private universe was certainly alienating, since it separated you from others, but it also reaped a symbolic benefit from alienation, which is that alterity can be played for better or worse. Thus was consumer society experienced under the sign of alienation, as the society of the spectacle; but in truth, spectacle is still spectacle, it is never obscene, since obscenity begins when there is no more scene, when everything becomes inexorably transparent.

Marx already denounced the obscenity of merchandise bound to the abject principle of its free circulation. The obscenity of merchandise derives from that which is abstract, formal and insubstantial, opposed to the weight and density of the object. Merchandise is readable: contrary to the object, which never entirely divulges its secret, merchandise always manifests its visible essence, which is its price. It is the formal locus of the transcription of all possible objects: through it, all of them communicate — it is the first great medium of communication in the modern world. But the message it delivers is extremely simplified, and it is always the same: exchange value. Thus, fundamentally the message already no longer exists — it is the medium which imposes itself in its pure circulation.

You only have to extend this analysis by Marx of the obscenity of merchandise to decipher the universe of communication.

It is not only the sexual which becomes obscene in pornography; there is today a whole pornography of information and communication, of circuits and networks, a pornography of functions and objects in their readability, their fluidity, their availability, their regulation, their polyvalence, in their forced signification, in their free expression . . . It is the obscenity of that which is entirely soluble in communication.

Black obscenity is succeeded by white obscenity — hot obscenity is succeeded by cold obscenity. The two imply a form of promiscuity: the former concerns that of viscera in a body, of objects hoarded in a private universe, of what proliferates in the silence of repression, an organic, visceral and carnal promiscuity — whereas the latter concerns that of superficial saturation, of incessant solicitation, of the extermination of interstitial space.

I lift my telephone receiver and there it is, a whole accessory network ensnaring me, harassing me with the insufferable good faith of all this pretence at communication. Free radio: it speaks, it sings, it expresses — well done! but it's all a fantasy of content. In terms of the medium, the result is this: a space, like the FM band, becomes saturated, the stations intermingle and blur, to the point that nothing is communicated. Something once free ends up being not so at all — I don't know what I want any longer, and the more saturated is the space, the stronger is the pressure from everything clamouring to be heard.

I sink into the negative ecstasy of radio.

To be sure, there is a specific state of fascination linked to this frenzy of communication, and thus a unique pleasure. If one follows Caillois in his classification of games — games of expression, games of competition, games of chance, vertiginous games — then the whole tendency of our contemporary culture would lead us from the relative disappearance of the forms of expression and competition in favour of the forms of chance and vertigo, which are no longer games of the scene, the mirror, challenge or the duel, but rather ecstatic, solitary and narcissistic games, whose pleasure is not at all the scenic, aesthetic or exoteric pleasure of meaning, but the aleatory and psychotropic pleasure of pure fascination. And this is not a negative judgment. There is certainly a novel mutation in the forms of perception and pleasure, whose consequences we find hard to guage. In wanting to apply our old criteria and reflexes of sensibility, undoubtedly we misjudge the possibilities of this new sensory sphere.

One thing is certain: the scene impassions us, while the obscene fascinates us. With fascination and ecstasy, passion disappears. Investment, desire, passion, seduction, or again following Caillois, expression and competition: that's the hot universe. Ecstasy, obscenity, fascination, communication, or again following Caillois, chance and vertigo: that's the cold, 'cool' universe (intoxication [*vertige*] is cold, even with drugs).

In any event, we will have to endure this enforced extraversion of all interiority and this enforced irruption of all exteriority strictly indicated by the categorical imperative of communication. Do we need to avail ourselves of pathological metaphors? If hysteria was the pathology of the exacerbated staging of the subject, the pathology of the expression as well as the theatrical and operatic conversion of the body; if paranoia was the pathology of the organisation as well as the inflexible and jealous structuration of the world — then, with communication and information, with the immanent promiscuity of networks, with this continuous connection, we would instead be in a new form of schizophrenia. No more hysteria, and no more projective paranoia strictly speaking, but that specific state which comprises the terror of the schizophrenic: the too great proximity of everything, the indecent promiscuity of all those things which contact, invest, and penetrate him with no resistance: no protective halo, not even his own body envelops him anymore. The schizo is deprived of the whole scene, open despite himself to everything in the greatest confusion. He is himself obscene, the obscene prey of the world's obscenity. What characterises him is less an estrangement from the real by light-years, a total separation, than the total proximity and instantaneity of things, with no defence, without retreat, the end of interiority and privacy, the overexposure and transparency to the world, which pierces him with no possibility of deflecting it. This is because he can no longer create limits for his own being, and can no longer reflect himself: he is nothing more than an absorbent screen, an insensible turntable for all networks of influence.

We are all potentially him.

If it was true, if it was possible, then this obscene and universal ecstasy of all functions would indeed be a desirable state of transparency, a state of reconciliation of the subject with the world — it would fundamentally be for us the Last Judgment, and it would already have taken place.

Two eventualities, perhaps equal: nothing has happened as yet, our unhappiness fundamentally derives from nothing having truly begun (liberation, revolution, progress . . .) — the finalist utopia. The other eventuality is that everything has already happened. We are already beyond the end. Everything that was metaphor has already materialised, caved in to reality. This is our destiny: the end of the end. We are in a transfinite universe.

NOTES

1. But 'deficit' management of the social leads, as we know, to all sorts of impasses. Here is an allegory of this: everywhere in the United States sidewalks have been adapted for the mobility of the handicapped. But the blind who try to manoeuver around the ramps become disorientated and are frequently run over. From this came the idea of installing rails for the blind at the major intersections. But then the wheelchairs of the handicapped became caught in the rails . . .

2. One might observe that the pathology associated with the metaphoric body, with its division and repression, no longer operates in this metastatic phase. This other body, that of the obese, clones and cancer, is a prosthesis, a metastasis, an ex-crescence — it is no longer a scene, since the phantasm and repression no longer have value for it. It no longer has an unconscious in a sense, and this is the end of psychoanalysis. But it is doubtless the beginning of another pathology: we are familiar with this clonal (chronic) melancholy of infinitely divisible beings, that of sexless fissiparous protozoa, which proceed by extension and expulsion, and not by drives and intensity, which no longer proceed by growth, but by excrescence, which no longer proceed by seduction, but by transduction (that of bodies become networks and extending across a web of networks). We are familiar with this melancholy of being in a narcissistic society — narcissistic by indivisibility and indefinition — about which analysis can do nothing. In any event, this analysis, psychoanalysis, only has something to say in the field of metaphor, which belongs to the symbolic order. It has nothing to say in a different order, neither in that of metamorphosis, nor, at the other extreme, in that of metastasis.

3. The abstraction of orbital surveillance should not conceal from us that this balance of terror is present at the infinitessimal or individual level: we are made responsible for the order which reigns within us. If this order were to be seriously threatened, we are psychologically programmed to self-destruct . . .